# Full Stack FastAPI, React, and MongoDB

Build Python web applications with the FARM stack

**Marko Aleksendrić**

BIRMINGHAM—MUMBAI

# Full Stack FastAPI, React, and MongoDB

**Group Product Manager**: Pavan Ramchandani

**Publishing Product Manager**: Jane D'Souza

**Senior Editor**: Aamir Ahmed

**Technical Editor**: Simran Udasi

**Copy Editor**: Safis Editing

**Project Coordinator**: Manthan Patel

**Proofreader**: Safis Editing

**Indexer**: Rekha Nair

**Production Designer**: Alishon Mendonca

**Marketing Coordinator**: Anamika Singh

First published: August 2022

Production reference: 1290822

Published by Packt Publishing Ltd.

Livery Place

35 Livery Street

Birmingham

B3 2PB, UK.

ISBN 978-1-80323-182-2

www.packt.com

# Contributors

## About the author

**Marko Aleksendrić** is a graduate of the University of Belgrade, Serbia, with a Ph.D. and also a Master's degree in control engineering. He is a self-taught full-stack developer and former scientist and works as an analyst in a trade promotion agency.

He started his programming journey with Visual Basic and Fortran 77 for numeric simulations. Upon discovering Python (version 2.3), he started using it for all kinds of automation tasks: building reporting pipelines and exporting measurement data from instruments into Excel or similar user-friendly reporting tools. Nowadays, he splits his time between business consulting and analytics, full-stack web development, and data visualization.

*I want to thank the people who have been close to me and supported me: first and foremost, my family, but also the incredibly professional and friendly Packt Publishing team – first and foremost, Aamir Ahmed, but also Jane D'Souza, Apeksha Shetty, and all the others. They have really welcomed me as family and guided me through this incredible journey.*

*To my daughter Tara and to my son Luka, for being my driving force and my guiding light. To my wife Tanja, for being my loving life partner.*

*– Marko Aleksendrić*

# 3

# Getting Started with FastAPI                                            57

# 4

# Setting Up a React Workflow                                             89

# Table of Contents

# About the reviewer

**Eleke Great** (BEng) is a senior Python developer with hands-on experience with the Django REST framework and FastAPI for creating both large- and small-scale APIs for high-profile organizations and startup companies in the US and Europe. Other areas of expertise are React.js, Next.js, Tailwind CSS, Google Cloud Platform, CI/CD, MongoDB, PostgresDB, system design, and database architecture. He is also a full-stack blockchain developer with hands-on experience with web3 with solidity, web4, and web5 with Rust on Solana.

*This book is a complete zero-to-hero guide to the FARM stack. The author took the time to break down React hooks, FastAPI routes and file structure, and MongoDB to the point that someone from a non-programming background can understand it and get up and running.*

**Parth Patel** is a Security DevOps Engineer living and working in Toronto, Canada. Over the past six years, he has worked for companies delivering software in a variety of languages such as Python, C#, and JavaScript. He has been working with Python since 2018 and is one of the early adopters of FastAPI. Currently, he works as Team Lead at a financial institution in Toronto delivering innovative solutions to improve the security posture of the institution. In his free time, he likes to enjoy traveling, hiking, and watching movies with his family and friends.

*I would personally like to thank my parents for believing in me and giving me an opportunity to pursue the education I want.*

# Part 2 – Parts of the Stack Working Together

## 5

## 6

## 7

# Part 3 – Deployment and Final Thoughts

## 8

## Server-Side Rendering and Image Processing with FastAPI and Next.js    197

## 9

## Building a Data Visualization App with the FARM Stack    243

## 10

## Caching with Redis and Deployment on Ubuntu (DigitalOcean) and Netlify    279

# 11

## Useful Resources and Project Ideas    297

# Preface

*FastAPI* is a Python-based asynchronous web framework for building fast and performant APIs (REST or GraphQL) that has seen great growth in popularity over the last couple of years. It enables developers to create flexible and powerful standards-compliant APIs as it is based on Python type hinting, it provides automatic documentation out of the box, and its performance is comparable to APIs developed in Go or Node.js.

*React* is arguably still the most popular solution for building user interfaces on the web. It is a library that adopts a declarative approach and simplifies the workflow by allowing developers to use only JavaScript or JSX, without a templating engine. With frameworks such as Next.js and a Node.js server, React enables us to create server-side generated or statically created web pages, while it is relatively easy to reuse an existing code base in React Native (for native applications), and with the plethora of third-party libraries, one of the strongest online communities, and the introduction of the Hooks mechanism, it has you covered whatever your specific need might be.

*MongoDB* is the most popular NoSQL database solution and offers numerous benefits – it is flexible and schemaless, it's ideal for rapid prototyping, and it is also highly scalable and fast.

Combined together, these technologies blend very well, and though they bear a funny acronym (the FARM stack), they allow for a pleasant and fast developer experience, offer speed and flexibility, but most importantly, the opportunity to peruse the wide Python ecosystem, which is suitable for the most diverse problems – from data science and machine learning to analytics and image processing, task automation, and more.

This book aims to teach you how to design, build and deploy fast, scalable, standards-compliant, and flexible full-stack applications in an efficient and, hopefully, fun way. By the end of this book, you should be comfortable modeling the most diverse business problems with fluid requirements through a set of modern technologies and online services.

## Who this book is for

This book is for backend and frontend JavaScript and Python developers or really anyone who wants to or needs to create web applications or sites within a flexible environment – websites that can include data processing or automation pipelines, but also simple websites for structured content. Basic knowledge of Python and JavaScript is assumed, while a general knowledge of the basics of the HTTP protocol and REST API concepts will be beneficial but is not mandatory. Minimal knowledge of CSS and HTML will be helpful.

# What this book covers

*Chapter 1, Web Development and the FARM Stack*, starts with a brief introduction to the problems of the modern web and provides an analysis of the components of the stack and their benefits.

*Chapter 2, Setting Up the Document Store with MongoDB*, provides a quick but operative introduction to MongoDB through simple illustrative examples that will enable you to start prototyping quickly.

*Chapter 3, Getting Started with FastAPI*, explores the basics of the FastAPI framework, as well as the foundations upon which it is built: types, its asynchronous nature, and how it handles typical web-related tasks.

*Chapter 4, Setting Up a React Workflow*, is a very basic introduction to the React library and its basic features that enable developers to create simple or complex user interfaces. A brief introduction to JSX, React Hooks, and the handling of state and events is provided.

*Chapter 5, Building the Backend for Our Application*, teaches you how to create a basic backend with CRUD functionality using FastAPI and MongoDB and how to make it available through a Heroku deployment.

*Chapter 6, Building the Frontend of the Application*, continues the previous example and shows how to build a minimal React-based frontend for our application using the latest version of React Router for navigation.

*Chapter 7, Authentication and Authorization*, provides a practical introduction to **JWT (JSON Web Token)** based authentication and its implementation with FastAPI and React.

*Chapter 8, Server-Side Rendering and Image Processing with FastAPI and Next.js*, provides an introduction to the Next.js framework and its various page rendering methods as well as an image processing pipeline based on Cloudinary and the Python Pillow module. Finally, it shows how an application can be deployed on Vercel.

*Chapter 9, Building a Data Visualization App with the FARM Stack*, shows how to achieve various functionalities that might be needed in a modern web application – sending emails, displaying charts or dashboards based on data, creating reports, and more.

*Chapter 10, Caching with Redis and Deployment on Ubuntu (DigitalOcean) and Netlify*, provides an in-depth guide to deployment of FastAPI on a Ubuntu server with Nginx on a popular platform and the use of Netlify for the frontend.

*Chapter 11, Useful Resources and Project Ideas,* concludes with some useful tips and considerations regarding the various stack components and provides some project ideas for further development.

# To get the most out of this book

You will need Python 3.6 or later installed on your computer, as well as Node.js 16 (or later). You should also have the basic knowledge needed to install packages with pip (Python) and npm or yarn (Node.js).

| Software/hardware covered in the book | Operating system requirements |
|---|---|
| Node.js 16 | Windows, macOS, or Linux |
| Python 3.6 or later | Windows, macOS, or Linux |
| Visual Studio Code | Windows, macOS, or Linux |
| React 18 or later | Windows, macOS, or Linux |
| MongoDB 5 or later | Windows, macOS, or Linux |
| Next.js 12 or later | Windows, macOS, or Linux |

For the deployment of the projects, you will need to create accounts on MongoDB, Heroku, Vercel, Netlify, and Cloudinary (free). For the deployment on DigitalOcean, the cheapest solution is suggested (at the time of writing, 5 USD per month). I have tried to use the cheapest and, where possible, free tiers of the services so you can try before you find a solution that works well for you.

**If you are using the digital version of this book, we advise you to type the code yourself or access the code from the book's GitHub repository (a link is available in the next section). Doing so will help you avoid any potential errors related to the copying and pasting of code.**

## Download the example code files

You can download the example code files for this book from GitHub at `https://github.com/PacktPublishing/Full-Stack-FastAPI-React-and-MongoDB`. If there's an update to the code, it will be updated in the GitHub repository.

We also have other code bundles from our rich catalog of books and videos available at `https://github.com/PacktPublishing/`. Check them out!

## Download the color images

We also provide a PDF file that has color images of the screenshots and diagrams used in this book. You can download it here: `https://packt.link/Qat1m`.

## Conventions used

There are a number of text conventions used throughout this book.

`Code in text`: Indicates code words in text, database table names, folder names, filenames, file extensions, pathnames, dummy URLs, user input, and Twitter handles. Here is an example: "Let's open our `.env` file and set up *Cloudinary*."

A block of code is set as follows:

```
from fastapi import FastAPI
app = FastAPI()
@app.get("/")
async def root():
    return {"message": "Hello FastAPI"}
```

When we wish to draw your attention to a particular part of a code block, the relevant lines or items are set in bold:

```
import shutil
from fastapi import FastAPI, Form, File, UploadFile
app = FastAPI()
```

Any command-line input or output is written as follows:

```
uvicorn chapter3_first_endpoint:app --reload
```

**Bold**: Indicates a new term, an important word, or words that you see onscreen. For instance, words in menus or dialog boxes appear in **bold**. Here is an example: "You must explicitly set that on your **Cloudinary** settings page, under the **Uploads** tab – **Enable unsigned uploading**."

> **Tips or important notes**
> Appear like this.

## Get in touch

Feedback from our readers is always welcome.

**General feedback**: If you have questions about any aspect of this book, email us at `customercare@packtpub.com` and mention the book title in the subject of your message.

**Errata**: Although we have taken every care to ensure the accuracy of our content, mistakes do happen. If you have found a mistake in this book, we would be grateful if you would report this to us. Please visit www.packtpub.com/support/errata and fill in the form.

**Piracy**: If you come across any illegal copies of our works in any form on the internet, we would be grateful if you would provide us with the location address or website name. Please contact us at copyright@packt.com with a link to the material.

**If you are interested in becoming an author**: If there is a topic that you have expertise in and you are interested in either writing or contributing to a book, please visit authors.packtpub.com.

## Share Your Thoughts

Once you've read *Full Stack FastAPI, React, and MongoDB*, we'd love to hear your thoughts! Scan the QR code below to go straight to the Amazon review page for this book and share your feedback.

https://packt.link/r/1-803-23182-3

Your review is important to us and the tech community and will help us make sure we're delivering excellent quality content.

# Part 1 – Introduction to the FARM Stack and the Components

In this part, we will cover the basics of MongoDB, FastAPI, and React, explore the difference between other options, and learn how to start with each of the technologies covered.

This part includes the following chapters:

- *Chapter 1, Web Development and the FARM Stack*
- *Chapter 2, Setting Up the Document Store with MongoDB*
- *Chapter 3, Getting Started with FastAPI*
- *Chapter 4, Setting Up a React Workflow*

# 1
# Web Development and the FARM Stack

Websites are built using a set of technology that is often called a *stack* – every component of the stack is responsible for one layer of the app. Although, in theory, you could combine any type of frontend technology with any type of background technology and, thus, end up with a custom stack, some have proven their worth in terms of agility and reduced development time, and they have strong communities and companies backing them.

In this chapter, we will provide an overview of today's web development landscape in terms of the available technologies and demands, and we make the case for the **FARM** stack – a combination of *FastAPI* for the REST API layer, *React* for the frontend, and *MongoDB* as the database.

If you are a web developer, an analyst who must put some data online from time to time, or if you just want to broaden your developer's horizon, this chapter should give you some perspective on this set of tools, the choices that tend to it, and how it compares to alternative technologies.

I will try to give a broad overview of the high-level concepts of the technologies that constitute the FARM stack, and I will discuss the ways that your next web development project might benefit from using this set of tools. For now, we will not go into details or concrete examples, but rather compare the selected stack components (MongoDB, FastAPI, and React) with their possible counterparts and make the case for the FARM stack.

As someone who has begun their journey through web development in what is considered the early days of yore, I remember Microsoft Frontpage and the possibility of turning Word documents into web pages. I remember using tables for layouts, and I remember animated GIF banners popping up everywhere. I also remember the excitement of putting a page online for the world to see.

Today, we have so many options for building websites and apps that it can become overwhelming to navigate and try to figure out the tools that satisfy often contradictory criteria. Websites aren't just websites anymore – they are living creatures of the web that might evolve into, say, a mobile app or a lightweight CRM solution. Rapid tools such as React Native enable us to reuse the same (backend) code base and deliver a pretty good mobile app with almost all the native app features. Maybe the web app will need to provide some type of analytics that involves some heavy math – statistical analysis (a Spanish political party made great use of a simple statistical mobile app a couple of years ago and made a real impact by enabling its members to participate more directly in the decision-making process at all levels) or a simple recommendation algorithm. Maybe we want to add some fancy interactive charts and graphs displaying the many advanced metrics of our favorite NBA player's statistics?

In this chapter, we will cover the following topics:

- What is the FARM stack and how does it fit together?
- Why use MongoDB for data storage?
- What is FastAPI?
- The frontend with React

By the end of this chapter, you will have a good understanding of the benefits that individual FARM stack components bring to a development project, how they relate to each other, and why this particular set of technologies might be a great fit for web apps that have fluid specifications – both in terms of the data handled and desired functionalities.

## What is the FARM stack and how does it fit together?

It is important to understand that stacks aren't really special – they are just sets of technologies that cover different parts of a modern web app, blend well together, and enable us to satisfy certain criteria while building web apps. To have a functional web application or site, we need to have a system consisting of the following:

- **An operating system**: Usually, this is Unix/Linux-based.
- **A database layer**: A SQL or NoSQL solution. In our case, we will use MongoDB.
- **A web server**: Apache and Nginx are quite popular, but we will talk about Python solutions for FastAPI, such as Uvicorn or Hypercorn.
- **A development environment**: PHP, Node.js/JavaScript, .NET, or Python.

Optionally, and more often than not, we could also add a frontend library or framework (such as Vue.js, Angular, React, or Svelte) since the vast majority of web development companies benefit from adopting one in terms of consistency, development speed, and standards compliance. And let's face it – it is 2022, and you just cannot afford to handcraft your user interfaces without a library or a framework.

Let's list the most famous stacks or, at the very least, some of those that have a popular acronym:

- **MERN**: MongoDB + Express.js + React + Node.js is still probably one of the most popular ones today. Developers can be comfortable and never leave JavaScript, except when they need to write some style sheets. With the addition of React Native for mobile apps and something like Electron.js for desktop apps, a product can encompass virtually every platform while relying solely on JavaScript.

- **MEAN**: MongoDB + Express.js + Angular.js + Node.js is similar to the previously mentioned MERN, with Angular.js managing the frontend in a more structured **Model–View–Controller (MVC)** way.

- **PERN**: Postgres + Express.js + React + Node.js is for those who want the stability and features of a Postgres relational database. Often, it is used in conjunction with an object-relational mapper.

- **LAMP**: Linux + Apache + MySQL + PHP is probably the first acronym to gain popularity and one of the most perused in the past 20 years.

The first three stacks run on the Node.js platform (a server-run JavaScript V8 engine) and have a web framework in common – although Express.js is the most popular, there are excellent alternatives in the Node.js universe, such as Koa.js, Fastify.js, or some more structured ones such as Nest.js.

One popular, and very interesting, Python-based combination is using the Django web framework and the excellent **Django REST Framework** (**DRF**), which is a toolkit for building REST APIs in a modern and logical way. Django itself is very mature and popular among Python developers and offers flexibility and development speed along with some typical Django goodies: an admin site, the possibility of customizing and serializing REST responses, the option to choose between functional and class-based views, and more.

The choice of the stack should be heavily conditioned by the type and the scope of the project at hand. Startups, but also small internal tools, can often benefit from agile, rapid development with flexibility and potential scalability down the road. Additionally, time-to-market, the availability of developers (the talent pool), and the maintainability and support of individual layers play a key role in the process of stack selection.

**FARM** is a new acronym, and there aren't many resources covering it as a whole, though there are excellent resources on MongoDB and React, which have a great degree of adoption and maturity. On the other hand, FastAPI is much newer but provides excellent online documentation.

Let's dissect this funny acronym. **FA** stands for FastAPI – a very interesting and, in technology years, brand-new Python web framework. **R** stands for React, which is, arguably, the most popular UI library, while **M** denotes the data layer – MongoDB, which is, arguably, the most popular NoSQL database available today. I honestly don't know if the acronym started as a joke, but it sure sounds great.

The main objective of this chapter is to get you acquainted with the included technologies at a high level and compare them with the alternatives. We will try to set the ground for a simple project that we will be building throughout the book – a used automobile sales website – and then add some functionality while trying to implement some of the best practices in all of the areas. At the end of the chapter, you should hopefully become interested (maybe even excited!) in the proposed technology mix and be able to evaluate whether this type of setup could benefit your future projects and whether it is something useful to add to your web developer's toolkit.

The following diagram provides a high-level overview of the moving parts involved in the FARM stack:

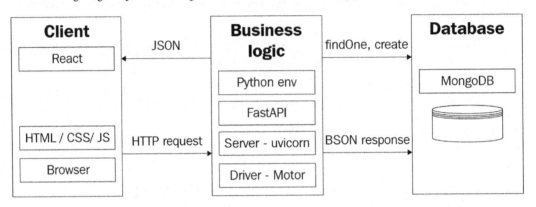

Figure 1.1 – A Diagram of the FARM stack with its components

As you can see from the preceding diagram, the FARM stack is composed of three layers. The user performs an action using the client, which, in our case, will be based on React – this ultimately creates a bundle of HTML, CSS, and JavaScript. This user action (a mouse click, a form submit, or some other event) then triggers an HTTP request (such as GET, POST, PUT, or another HTTP verb with a payload) that gets processed by our REST API service (FastAPI).

The Python part is centered around FastAPI and optional dependencies and is served by *uvicorn* – a fast Python-based server. The backend is responsible for dispatching the appropriate database calls to MongoDB using various commands - queries (such as `findOne`, `find`, `create`, `update`, and more) and leveraging the MongoDB aggregation framework. The results obtained from the database are interpreted by FastAPI through the Python driver of choice (*Motor*), converted from BSON into appropriate Python data structures, and finally, output from the REST API server in the form of plain JSON.

Since we will use Motor, which is an *asynchronous Python driver for MongoDB*, these calls will be handled asynchronously. Finally, returning to the diagram and the arrow denoted by *JSON*, the data is fed to the UI where it is handled by React and used to update the interface, render the necessary components, and synchronize the UI with React's virtual DOM tree.

In the following sections, we will go over the motivations behind the birth of the FARM stack. Additionally, we will go over each component and the features that make it a good fit in more detail. After a brief introduction to the benefits of the stack as a whole, I will provide a high overview of each choice and underline the benefits that it can provide to a modern web development workflow.

## Why the FARM stack?

I truly believe that the flexibility and simplicity of the stack, along with the components comprising it, could give you a real boost in terms of development speed, extensibility, and maintainability while allowing for scalability (due to the distributed nature of MongoDB on the one hand and the async nature of FastAPI on the other hand) down the road, which might prove crucial should your product need to evolve and become bigger than it was initially supposed to be. The ideal scenario would probably be a small-to-medium-scale web app that you could play with and find the time to experiment with a bit. Finally, I believe that developers and analysts alike could greatly benefit from Python's ecosystem and extensibility through a rich ecosystem of modules that encompasses virtually every human activity that includes some type of computing.

## Evolution in Web Development

The beginning of the 2020s saw an interesting blurring of the borders between classical web development and other types of computing. Data science has lost some of its mystique, much of the science of it has been turned into a craft, and it has descended into the plebs and the not-so-scientifically inclined developers. Now, algorithms such as linear regressions, clustering, even neural networks, and ensemble methods are very easy to embed even in the most mundane systems in order to gain a feature, to achieve a slight performance gain, or add a simple recommendation engine. The visualization toolbox has moved online and classical workhorses such as Ggplot2 (for R) and D3.js, which require a thorough understanding of the underlying technologies, are now being given a run for their money by various combinations of D3.js and Svelte or React, SVG or Canvas - based solutions and more; for example, full-blown Python and React web application frameworks specialized for data visualization such as Plotly - Dash, Streamlit, or simple yet powerful solutions such as Chart.js.

Alternatively, if you just need to create a company or portfolio website with structured content, you can choose from the plethora of popular JAMstack solutions. JAMstack is a relatively new web development paradigm based on not-so-new components – **JavaScript, API(s), and Markup** (**JAM**) – and enables developers to develop faster web solutions, achieving blazing performance and a non-techie-friendly admin interface.

Additionally, web hosting costs have rapidly decreased in the last decade and several cloud-based companies have drastically lowered the technical barrier to web development and the creation of internet-based products. In this book we will examine many cloud-based systems that can handle parts of the system well.

Having provided a brief introduction to the contemporary and novel challenges of modern web development, it is time to introduce our database system of choice – MongoDB.

# Why use MongoDB?

In the following paragraphs, we will go through the main features of our selected database system – MongoDB – and give a high-level overview of the features that make it an excellent fit for our FARM stack. After a brief introduction of some specificities of the database, in the following chapter, we will go over the setup and create a working database environment that will enable us to showcase some basic methods.

MongoDB is the database of choice in the FARM stack. It is a fast, scalable, and document-oriented database that enables flexible schemas and, thus, iterative and rapid development. MongoDB is able to accommodate data structures of varying complexities, and its querying and aggregation methods make it an excellent choice for a flexible REST API framework such as FastAPI, coupled with an official Python driver. It has a high level of adoption and maturity and is one of the pillars of the NoSQL data storage movement that took the web development world by storm a decade ago.

The main features that make MongoDB an ideal candidate for a flexible and fast-paced development environment, prototyping, and iterative development are listed as follows:

- **Easy and cheap**: It is easy and fast to set up using an online cloud service that offers a generous free tier, while local installation is always an option.

- **Flexibility**: The NoSQL nature of the database enables extremely flexible models and fast iterations and modifications on the fly.

- **Web-friendly format**: The native data format – BSON – is practically a binary version of JSON, which, in turn, is the de facto data format of the modern web, so no complex parsing or transformations are necessary.

- **Complex nested structures**: MongoDB documents allow other documents and arrays of documents to be embedded, which naturally translates into the data flow of a modern data web app (for example, we can embed all of the comments into the blog post they refer to). Denormalization is encouraged.

- **Simple intuitive syntax**: The methods for performing basic **CRUD** operations (that is, **create, read, update, and delete**), coupled with powerful aggregation frameworks and projections, allow us to achieve mostly all data reads relatively simply through the use of drivers, and the commands should be intuitive for anyone with a bit of SQL experience.

- **Built with scalability in mind**: MongoDB is built from the ground up with several objectives – scalability, speed, and the ability to handle huge (huMONGOus) amounts of data.

- **Community and documentation**: Lastly, MongoDB is backed by a mature company and a strong community, and it offers various tools to facilitate the development and prototyping process. For instance, Compass is a desktop application that enables users to manage and administer databases. The framework of the serverless functions is constantly being updated and upgraded, and there are excellent drivers for virtually every programming language.

I believe that in some cases – and this includes a lot of cases – MongoDB should be your first choice, especially when you are designing something that still has a very fluid or vague specification, and let's be honest, that happens a lot more than we would like to admit.

Of course, MongoDB is not a silver bullet, and some drawbacks are worth noticing upfront. On the one hand, the schemaless design and the ability to insert any type of data into your database might be a bit panic-inducing but translates to the need for stronger data integrity validation on the backend side. We will see how Pydantic – an excellent Python validation and type-enforcement library – can help us with that. The absence of complex joins, which are present in the SQL world, might be a dealbreaker for some types of applications. For analytics-intensive applications that require numerous complex queries, relational databases are a better, and often the only possible, solution. Finally, for mission-critical applications that require adherence to the **ACID** principles (that is, **atomicity, consistency, isolation**, and **durability**) of transactions, MongoDB or any NoSQL database system might not be the right solution.

Now that we understand what MongoDB brings to the table in terms of scalability, but especially flexibility with its schema-less approach, let us take a look at the REST API framework of choice, FastAPI, and learn how it can help us leverage that schema-less approach and simplify our interactions with the data.

## Introducing FastAPI

Now we will look at a brief introduction to the Python REST-API framework of choice – **FastAPI**. Additionally, we will go over a high-level overview of the features that make it a protagonist in our FARM stack. I will try to compare FastAPI with Python and JavaScript alternatives and explain why it can be a great fit for a modern and flexible stack.

### REST APIs

What is an API? Technically, **API** stands for **Application Programming Interface**. APIs are used to enable some kind of interaction between different pieces of software and different systems, and they communicate using **HTTP** (short for **Hypertext Transfer Protocol**) through a cycle of requests and responses. In the last couple of decades, APIs have become the standard protocol for communication between various servers and heterogeneous clients, and they can be seen as a sort of vascular system that is fundamental to information exchange on the web.

There are many definitions, more or less formal ones, and application programming interfaces can mean many things, but I like to view them as wirings that expose the business logic through a uniform interface, allowing us to use them from another realm.

An API is, as its name suggests, an interface. It is a way for a human or a machine to interact with an application or a service through an interface. Every API provider will provide an interface that is well-suited for the type of data that they provide, for instance, a weather forecasting station will provide an API that lists the temperatures and humidity levels for a certain period and a certain location. Some sports sites will provide statistical data about the games that are being played and a pizza delivery API will provide you with the selected ingredients, the price, and the estimated time of arrival. APIs are everywhere – inside your TV, your wallet, and, heck, your favorite news site probably uses at least a dozen of them. With the adoption of the Internet of Things, APIs will enter even more aspects of our lives, transmitting biometric and medical data, enabling fast communications between factory machines, tractors in the fields, traffic frequencies, traffic light control systems, and more. APIs are what makes today's web turn, what generates traffic, and ultimately, what generates revenue. Put simply, we can think of an API as a standardized way of information exchange, with usability, performance, and scalability in mind.

We will not go over the rigorous definitions of REST APIs, but just list some of the most important ones:

- **Statelessness**: REST APIs are said to be *stateless*, which means that neither the client nor the server stores any states in-between. All the requests and responses are handled by the API server in isolation and without information about the session itself.

- **Layered structure**: In order to keep the API scalable and understandable, a RESTful architecture implies a layered structure. The different layers form a hierarchy and communicate with each other but not with every component, thus improving overall security.

- **Client-server architecture**: APIs should be able to connect different systems/pieces of software without limiting their own functionalities – the server (the system that provides the response) and the client (the system making the request) have to stay separate and independent from each other.

We will be using FastAPI for our REST API layer, and we could say that it checks all the required boxes and then some more.

## What is FastAPI?

FastAPI is a modern and performant web framework for building APIs. Built by *Sebastian Ramirez*, it uses, to best avail, the newest features of the Python programming language, such as type hinting and annotations, the `async - await` syntax, Pydantic models, web socket support, and more.

There are numerous reasons why FastAPI, though relatively new, will probably see a wider spread in the web development world in the future, so let's list some of them:

- **High performance**: FastAPI is able to achieve very high performance, especially compared to other Python-based solutions. By using Starlette under the hood, FastAPI's performance reaches levels that are usually reserved for Node.js and Go.

- **Data validation and simplicity**: Being heavily based on Python types and Pydantic brings numerous benefits. Since Pydantic structures are just instances of classes the developers define, we can perform complex data validations, deeply nested JSON objects, and hierarchical models (using Python lists and dictionaries), and this relates very well with the nature of MongoDB.

- **Faster development**: Development becomes more intuitive, with strong **integrated development environment (IDE)** support, which leads to faster development time and fewer bugs.

- **Standards compliance**: FastAPI is standard-based and fully compatible with open standards for building APIs – OpenAPI and JSON schemas.

- **Logical structuring of apps**: The framework allows for structuring of APIs and apps into multiple routers and allows granular request and response customization. and easy access to every part of the HTTP cycle.

- **Async support**: FastAPI uses an **Asynchronous Server Gateway Interface (ASGI)** and, with the use of an ASGI-compatible server, such as Uvicorn or Hypercorn, is able to provide a truly asynchronous workflow without actually having to import the Async.io module into Python.

- **Dependency injection**: The dependency injection system in FastAPI is one of its biggest selling points. It enables us to create complex functionalities that are easily reusable across our API. This is a pretty big deal and probably the feature that makes FastAPI ideal for hybrid web apps – it gives developers the opportunity to easily attach different functionalities to the REST endpoints.

- **Great documentation**: The documentation of the framework itself is excellent and second to none. It is both easy to follow and extensive.

- **Automatic documentation**: Being based on OpenAPI, FastAPI enables automatic documentation creation, which essentially means that we get our API documented for free with Swagger.

In order to get at least a basic idea of what coding with FastAPI looks like, let's take a look at a minimal API:

```python
# main.py
from fastapi import FastAPI
app = FastAPI()


@app.get("/")
async def root():
    return {"message": "Hello World"}
```

The preceding few lines of code define a minimal API with a single endpoint (/) that responds to a GET request with the message "Hello world". We instantiate a FastAPI class and use decorators to tell the server which HTTP methods should trigger which function for a response, just like with the Flask microframework, for example.

## Python and REST APIs

Python has been used to build REST APIs for a very long time. While there are many options and solutions, DRF and Flask seem to be the most popular ones, at least until recently. If you are feeling adventurous, you can Google less popular or older frameworks such as bottle.py and CherryPy. DRF is a plug-in system for the Django web framework and enables a Django system to create highly customized REST API responses and generate endpoints based on the defined models. DRF is a very mature and battle-tested system. It is regularly updated, and its documentation is very detailed. Flask, Python's lightweight microframework, is a real gem among the web-building Python tools and can create REST APIs in a lot of different ways. You can use pure Flask and just output the appropriate format (i.e., JSON instead of HTML) or use some of the extensions developed to make the creation of REST APIs as straightforward as possible. Both of these solutions are fundamentally synchronous, although there seems to be active development in the direction of enabling async support.

There are also some very robust and mature tools, such as Tornado, which is an asynchronous networking library (and a server) that is able to scale to tens of thousands of open connections. Finally, in the last couple of years, several new Python-based solutions have been created.

One of these solutions, and arguably the fastest, is Starlette. Dubbed as a lightweight ASGI framework/toolkit, it is ideal for building high-performance async services.

Like Flask was built on top of a couple of solid Python libraries – Werkzeug and Jinja2 – 10 or more years ago, Sebastian Ramirez built FastAPI on top of Starlette and Pydantic, while also adding numerous features and goodies by using the latest Python features, such as type hinting and async support. According to some recent surveys, FastAPI is quickly becoming one of the most popular and most loved web frameworks.. Undeniably, it is gaining in popularity, and it looks like it is here to stay, at least for the foreseeable future.

In *Chapter 3*, *Getting Started with FastAPI*, of this book, we will go over the most important features of FastAPI, but at this point, I just want to stress the significance of having a truly async Python framework as the glue for the most diverse components of a system. In fact, besides doing the *usual web framework stuff*, such as communicating with a database or, in our case, a MongoDB store, spitting out data to a frontend, and managing authentication and authorization, this Python pipeline enables us to quickly integrate and easily achieve frequently required tasks such as background jobs, header and body manipulation, response and request validation, and more through the dependency injection system.

We will try to cover the absolute minimum necessary for you to be able to build a simple FastAPI system. I will make frequent trips to the official documentation site and try to find the simplest solutions. Lastly, we will consider various web server solutions and deployment options (such as Deta, Heroku, and Digitalocean) for our FastAPI Python-based backend, while trying to opt for free solutions.

So, to cut a long story short, we choose FastAPI because we ideally want the ability and speed to handle requests asynchronously as if we were using a Node.js server while having access to the Python ecosystem. Additionally, we want the simplicity and development speed of a framework that automatically generates documentation for us.

After reviewing the backend components, it is time to finalize our stack and put a face on it. We will now look at a minimal introduction to React and discuss what distinguishes it from other (also valid) solutions.

# The frontend – React

Let's start with a bit of context here. Perhaps the changes in the world of the web are most visible when we talk about the frontend – the part of the website that is facing the users. Tim Berners-Lee made the first HTML specification public in 1991, and it consisted of text and under 20 tags. In 1994, we got cascading style sheets and the web started looking a little nicer. Legend has it that a new browser scripting language called Mocha was created in just 10 days – that was in 1995. Later, this language went through numerous changes and became what we know today as JavaScript – a powerful and fast language that, with the advent of Node.js, was able to conquer the servers, too.

Another important concept that has left a strong mark in the development of the frontend is the extensive use of **Asynchronous JavaScript and XML (AJAX)** – you might remember all those rounded corner web apps with vowel-based URLs. The technology of making asynchronous HTTP requests was known well before the arrival of Web 2.0 but was mostly underutilized. Libraries such as jQuery, but also Scriptaculous, MooTools, and more, began using AJAX and offering desktop-like interactivities in the browser.

One problem that quickly arose was the handling of data across shared views. Backbone, Knockout, and Ember were the most popular libraries that mitigated to solve that problem. In 2010, AngularJS came to light; this was a complex **Model View Controller** (**MVC**)-based framework with a very specific and prescribed way of doing things.

In May 2013, React was presented in the US and the web development world was able to witness numerous innovations – virtual DOM, one-way data flow, the Flux pattern, and more.

This is a bit of history to just try and provide some context and continuity because web development, like any other creative human activity, rarely moves in quantum leaps. Usually, it moves in steps that enable users to resolve the issues that they are facing in an, often, suboptimal way. It would be unfair not to mention Vue.js, which is an excellent choice for building frontends that also sports an entire ecosystem of libraries, and Svelte.js, which offers a radical shift in building UIs in the sense that the UI is compiled and the bundled size is significantly smaller.

## Why use React?

As of 2022, interactive, attractive, fast, and intuitive UIs are a necessity for any public-facing web application. It is possible, though very difficult, to achieve most or every functionality that even a simple web is expected to provide using just plain JavaScript. FastAPI is more than capable of serving HTML (and static files, such as JavaScript or CSS) using any compatible templating engine (the most widely used in the Python world is probably Jinja2), but we and the users want more:

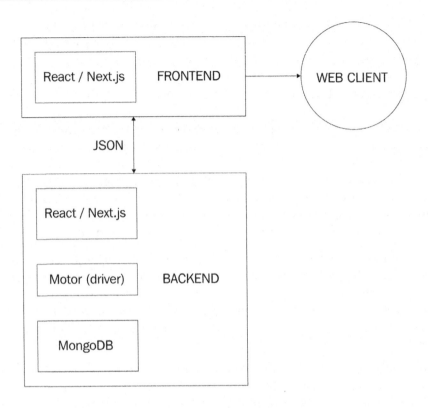

Figure 1.2 – The FARM stack

First of all, we want a streamlined and structured way of building UIs. React enables the developers to create dynamic applications in a much easier way by relying on JSX – a mix of JavaScript and XML that has an intuitive tag-based syntax and provides developers with a way to think of the application in terms of components that go on to form other, more complex, components, thus breaking the process of crafting complex user interfaces and interactions into smaller, more manageable steps.

The main benefits of using React as a frontend solution can be summarized as follows:

- **Performance**. By using the React virtual DOM, which operates in memory, React apps provide smooth and fast performance.

- **Reusability**: Since the app is built by using components that have their own properties and logic, we can write out components once and then reuse them as many times as needed, cutting down development time and complexity.

- **Ease of use**: This is always a bit subjective, but React is easy to get started. Advanced concepts and patterns require some level of proficiency, but even novice developers can reap immediate benefits just from the possibility of splitting the application frontend into components and then using them like LEGO bricks.

- **SPAs or SSR**: React and frameworks based on React empower us, the developers, to create Single-Page Applications that have a desktop-like look and feel but also server-side rendering that is beneficial for search engine optimization.

- **React-based frameworks**: Knowing our way around React enables us to benefit from some of today's most powerful frontend web frameworks such as Next.js, static site generators (such as Gatsby.js), or exciting and promising newcomers (such as React Remix).

- **Hooks system**: In version 16.8, the React library introduced *hooks* that enable the developers to use and manipulate the state of the components, along with some other features of React without the need to use classes. This is a big change that tackles (successfully) different issues: it enables the reusability of stateful logic between components and simplifies the understanding and management of complex components.

The simplest React hook is probably the `useState` hook – it enables us to have and maintain a stateful value (such as an object, array, or variable) throughout the life cycle of the component, without having to resort to old-school class-based components.

For instance, a very simple component that could be used for filtering search results when a user is trying to find the right car might contain the desired brand, model, and some production year range. This functionality would be a great candidate for a separate component – a search component that would need to maintain the state of different input controls – probably implemented as a series of dropdowns. Let's just see the simplest possible version of this implementation. We will create a simple functional component with a single stateful string value – an HTML select element that will update the stateful variable named brand:

```
import { useState } from "react";

const Search = () => {
  const [brand, setBrand] = useState("");
  return (
    <div>
      <div>Selected brand: {brand}</div>
      <select onChange={ (ev) =>
          setBrand(ev.target.value)}>
        <option value="">All brands</option>
        <option value="Fiat">Fiat</option>
        <option value="Ford">Ford</option>
        <option value="Renault">Renault</option>
        <option value="Opel">Opel</option>
      </select>
```

```
        </div>
     );
  };


  export default Search;
```

The bold line is where the hook magic happens, and it must be within the body of a function. The statement simply creates a new state variable, called brand, and provides us a setter function that can be used inside the component to set the desired value.

There are many hooks that solve different problems, and in this book, we will go over the fundamental ones. In this example, the state variable brand is available inside the component, and it could be tied to a query string that would enable the API to only return the results that conform to the filter defined by the state variable.

- **Declarative views**: In React, we do not have to worry about transitions or mutations of the DOM. React handles everything, and the only thing the developer has to do is to declare how the view looks and reacts.

- **No templating language**: React practically used JavaScript as a templating language (through JSX), so all you have to know in order to be able to use it effectively is some JavaScript, such as array manipulation and iteration.

- **Rich ecosystem**: There are numerous excellent libraries that complement React's basic functionality – from routers to custom hooks, external library integrations, CSS framework adaptations, and more.

In this book, we will not dive deep into React. Why not? Well, I believe that the UI is as important as any other part of the app – if your app is not user-friendly or downright ugly, nobody will want to have anything to do with it, no matter how much value it brings. However, that is not the emphasis of this book. The idea is just to get the ball rolling and see how all the different parts connect and fit within the bigger picture. So, we will keep the frontend part to a minimum. Another reason to choose React is because of its great community, so you are bound to have to deal with it someday if you haven't already, and to be quite honest, with the addition of React Hooks, at least for me, it has become very pleasant to work with. Hooks provide React with a new way of adding and sharing stateful logic across components and can even replace (in simpler cases) the need for Redux or other external state management libraries. We will make use of the Context API – a React feature that enables us to pass objects and functions down the component tree without the need of passing props through components that do not need it. Coupled with a hook – the useContext hook – it provides a straightforward way of passing and maintaining stateful values in every part of the app. Just being able to create declarative reusable components and parametrize them into functions was what got me interested – treating visual and UI components like functions with a state if you will. Compared to other frameworks, React is small.  It isn't even considered a framework but a library – actually, a couple of libraries. Still, it is a mature product with over 10 years of development behind it, created for the needs of Facebook, and the biggest internet companies such as Uber, Twitter, and Airbnb use and rely upon it.

Like FastAPI, which is based on the newest and coolest Python features and, thus, makes maximum use of what the language has to offer, React uses (although it is not imperative) the newest features of functional JavaScript, ES6, and ES7, particularly when it comes to arrays. As someone said, working with React improves our understanding of JavaScript, and a similar thing could be said of FastAPI and modern Python.

The final piece of the puzzle will be the choice of a CSS library or framework. In 2022, there are dozens of CSS libraries that play nice with React, ranging from Bootstrap, Material UI, Bulma, and more. Many of these libraries merge with React to become meaningful frameworks of prebuilt customizable and parametrized components. We will use Tailwind CSS as it is simple to set up – all the cool kids are using it, and it is intuitive once you get the hang of it, but more on that later.

Keeping the React part to a bare minimum should allow you, the reader, to focus more on the true protagonists of the story – FastAPI and MongoDB and their dance – and easily replace the React part, should you wish to do so, with anything else that rocks your boat, be it Svelte.js, Vue.js, or vanilla handcrafted ECMAScript.

However, you should know that by embracing or, at the very least, learning the basics of React (and Hooks), you are embarking on a wonderful web development adventure that will enable you to use and understand many tools and frameworks built on top of React.

Arguably, Next.js is the feature-richest server-side rendering React framework that enables fast development, filesystem-based routing, and more. Gatsby, a React-based static site generator, is a great tool for crafting blazingly fast sites and, coupled with a headless CMS, enables us to create simple and streamlined workflows suited for non-technical staff. React-Remix seems to be an interesting project, with a lot of the new React features baked in. Lastly, learning one major frontend framework, be it React, Svelte, or Vue, enables you to switch to another much easier one – the problems they are trying to solve are pretty much the same, and the solutions and underlying philosophies have many things in common even if the implementations might differ drastically.

## Summary

In this chapter, we laid the background for the FARM stack, from describing the role of each component to their strengths. Hopefully, I have managed to get you interested in exploring the FARM stack. Now you understand how to make a conscious and informed decision and adopt the FARM stack for your next project, and you can justify your choice within the context of a flexible and fluid web development project specification. In the next chapter, we will provide a fast-paced, concise, and actionable overview of MongoDB and its querying and aggregation functionalities, with emphasis on the Python ecosystem.

# 2

# Setting Up the Document Store with MongoDB

In this chapter, we are going to address some of the main features of MongoDB, building upon what was mentioned in the introductory chapter, and then we will dive into a practical introduction through several simple yet illustrative examples. After reviewing the process of installation on a local machine, using Windows or Ubuntu (which is probably the most popular Linux distribution today), and creating an online account on Atlas, we will be covering the basic commands of the MongoDB querying framework that enable us to start as quickly as possible. We will walk you through the essential commands (methods) that will enable you to insert, manage, query, update, and wrangle your data. The aim of this chapter is not to make you a MongoDB expert or even a proficient user, but just to help you see how easy it can be to set up a system—be it on your local machine or on the cloud—and perform the operations that might arise in a fast-paced web development process.

In this chapter, we will cover the following topics:

- The structure of a MongoDB database
- Installing MongoDB and friends
- MongoDB querying and CRUD operations
- Aggregation framework

By the end of this chapter, you will be able to set up a MongoDB database in a local or online environment, and you will know the basics of data modeling with the most popular NoSQL database. Topics such as querying (through MongoDB methods and aggregation) are best learned through playing around with data. In this chapter, we have provided a simple yet interesting real-life dataset that will be your starting point. Finally, this chapter should enable you to import your own data and apply the principles from the following pages, building upon them and coming up with your own queries, aggregations, and data insights.

# Technical requirements

MongoDB's latest version (version 5) requires Windows 10 64-bit or Windows Server 2019 or later. When it comes to Linux, the last three versions of Ubuntu (Debian) are supported. Any decent PC or laptop with at least 8 GB of RAM and a CPU not more than 5 years old should be more than enough to get you started. However, for full-stack development—which means having a couple of processes running simultaneously, compiling the frontend, maybe some CSS processor, having an editor (we will use VS Code), and a browser with a dozen tabs open—if possible, we would recommend 16 GB of RAM and a big screen (protect your eyes because unfortunately, they are not upgradeable!).

The supporting files for this chapter can be found at the following link: `https://github.com/PacktPublishing/Modern-Web-Development-with-the-FARM-Stack`.

# The structure of a MongoDB database

MongoDB is arguably the most used NoSQL database today – its power, ease of use, and versatility make it an excellent choice for large and small projects; its scalability and performance enable us to be certain that at least the data layer of our app has a very solid foundation.

In the following sections, we will take a deeper dive into the basic units of MongoDB: the document, the collection, and the database. Since this book is taking a bottom-up approach, we would like to start from the very bottom and present an overview of the simplest data structures available in MongoDB and then take it up from there into documents, collections, and so on.

## Documents

We have repeated numerous times that MongoDB is a document-oriented database, so let's take a look at what that actually means. If you are familiar with relational database tables (with columns and rows), you know that one unit of information is contained in a row, and we might say that the columns describe that data.

In MongoDB, we can make a rough analogy with the relational database row, but, since we do not have to adhere to a fixed set of columns, the model is much more flexible. In fact, it is as flexible as you want it to be, but you might not want to take things too far in that direction if you want to achieve some real functionality. This flexible document really is just an ordered set of keys and corresponding values. This structure, as we will explore later, corresponds with data structures in every programming language; in Python, we will see that this structure is a dictionary and lends itself perfectly to the flow of data of a web app or a desktop application.

The rules for creating documents are pretty simple: the key must be a string, a UTF-8 character with a few exceptions, and the document cannot contain multiple keys. We also have to keep in mind that MongoDB is case sensitive. Let's take a look at the following relatively simple valid MongoDB document, similar to the ones that we will be using throughout the chapter:

```
{
        {"_id":{"$oid":"62231e0a286b06fd01be579e"},
        "brand":"Hyundai",
        "make":"ix35",
        "year":2012,
      "price":9000,
      "km":143500
}
```

Apart from the first field, denoted by _id, which is the unique ID of the document, all of the other fields correspond to simple **JavaScript Object Notation (JSON)** fields—brand and make are strings (Hyundai, i35), whereas year, price and km (denoting the year of production, the price of the vehicle in euros, and the numbers of kilometers on the meter) are numbers (integers, to be precise).

So, what data types can we use in our documents? One of the first important decisions when designing any type of application is the choice of data types—we really do not want to use the wrong tools for the job at hand. Let's look at the most important data types in the following sections.

### Strings

Strings are probably the most basic and universal data type in MongoDB, and they are used to represent all text fields in a document. Bear in mind that text fields do not have to represent only strictly textual values; in our case, in the application that we will be building, most text fields will, in fact, denote a categorical variable, such as the brand of the car or the fact that the car has a manual or automatic transmission. This fact will come in handy if you are designing a data science application that has categorical or ordinal variables. As in JSON, text fields are wrapped in quotes. JSON files follow a dictionary-like structure with a string, numbers, arrays, and Booleans of key-value pairs. An example of a string variable called name encoded in JSON would be the following:

```
"name":"Marko"
```

Text fields can be indexed in order to speed up searching and they are searchable with standard regular expressions, which makes them a powerful tool able to process even massive amounts of text.

### Numbers

MongoDB supports different types of numbers:

- **int**: 32-bit signed integers
- **decimal**: 128-bit floating point
- **long**: 64-bit unsigned integer
- **double**: 64-bit floating point

Every MongoDB driver takes care of transforming data types according to the programming language that is used to interface, so we shouldn't worry about conversions except in particular cases that will not be covered here.

### Booleans

This is the standard Boolean true or false value; they are written without quotes since we do not want them to be interpreted as strings.

### Objects or embedded documents

This is where the magic happens. Object fields in MongoDB represent nested or embedded documents and their values are other valid JSON documents. These embedded documents can have other embedded documents inside, and this seemingly simple capability allows for complex data modeling. An example would be if we wanted to embed the salesman responsible for a particular car, added in bold in the following example:

```
{
        {"_id":{"$oid":"62231e0a286b06fd01be579e"},
        "brand":"Hyundai",
        "make":"ix35",
        "year":2012,
        "price":9000,
        "km":143500,
        "salesman":{
                "name":"Marko",
                {"_id":{"$oid":"62231e0a286b87fd01be579e"},
                "active":true
                        }
}
```

## Arrays

Arrays can contain zero or more values in a list-like structure. The elements of the array can be any MongoDB data type including other documents. They are zero-based and particularly suited for making **embedded relationships** – we could, for instance, store all of the post comments inside the blog post document itself, along with a timestamp and the user that made the comment. In our example, a document representing a car could contain a list of salesmen responsible for that vehicle, a list of customer requests for additional information regarding the car, and so on. Arrays can benefit from the standard JavaScript array methods for fast editing, pushing, and others.

## ObjectIds

Every document in MongoDB has a unique 12-byte ID that is used to identify it, even across different machines, and serves as a primary key. This field is autogenerated by MongoDB every time we insert a new document, but it can also be provided manually – something that we will not do. These ObjectIds are extensively used as keys for traditional relationships – for instance, every salesperson in our application could have a list of ObjectIds, each corresponding to a car that the person is trying to sell. ObjectIds are automatically indexed.

## Dates

Though JSON does not support date types and stores them as plain strings, MongoDB's BSON format supports date types explicitly. They represent the 64-bit number of milliseconds since the Unix epoch (January 1, 1970). All dates are stored in UTC and have no time zone associated.

## Binary data

Binary data fields can store arbitrary binary data and are the only way to save non-UTF-8 strings to a database. These fields can be used in conjunction with MongoDB's GridFS filesystem to store images, for example. Although, there are better and more cost-effective solutions for that, as we will see.

Other data types worth mentioning are null – which can represent a null value or a nonexistent field, and we can store even JavaScript functions.

When it comes to nesting documents within documents, MongoDB supports 100 levels of nesting, which is a limit you really shouldn't be testing in your designs, at least in the beginning.

Documents in MongoDB are the basic unit of data and as such, they should be modeled carefully when trying to use the database-specific nature to our advantage. Documents should be as self-contained as possible and MongoDB, in fact, encourages a good amount of data denormalization. As MongoDB was built with the purpose of providing developers with a flexible data structure that should be able to fit the processes of data flow in a web application as easily as possible, you should think in terms of objects and not tables, rows, and columns.

If a certain page needs to perform several different queries in order to get all the data needed for the page and then perform some combine operation, your application is bound to slow down. On the other hand, if your page greedily returns a bunch of data in a single query and the code then needs to go over this result set in order to filter the data that is actually needed, memory consumption will likely rise, and this can lead to a potential problem and slow operations. So, like almost everywhere, there is a sweet spot; a locally optimal solution, if you will.

In this book, we will be using a simple example with automobiles for sale and the documents representing the unit (a car, really) are going to be rather straightforward.

We can think of a scenario where users can post comments or reviews on these cars and the SQL-ish way to do it would be to create a many-to-many relationship; a car can have multiple user comments and a user can leave comments or ratings on multiple cars. To retrieve all of the comments for a particular car, we would then have to perform a join by using that car's primary key, entering the relationship table, and finding all of the comment IDs. Finally, we would use these comment IDs to filter the comments from the table that stores all of the comments, find their IDs, authors, the actual comments, ratings, and so on.

In MongoDB, we can simply store the comments in an array of BSON objects embedded in the car document. As the user clicks on a particular car page, MongoDB performs one single find query and fetches the car data and all of the associated comments, ready to be displayed. Of course, if we want to make a user profile page and display all of the data and the comments and reviews made by the user, we wouldn't want to have to scan through all of the cars in the database and check if there are comments. In this case, it would probably be wise to have a separate collection that would store only users, their profiles, and the comments (storage is cheap!). **Data modeling** is the process of defining how our data will be stored and what relationships and types of relationships should exist between different documents in our data.

Now that we have an idea of what type of fields are available in MongoDB and how we might want to map our business logic to a (flexible) schema, it is time to introduce collections – groups of documents and a counterpart to a table in the SQL world.

## Collections and databases

With the notion of the schema flexibility already repeated several times, you might be asking yourself if multiple collections are even necessary? Indeed, if we can store any kind of heterogeneous documents in a single collection (and MongoDB says we can), why bother with separate collections? There are several reasons as follows:

- Different kinds (structures) of documents in a single collection make development very difficult. We could add fields denoting different kinds of documents, but this just brings overhead and performance issues. Besides, every application, whether web-based or not, needs to have some structure.

- It is much faster (by orders of magnitude) than querying for the document type.

- **Data locality**: Grouping documents of the same type in a collection will require less disk seek time, and considering that indexing is defined by collection, the querying is much more efficient.

Although a single instance of MongoDB can host several databases at once, it is considered good practice to keep all of the document collections used in an application inside a single database. When we install MongoDB, there will be three databases created and their names cannot be used for our application database: admin, local, and config. *They are built-in databases that shouldn't be replaced, so avoid accidentally naming your database the same way.*

After reviewing the basic fields, units, and structures that we are able to use in MongoDB, it is time to learn how to set up a MongoDB database server on our computer and how to create an online account on MongoDB.com. The local setup is excellent for quick prototyping that doesn't even require an internet connection (though in 2022 that shouldn't be a problem) and the online database-as-a-service Atlas provides several benefits.

First, it is easy to set up, and, as we will see, you can get up and running literally in minutes with a generous free tier database ready for work. Atlas takes away much of the manual setup and guarantees availability. Other benefits include the involvement of the MongoDB team (which tries to implement best practices), high security by default with access control, firewalls and granular access control, automated backups (depending on the tier), and the possibility to be productive right away.

## Installing MongoDB and friends

The MongoDB ecosystem is composed of different pieces of software, and I remember that when I was starting to play with it, there was some confusion. It is, in fact, quite straightforward as we will see. Let's examine the following various components that we will be installing or using in the following part:

- **MongoDB Community Edition** – a free full-fledged version of MongoDB that runs on all major operating systems (Linux, Windows, or macOS) and it is what we are going to use to play around with data locally.

- **MongoDB Compass** – a **graphical user interface** (**GUI**) for managing, querying, aggregating, and analyzing MongoDB data in a visual environment. Compass is a mature and useful tool that we'll be using throughout our initial querying and aggregation explorations.

- **MongoDB Atlas** – the *database-as-a-service* solution from MongoDB. To be honest, this is one of the main reasons MongoDB is a huge part of the FARM stack. It is relatively easy to set up and it relieves us from manually administering the database.

- **MongoDB Shell** – a command-line shell that we can use not only to perform simple **Create, Read, Update, Delete (CRUD)** operations on our database, but also to perform administrative tasks such as creating and deleting databases, starting and stopping services, and similar jobs.

- **MongoDB Database Tools** – several command-line utilities that enable administrators and developers to export or import data to and from a database, provide diagnostics, or enable manipulation of files stored in MongoDB's GridFS system.

The MongoDB ecosystem is constantly evolving, and it is quite possible that when you read these pages, the latest version numbers will be higher or some utility might have changed its name. MongoDB recently released a product called *Realm*, which is a real-time development platform useful for building mobile apps or **Internet of Things (IoT)** applications, for instance. We will not cover all of the steps necessary to install all the required software as we do not find a huge stack of screenshots particularly inspiring. We will instead focus on the overall procedure and try to pinpoint the key steps that are necessary in order to have a fully functional installation.

## Installing MongoDB and Compass on Windows

We will be installing the latest version of MongoDB Community Edition, which at the time of writing is 5.0.6. The minimum requirements listed on the website for the Windows edition are Windows 10 or later, 64-bit editions, or Windows Server 2019. It is important to note that MongoDB supports *only 64-bit* versions of these platforms. To install MongoDB and Compass, you can refer to the following steps, although we strongly advise you to look at the instructions on the MongoDB website as well, as they might slightly change:

1.  To download the installer, head over to the download page at `https://www.mongodb.com/try/download/community`, select the **Windows** version, and click on **Download** as follows:

Figure 2.1 – Selecting the latest Windows 64-bit installer from the MongoDB download page

2.  When the file is downloaded, locate it on your computer and execute it. If a security prompt asks **Open Executable File**, select **Yes** and proceed to the MongoDB setup wizard. The wizard will open the following page:

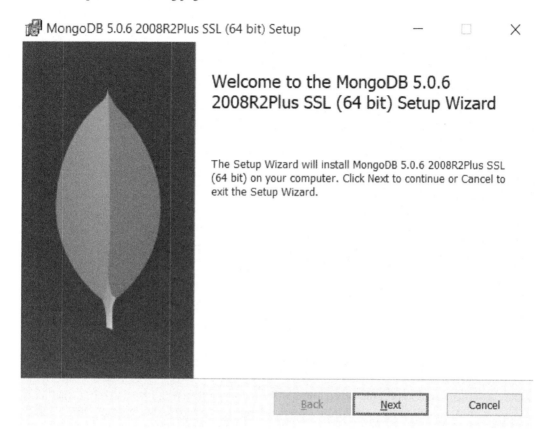

Figure 2.2 – Starting the MongoDB installer

3.  Read the license agreement, select the checkbox, and then click on **Next**.

4.  This is an important screen. When asked which type of setup to choose, select **Complete**, as follows:

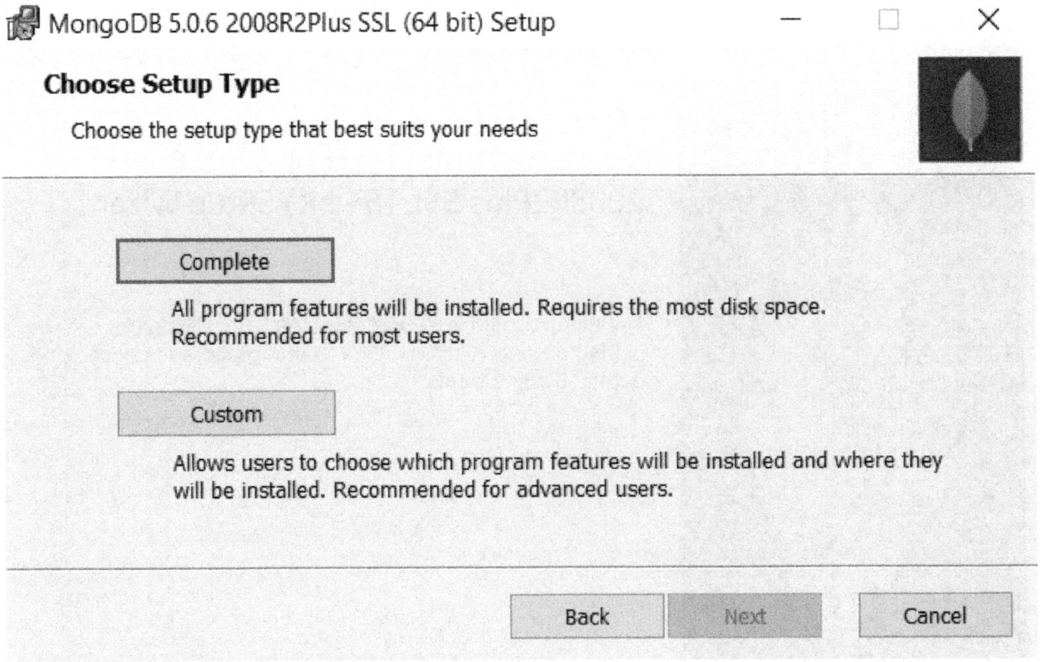

Figure 2.3 – Selecting the Complete installation – click Complete, then Next

5.  Another rather important screen follows. The following screen allows us to select whether we want MongoDB to run as a Windows network service (we do) and we can select the data and log directories. We will leave the default values as follows:

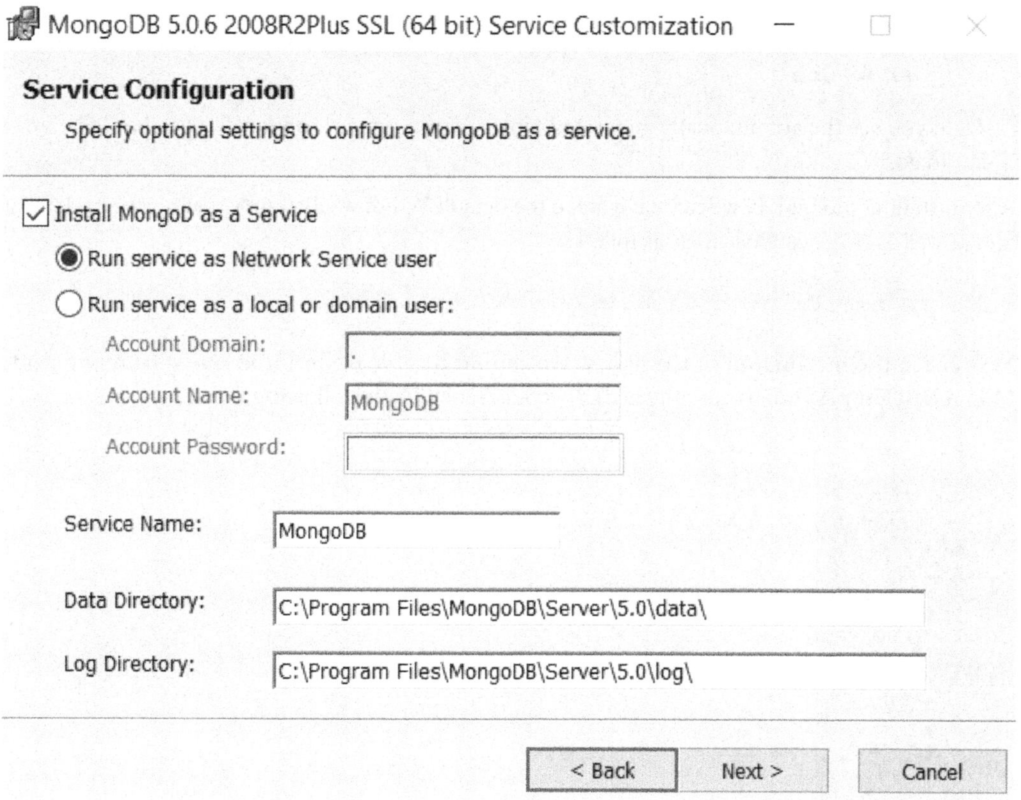

Figure 2.4 – The MongoDB service customization screen with the desired (default) values

*Figure 2.4* shows that we want to select **Install MongoDB**—the MongoDB daemon—as a Windows service, which basically means that we will not have to start it manually. The rest of the settings are left as default as well as **Data Directory** and **Log Directory**.

6. Another screen will ask you if you want to install Compass, MongoDB's GUI tool for database management. Please check the checkbox and proceed to install it.

7. Finally, the **User Account Control** (**UAC**) Windows warning screen will pop up, and you should select **Yes**.

8. At this point, we should be able to test whether MongoDB is running (as a service), so enter the following command in the command prompt of your choice (we like to use *cmder*, available at `https://cmder.app`) and type the following:

```
mongo
```

9.    You should see various notifications and a tiny prompt denoted with >. Try typing the following:

```
show dbs
```

If you see the automatically generated tables *admin*, *config*, and *locals*, you should be good to go.

After installing MongoDB, we can navigate to the default Windows directory that hosts our database files as well as the executable files, as follows:

```
C:\Program Files\MongoDB\Server\5.0
```

Let's check the installation of Compass. We should be able to find it in our start menu under **MongoDBCompass** (all words attached). It should look like the following:

Figure 2.5 – The initial screen of MongoDB Compass

If we just click the *green* **Connect** button, without pasting or typing in any connection string, Compass will connect to the local MongoDB service and we should be able to see all of the databases that we saw when we used the command line with MongoDB: admin, db, and local.

The last local installation that we can and should execute is for a group of utilities called **MongoDB Database Tools**. You should just head over to https://www.mongodb.com/try/download/database-tools and select the latest version (at the time of writing, it is 100.5.2). The actual download page contains all of the MongoDB-related files and looks like the following:

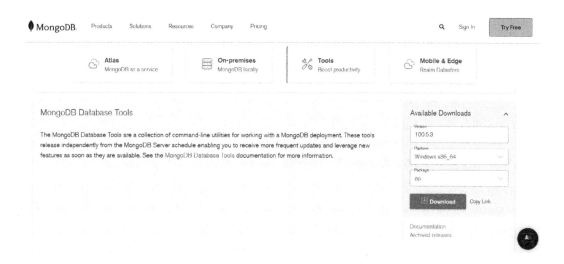

Figure 2.6 – The MongoDB downloads page

Once you have scrolled to the **MongoDB Database Tools** tab, you will be presented with a small box on the right – titled **Available Downloads**. You should choose the latest version, check your platform (in our case it is **Windows x86_64**) and the .msi Windows package installer, as follows:

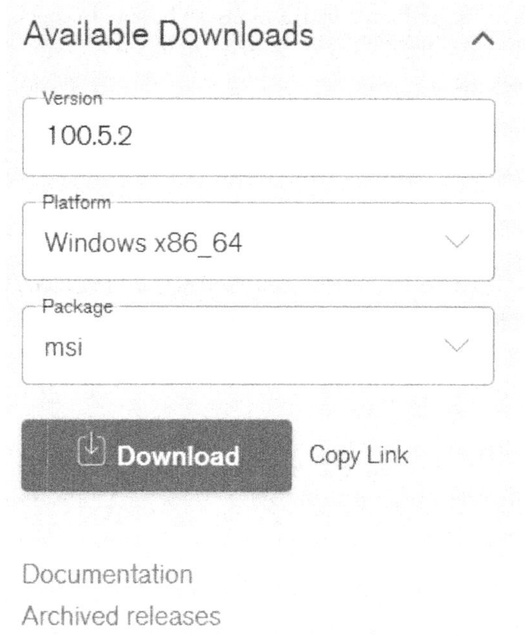

## Available Downloads ⌃

Version
100.5.2

Platform
Windows x86_64

Package
msi

⬇ Download    Copy Link

Documentation
Archived releases

Figure 2.7 – The MongoDB Database Tools download page

Be careful to select the `.msi` package and run the installer using the standard procedure (accept the agreement, confirm the UAC popup, and so on).

The only modification that you should do, although it is not mandatory, is to select the `bin` directory in the previously installed MongoDB folder. This will facilitate the use of the utilities, although we will mostly use Compass to start playing with some data.

Now we will go through the process of installing MongoDB on a standard Linux distribution.

## Installing MongoDB and Compass on Linux – Ubuntu

Linux offers numerous benefits for the development and management of local servers, but most importantly, should you decide that the database-as-a-service of MongoDB isn't what you want to use anymore, you will probably be going to work on a Linux-based server.

In this book, we will go over the installation process on Ubuntu version 20.4 LTS (Focal), while the MongoDB version supports the last three **long-term support** (**LTS**) versions on x86_64 architecture (Focal, Bionic, and Xenial). As in the earlier paragraph for Windows 10, we will list the necessary steps here, but you should always check the MongoDB Ubuntu installation page for last-minute changes. The process, however, shouldn't change.

The following actions are to be performed in a Bash shell. We are going to download the public key that will allow us to install MongoDB, then we will create a list file and reload the package manager. Similar steps are required for other Linux distributions, so be sure to check them on your distribution of choice's website. Finally, we will perform the actual installation of MongoDB through the package manager and start the service.

It is always preferable to skip the packages provided by the Linux distribution as they are often not updated to the latest version. Perform the following steps to install MongoDB on Ubuntu:

1. You should import the public key used by the package manager as follows:

```
wget -qO - https://www.mongodb.org/static/pgp/server-5.0.asc | sudo apt-key add -
```

2. After the preceding step has finished installing, you have to create a list file for MongoDB as follows:

```
echo "deb [ arch=amd64,arm64 ] https://repo.mongodb.org/apt/ubuntu focal/mongodb-org/5.0 multiverse" | sudo tee /etc/apt/sources.list.d/mongodb-org-5.0.list
```

3. Reload the package manager as follows:

```
sudo apt-get update
```

4.  Finally, install MongoDB as follows:

```
sudo apt-get install -y mongodb-org
```

If you follow these instructions and install MongoDB through the package manager, the `/var/lib/mongodb` data directory and the `/var/log/mongodb` log directory will be created during the installation.

5.  Start the `mongod` process using the `systemctl` process manager as follows:

```
sudo systemctl start mongod
sudo systemctl daemon-reload
```

6.  You should be able to start using the MongoDB shell by typing the following command:

```
mongosh
```

If you have issues with the installation, our first advice would be to visit the MongoDB Linux installation page, but MongoDB isn't particularly different than any other Linux software when it comes to installation and process management.

## Setting up Atlas

**MongoDB Atlas**—a cloud service by MongoDB—is one of the strongest selling points of MongoDB. As their website puts it:

*Database-as-a-Service, is one of the many -as-a-Service web development stages that have been running in the Cloud over the last decade (we also have platforms as a service and others). It just means that all or most part of the database administration and installation work is offloaded to a cloud service in a highly simplified, customizable and optimized procedure. It allows for a fast start, but also offers sensible and often optimal defaults when it comes to security, scalability and performance.*

Atlas is a cloud database that manages all the hard work and abstracts the majority of operations such as deployment, management, and diagnostics while running on a provider of our choice (AWS, GCP, or Azure).

We believe that the processes of signing up and setting up a MongoDB Atlas instance are very well documented on the site at `https://www.mongodb.com/basics/mongodb-atlas-tutorial`.

After setting up the account (we used a Gmail address so we can log in with a Google account – it's faster), you will be prompted to create a cluster. You will select a **Shared Cluster**, which is free and you should select the **Cloud Provider & Region** as close to your physical location as possible in order to minimize latency. After a couple of minutes, you will be greeted by an administration page that can be a bit overwhelming at first. We will just walk you through the important screens. To set up Atlas, perform the following steps:

1.  Select a free M0 sandbox, as shown in the following screenshot:

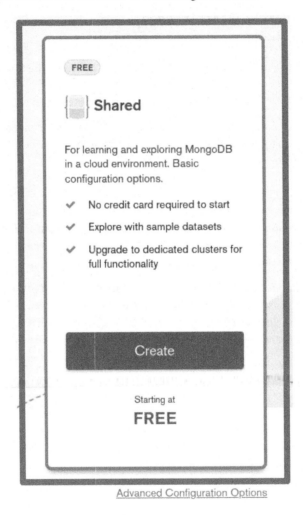

Figure 2.8 – Choose the Shared Cluster on MongoDB Atlas

2.  Give your cluster a meaningful name, choose the nearest location in order to minimize latency, and then choose the **Shared** option as follows:

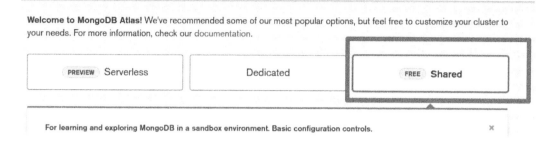

Figure 2.9 – Atlas deployment options

3.  In the menu, create a new database user, choose **Password** as the authentication method, and create them in the following fields. Later, you can let Atlas autogenerate a super secure password for you, but for now, choose something that will be easy to remember also when creating the connection string for Compass and the later Python connectors.

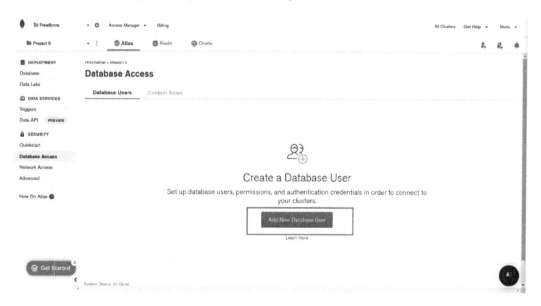

Figure 2.10 – The Database Access screen

4.  In this step, select a cloud provider and a region. It is advisable to select the region nearest to your geographical location in order to have the fastest response.

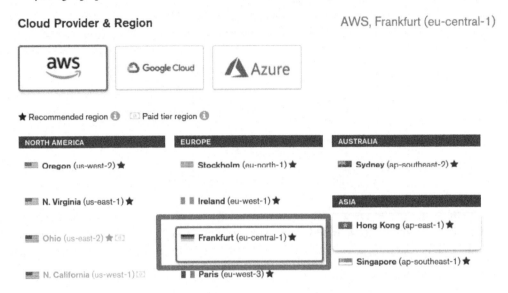

Figure 2.11 – The Cloud Provider & Region screen

5.  Finally, you should select the desired cluster tier. Since we want to begin with a free tier, you should select the **M0 Sandbox** option (shared RAM, 512 MB Storage). Do not worry, you can always change the plan later, and the free tier will be more than sufficient for your initial projects.

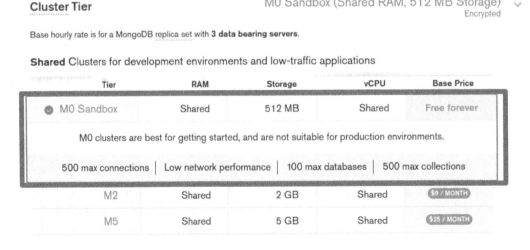

Figure 2.12 – Select the M0 Sandbox

6.   Then go ahead and add a name for the cluster as shown in the following screenshot:

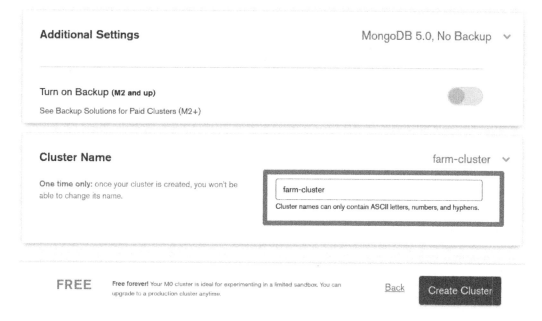

**Additional Settings**                                    MongoDB 5.0, No Backup ∨

Turn on Backup (M2 and up)

See Backup Solutions for Paid Clusters (M2+)

**Cluster Name**                                           farm-cluster ∨

One time only: once your cluster is created, you won't be       farm-cluster
able to change its name.
                                                          Cluster names can only contain ASCII letters, numbers, and hyphens.

FREE   Free forever! Your M0 cluster is ideal for experimenting in a limited sandbox. You can      Back      Create Cluster
       upgrade to a production cluster anytime.

Figure 2.13 – Type a meaningful name for your new cluster

The name isn't really important at this point, but soon you will have more clusters and it is wise to start naming them properly from the beginning.

7.   When you create a new database user, you will be presented with several options for authentication. In this phase, select **Password** as the authentication method (the first option). In the text boxes that will be underneath it, you should insert your username and password combination. These credentials will be used to access your online database.

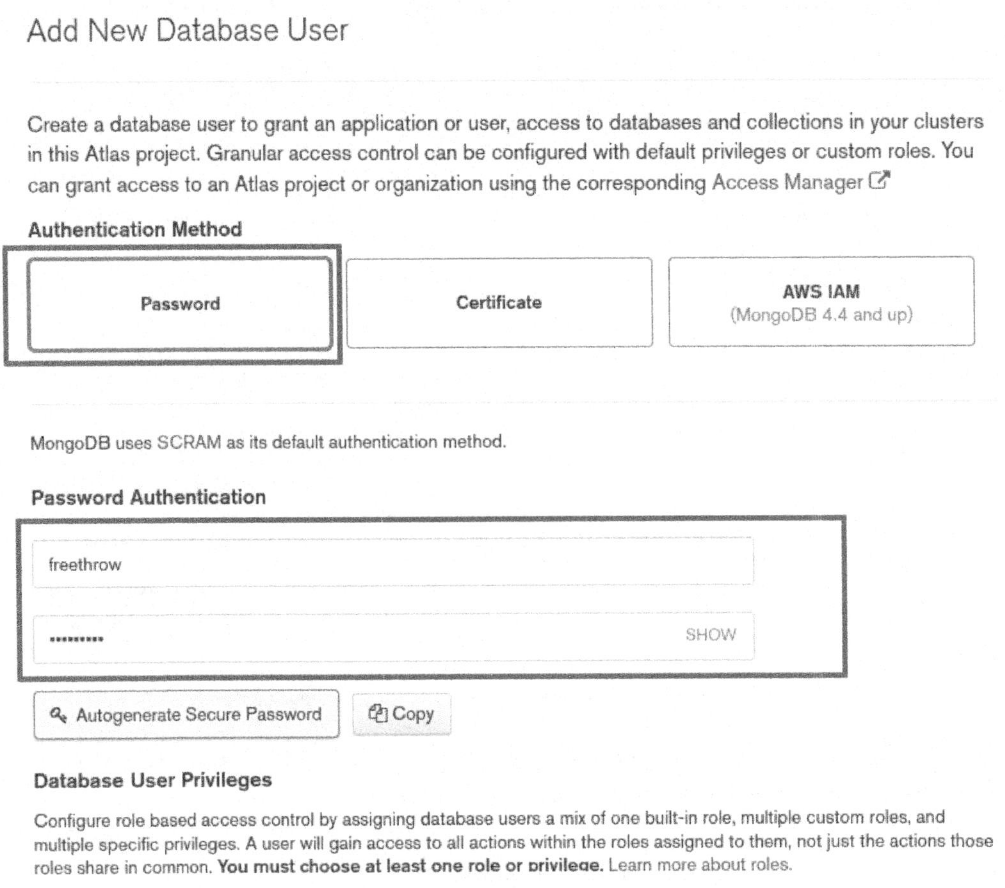

## Add New Database User

Create a database user to grant an application or user, access to databases and collections in your clusters in this Atlas project. Granular access control can be configured with default privileges or custom roles. You can grant access to an Atlas project or organization using the corresponding Access Manager 🗗

### Authentication Method

| Password | Certificate | AWS IAM (MongoDB 4.4 and up) |
|---|---|---|

MongoDB uses SCRAM as its default authentication method.

### Password Authentication

```
freethrow
```

```
••••••••                                                    SHOW
```

🔑 Autogenerate Secure Password      📋 Copy

### Database User Privileges

Configure role based access control by assigning database users a mix of one built-in role, multiple custom roles, and multiple specific privileges. A user will gain access to all actions within the roles assigned to them, not just the actions those roles share in common. **You must choose at least one role or privilege.** Learn more about roles.

Figure 2.14 – Choose a username and password

8    The created user won't be of much use if you do not give them the privileges to read and write, so check that in the built-in roles dropdown as follows:

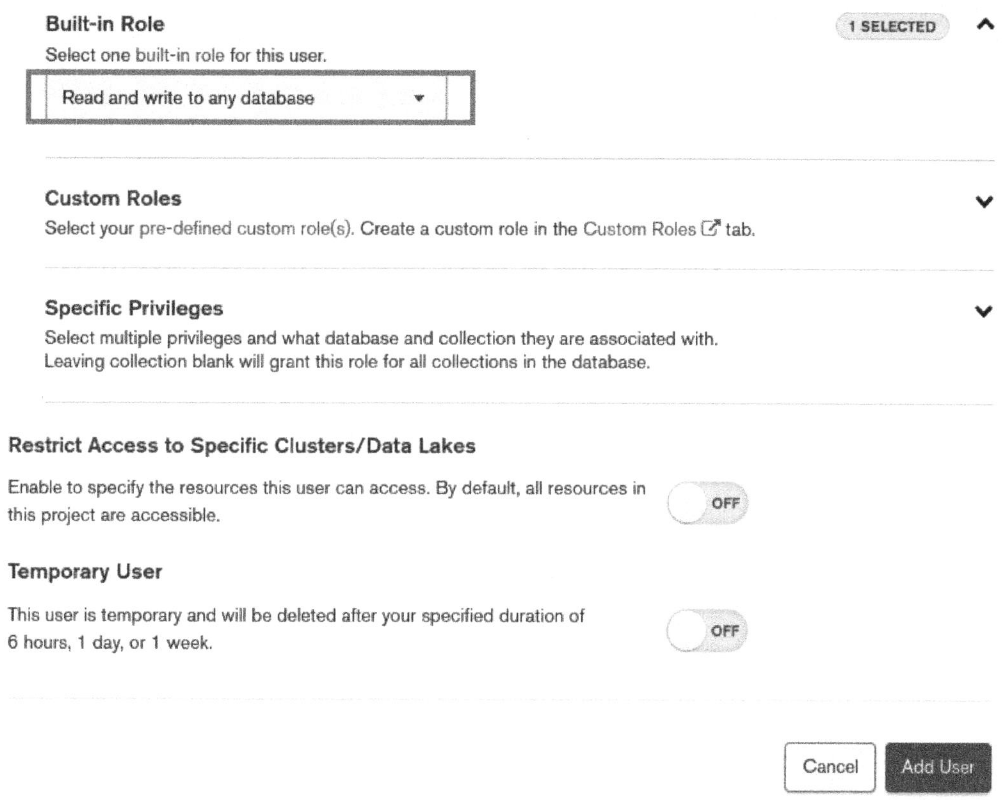

**Built-in Role**

1 SELECTED   ^

Select one built-in role for this user.

| Read and write to any database ▼ |

**Custom Roles**                                                                    ⌄

Select your pre-defined custom role(s). Create a custom role in the Custom Roles ⎘ tab.

**Specific Privileges**                                                             ⌄

Select multiple privileges and what database and collection they are associated with.
Leaving collection blank will grant this role for all collections in the database.

**Restrict Access to Specific Clusters/Data Lakes**

Enable to specify the resources this user can access. By default, all resources in      OFF
this project are accessible.

**Temporary User**

This user is temporary and will be deleted after your specified duration of            OFF
6 hours, 1 day, or 1 week.

Cancel     Add User

Figure 2.15 – Select read and write for the new user

## Importing (and exporting) data with Compass

Now, we cannot have even a vague idea of what we can or cannot do with our data if we don't have
any data to begin with. In the GitHub repository of the book, in the `chapter2` folder, you will find
a **comma-separated values** (**CSV**) file called `cars_data.csv`.

Download the file and save it somewhere handy. To understand the data importing and exporting
process, perform the following steps:

1. After you open Compass and click on **Connect**, *without entering a connection string*, you will
   be connected to the local instance of MongoDB that is running as a service on your computer.

2.  Click on the **Create Database** button and insert the database name `carsDB` and the collection name `cars`, as follows:

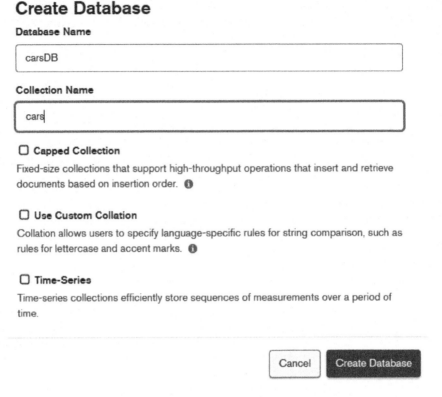

Figure 2.16 – The Create Database screen

3.  After this step, a new database should be available in the left-hand menu, called **carsDB**. Select this database on the left and you will see that we created a collection called **cars**. In fact, we cannot have a database without collections. There is a big **Import Data** button in the middle, and you will use it to open a dialog as follows:

Figure 2.17 – The Import Data button in Compass

4. After hitting the **Import Data** button, locate the previously downloaded CSV file and you will be presented with the opportunity to tune the types of the individual columns as follows:

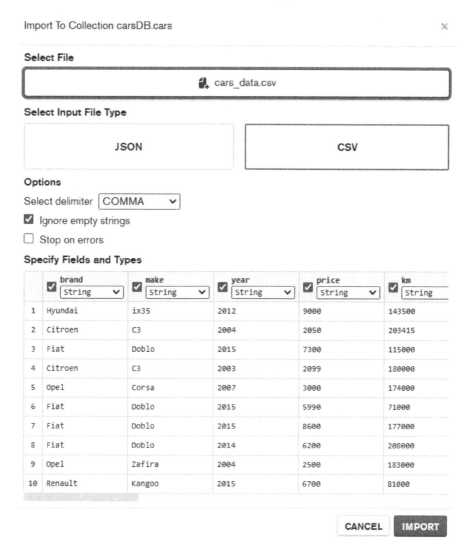

Figure 2.18 – The screen for selecting the file to be imported

This is important, especially because we're importing initial data and we do not want to have integers or floating numbers being interpreted as strings. The MongoDB drivers, such as Motor and PyMongo, that we will be using are "smart" enough to figure out the appropriate data types; however, when dealing with Compass or similar GUI database tools, it is imperative that you take the time to examine all of the data columns and select the appropriate data types.

This particular file that we imported contains data about 7,323 cars and the default for all the fields is *string*. We made the following modifications when importing:

- Set the columns **year**, **price**, **km**, **kW**, **cm3**, and **standard** to **Number**

- Set the **imported** and **registered** columns to **Boolean**

The names of the columns are pretty self-explanatory, but we will examine them more later. Now, once you hit the **Import** button, you should have a pretty decent collection with a little over 7,000 documents, each having an identical structure that we believe will facilitate the understanding of the operations that we are going to perform later on.

Later, we will see how we can use Compass to run queries and aggregations and export the data in CSV or JSON formats in a pretty similar way to the import that we just did. We suggest that you play around with the interface and experiment a bit. You can always delete the collection and the database, and then redo our data import from the CSV file from the repository.

Now, we will show you how you can connect your Mongo Atlas online database instance to Compass and use the GUI in the exact same way in order to manipulate the online database that we created when we made the Atlas account. Perform the following steps:

1.   In order to make Compass connect to a local instance of MongoDB, you do not need to provide any connection string. To connect to an Atlas instance, however, you should head over to the **Database Deployments** page on Atlas and click on the **Connect** button as follows:

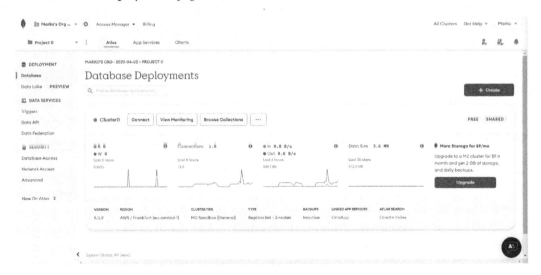

Figure 2.19 – Atlas and Compass connect popup page

2.   After clicking on the **Connect** button, select **Connect to Compass**, the latest version, and you will be presented with the following screen:

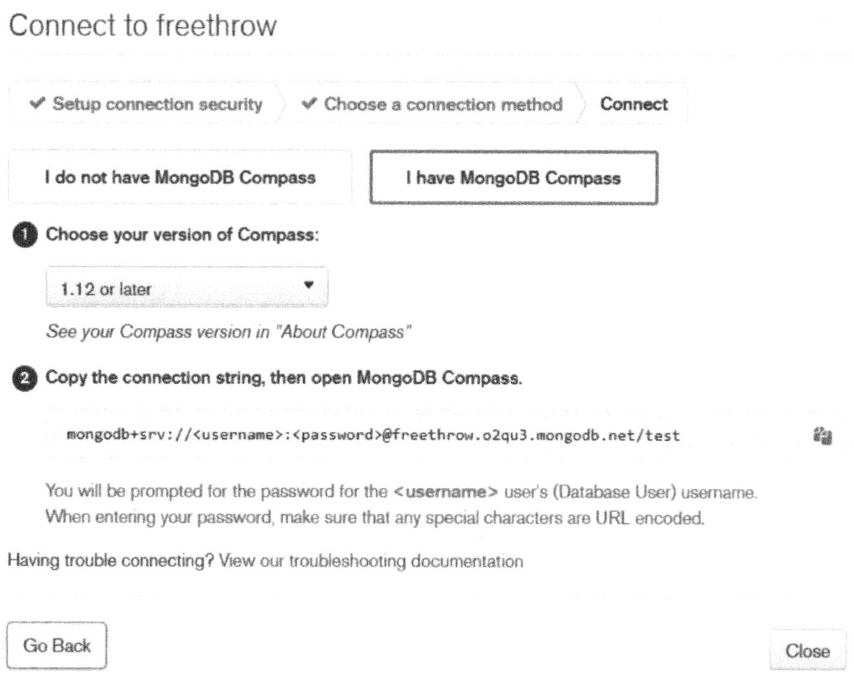

Connect to freethrow

✔ Setup connection security  〉 ✔ Choose a connection method  〉 **Connect**

I do not have MongoDB Compass          **I have MongoDB Compass**

**1** **Choose your version of Compass:**

1.12 or later                ▼

*See your Compass version in "About Compass"*

**2** **Copy the connection string, then open MongoDB Compass.**

mongodb+srv://<username>:<password>@freethrow.o2qu3.mongodb.net/test

You will be prompted for the password for the **<username>** user's (Database User) username.
When entering your password, make sure that any special characters are URL encoded.

Having trouble connecting? View our troubleshooting documentation

Go Back                                                Close

Figure 2.20 – Connection string

3.  The connection string, beginning with `mongodb+srv://`, will be at the bottom of the screen. You should copy it, replace the `<username>` and `<password>` with your actual username and password that you previously created, and paste it in the initial screen of Compass in the **New Connection** field. You should be able to connect!

Phew! We understand that this section was a bit overwhelming, but now you should have a fully functional instance of the world's most popular NoSQL database on your machine. You have also created an online account and managed to create your very own cluster, ready to take on most data challenges and power your web app. Now it is time to start exploring the bread and butter of MongoDB: querying, creating new documents, updating, and deleting.

## MongoDB querying and CRUD operations

After all this setting up, downloading, and installing, it is finally time to see MongoDB in action and try to get what all the fuss is about. In this section, we will show, through some simple examples, the most essential MongoDB commands. Though simple, these methods will enable us, the developers, to take control of our data, create new documents, query documents by using different criteria and conditions, perform simple and more complex aggregations, and output data in various forms. You might say that the real fun begins here!

Although we will be talking to MongoDB through our Python drivers (Motor and PyMongo), we believe that it is better to learn how to write queries directly. We will begin by querying the data that we have imported, as we believe that it is a more realistic scenario than just starting to make up artificial data, then we will go through the process of creating new data – inserting, updating, and so on. Let's first define our two options for executing MongoDB commands as follows:

- Compass interface
- MongoDB shell

We will now set up both options for working and executing commands on our local database and the cloud database on Atlas as well. Perform the following steps:

1.  In a shell session (Command Prompt on Windows or Bash on Linux), run the following command:

    ```
    mongo
    ```

2.  As earlier described when we were testing if the installation succeeded, we are going to be greeted with a minimal prompt: >. Let's see whether our *carsDB* database is still present and type the following command:

    ```
    show dbs
    ```

    This command should list all of the available databases: admin, carsDB (our database), config, and local.

3.  In order to use our database, let's type the following code:

    ```
    use carsDB
    ```

    The console will respond with „switched to db carsDB" and that means that now we can query and work on our database.

4.  To see the available collections inside the carsDB, try the following code:

    ```
    show collections
    ```

You should be able to see our only collection, *cars*, the one in which we dumped our 7,000+ documents from the downloaded CSV file. Now that we have our database and collection available, we can proceed and explore some querying options.

With Compass, we just have to start the program and click on the **Connect** button, without pasting the connection string. After that, you should be able to see all of the aforementioned databases in the left-hand menu and you can just select carsDB and then the cars collection, which resembles a folder inside the carsDB database.

Let's start with some basic querying!

## Querying MongoDB

As we mentioned earlier, MongoDB relies on a query language that is based on methods, rather than SQL. This query language has different methods that operate on collections and take parameters as JavaScript objects that define the query. We believe it is much easier to see how querying works, so let's try out some basic queries. We know we have over 7,000 documents in our carsDB database, and these are real documents that, at a certain point in time a couple of years ago, defined real ads of a used cars sales website. We chose this dataset, or at least a part of it, because we believe that working with *real data* with some *expected query results*, and not abstract or artificial data, helps reinforce the acquired notions and makes understanding the underlying processes easier and more thorough.

The most frequent MongoDB query language commands—and the ones that we will be covering—are the following:

- find(): A query for finding and selecting documents matching simple or complex criteria
- insertOne(): Inserts a new document into the collection
- insertMany(): Inserts an array of documents into the collection
- updateOne() and updateMany(): Update one or more documents according to some criteria
- deleteOne() and deleteMany(): Delete documents from the collection

As you can see, the MongoDB query methods closely match the HTTP verbs of a REST API!

We have over 7,000 documents, so let's take a look at them. To query for all the documents, type in the MongoDB shell the following command:

```
db.cars.find()
```

The preceding command will print several documents as follows:

```
{ "_id" : ObjectId("622c7b636a78b3d3538fb967"), "brand" :
"Fiat", "make" : "Doblo", "year" : 2015, "price" : 5700, "km"
: 77000, "gearbox" : "M", "doors" : "4/5", "imported" : false,
"kW" : 66, "cm3" : 1248, "fuel" : "diesel", "registered" :
true, "color" : "WH", "aircon" : "1", "damage" : "0", "car_
type" : "PU", "standard" : 5, "drive" : "F" }
{ "_id" : ObjectId("622c7b636a78b3d3538fb968"), "brand" :
"Fiat", "make" : "Doblo", "year" : 2015, "price" : 7500, "km"
: 210000, "gearbox" : "M", "doors" : "4/5", "imported" : false,
"kW" : 66, "cm3" : 1248, "fuel" : "diesel", "registered" :
false, "color" : "WH", "aircon" : "2", "damage" : "0", "car_
type" : "PU", "standard" : 5, "drive" : "F" }
{ "_id" : ObjectId("622c7b636a78b3d3538fb969"), "brand" :
```

```
"BMW", "make" : "316", "year" : 2013, "price" : 10800, "km" :
199000, "gearbox" : "M", "doors" : "4/5", "imported" : false,
"kW" : 85, "cm3" : 1995, "fuel" : "diesel", "registered" :
true, "color" : "VAR", "aircon" : "2", "damage" : "0", "car_
type" : "SW", "standard" : 6, "drive" : "B" }
{ "_id" : ObjectId("622c7b636a78b3d3538fb96a"), "brand" :
"Citroen", "make" : "C3", "year" : 2010, "price" : 3200, "km"
: 142000, "gearbox" : "M", "doors" : "4/5", "imported" : false,
"kW" : 50, "cm3" : 1398, "fuel" : "diesel", "registered" :
true, "color" : "WH", "aircon" : "2", "damage" : "0", "car_
type" : "HB", "standard" : 4, "drive" : "F" }
```

The console will print the message Type „it" for more as the console prints out only 20 items at a time. This statement could be interpreted as a classic SELECT * FROM TABLE in the SQL world. Let's see how we can restrict our query and return only cars made in 2019 (it should be the last available year, as the dataset isn't really fresh). In the command prompt, issue the following command:

```
db.cars.find({year:2019})
```

The results should now contain only documents that satisfy the condition that the year key is equal to 2019. This is one of the keys or CSV fields that, when importing, we have set to the numeric type.

The JavaScript object that we used in the previous query is a *filter*, and it can have numerous key-value pairs with which we define our query method. MongoDB has many operators that enable us to query fields with more complex conditions than plain equality, and their updated documentation is available on the MongoDB site at https://docs.mongodb.com/manual/reference/operator/query/.

We invite you to visit the page and look around some of the operators as they can give you an idea of how you might be able to structure your queries. We will try combining a couple of them to get a feel for it.

Let's say we want to find all Ford cars made in 2016 or later and priced at less than 7,000 euros. The following query will do the job:

```
db.cars.
find({year:{'$gt':2015},price:{$lt:7000},brand:'Ford'}).
pretty()
```

Notice that we used three filter conditions: `'$gt':2015` means "greater than 2015", we set the `price` to be less than 7000, and finally, we fixed the `brand` to be `'Ford'`. The `find()` method implies an AND operation, so only documents satisfying all three conditions will be returned. At the end, we added the MongoDB shell function called `pretty()`, which formats the console output in a bit more readable way. The result should look like the following:

```
{
        "_id" : ObjectId("622c7b636a78b3d3538fbb72"),
        "brand" : "Ford",
        "make" : "C Max",
        "year" : 2016,
        "price" : 6870,
        "km" : 156383,
        "gearbox" : "M",
        "doors" : "4/5",
        "imported" : true,
        "kW" : 92,
        "cm3" : 1596,
        "fuel" : "petrol",
        "registered" : false,
        "color" : "VAR",
        "aircon" : "2",
        "damage" : "0",
        "car_type" : "VAN",
        "standard" : 5,
        "drive" : "F"
}
{
        "_id" : ObjectId("622c7b646a78b3d3538fce03"),
        "brand" : "Ford",
        "make" : "Fiesta",
        "year" : 2016,
        "price" : 6898,
        "km" : 149950,
        "gearbox" : "M",
        "doors" : "4/5",
        "imported" : false,
```

```
        "kW" : 55,
        "cm3" : 1461,
        "fuel" : "diesel",
        "registered" : true,
        "color" : "BL",
        "aircon" : "2",
        "damage" : "0",
        "car_type" : "HB",
        "standard" : 6,
        "drive" : "F"
}
```

We have seen the find() method in action and we have seen a couple of examples where the find() operator takes a filter JavaScript object in order to define a query. Some of the most used query operators are $gt (greater than), $lt (less than), and $in (providing a list of values), but as we can see from the MongoDB website, there are many more – logical *and*, *or*, or *nor*, geospatial operators for finding the nearest points on a map, and so on. It is time to explore other methods that allow us to perform queries and operations.

findOne() is similar to find() and it takes an optional filter parameter but returns only the first document that satisfies the criteria.

Before we dive into the process of creating or deleting and updating existing documents, we want to mention a very useful method called **projection**, which allows us to limit and set the fields that will be returned from the query results. The find() (or findOne()) method accepts an additional object that tells MongoDB which fields within the returned document are included or excluded.

Building projections is easy; it is just a JSON object in which the keys are the names of the fields, while the values are *0* if we want to exclude a field from the output, or *1* if we want to include it. The ObjectId is included by default, so if we want to remove it from the output, we have to set it to 0 explicitly. Let's try it out just once; let's say that we want the top 5 oldest Ford Fiestas with just the year of production and the kilometers on the meter, so we type the following command:

```
db.cars.find({brand:'Ford',make:'Fiesta'},{year:1,km:1,_id:0}).
sort({'year':1}).limit(5)
```

We sneaked in two things here, the *sort* and the *limit* parts, but we did it on purpose so we can have a glimpse of the MongoDB aggregations (albeit the simplest ones) and to see how intuitive the querying process can be. The projection part, however, is hidden in the second JSON object provided for the find() method. We simply stated that we want the year and the km variable, and then we suppressed _id since it will always be returned by default.

Always reading and sorting the same documents can become a bit boring and quite useless in a real-life environment. In the next section, we will learn how to create and insert new documents into our database. Creating documents will be the entry point to any system that you will be building, so let's dive in!

## Creating new documents

The method for creating new documents in MongoDB is `insertOne()`. You can try inserting the following fictitious car into our database:

```
db.cars.insertOne({'brand':'Magic Car','make':'Green Dragon',
'year':1200})
```

MongoDB will now gladly accept our new car even though it doesn't look like the earlier imported cars and it will print out the following important message:

```
{
        "acknowledged" : true,
        "insertedId" : ObjectId("622da66da111a4265fd4f526")
}
```

The first part means that MongoDB acknowledged the insertion operation, whereas the second property prints out the `ObjectId`, which is the primary key that MongoDB uses and assigns automatically if not provided manually.

MongoDB, naturally, also supports inserting many documents at once with the `insertMany()` method. Instead of providing a single document, the method accepts *an array of documents*.

We could, for example, insert another couple of Magic Cars as follows:

```
db.cars.insertMany([{brand:'Magic Car',make:'Yellow
Dragon',year:1200},{brand:'Magic Car',make:'Red
Dragon',legs:4}])
```

Here we inserted two new highly fictitious cars and the second one has a new property, legs, which does not exist in any other car, just to show off MongoDB's schema flexibility. The shell acknowledges (reluctantly? We'll never know) and prints out the ObjectIds of the new documents.

## Updating documents

Updating documents in MongoDB is possible through several different methods that are suited for different scenarios that might arise in your business logic.

The `updateOne()` method updates the first encountered document with the data provided in the fields. For example, let's update the first Ford Fiesta that we find, add a `Salesman` field, and set it to `Marko` as follows:

```
db.cars.updateOne({make:'Fiesta'},{$set:{'Salesman':'Marko'}})
```

We can also update existing properties of the document as long as we use the `$set` operator. Let's say that we want to reduce the prices of all Ford Fiestas in a linear way (not something you would want to do in real life, though) by 200. You could try it with the following command:

```
db.cars.updateMany({make:'Fiesta'},{$inc:{price:-200}})
```

The preceding command updates many documents, namely all cars that satisfy the simple requirement of being a Fiesta (note that if another car producer, like Seat, decided to make a car named Fiesta, we would have to specify the brand as well) and makes use of the `$inc` operator (increment). Then, we pass the `price` field and the amount that we wish to increment the value. In our case, that would be minus 200 euros.

Updating documents is an atomic operation – if two or more updates are issued at the same time, the one that reaches the server first will be applied.

MongoDB also provides a `replaceOne` operator that takes a filter, like our earlier methods, but expects also an entire document that will take the place of the preceding one. It is worth mentioning that there is also a very handy method, within `updateOne()`, that enables us to check whether the document to be updated exists and then update it, but in the case that no such document exists, the method will create it for us. The syntax is the same as a standard `updateOne()` method, but with the `{"upsert":true}` parameter.

Updating single documents should generally involve the use of the document's ID.

## Deleting documents

Deleting documents works in a similar way to the `find` methods – we provide a filter specifying the documents to be deleted and we can use the `delete` or the `deleteMany` method to execute the operation. Let's delete all of our Magic Car automobiles under the pretext that they are not real, as follows:

```
db.cars.deleteMany({brand:'Magic Car'})
```

The shell will acknowledge this operation with a `deletedCount` variable equal to 3 – the number of deleted documents. The `deleteOne` method operates in a very similar way.

Finally, we can always drop the entire `cars` collection with the following command:

```
db.cars.drop()
```

> **Note**
> Make sure to import the data again from the CSV file if you delete all of the documents or drop the collection since there won't be any data left to play with!

## Cursors

One important thing to note is that the `find` methods return *a cursor* and not the actual results. The actual iteration through the cursor will be executed in a particular and customized way through the use of a language driver to obtain the desired results. The cursor enables us to perform some standard database operations on the returned documents, such as limiting the number of results, ordering by one or more keys ascending or descending, skipping records, and so on.

Since we are doing our MongoDB exploration using the shell (maybe you have been experimenting with Compass as well), we should point out that the shell automatically iterates over the cursor and displays the results. However, if we store the cursor in a variable, we can use some JavaScript methods on it and see that it exhibits, in fact, typical cursor behavior.

Let's create a cursor for the Ford Fiesta cars as follows:

```
let fiesta_cars = db.cars.find({'make':'Fiesta'})
```

Now you can play around with the `fiesta_cars` variable and apply various methods such as `next()`, `hasNext()`, and similar cursor operations. The point is that the query is *not sent* to the server immediately when the shell encounters a `find()` call, but it waits until we start requesting data. This has several important implications, but it also enables us to apply an array of methods that return the cursor itself, thus enabling the **chaining of methods**.

Very similarly to jQuery or D3.js if you ever used them, chaining enables a nifty way of applying several operations on a cursor and returning a fine-tuned result set. Let's see a simple example in action. We want the top 5 cheapest cars made in 2015, as follows:

```
db.cars.find({year:2015},{brand:1,make:1,year:1,_
id:0,price:1}).sort({price:1}).limit(5)
```

For simplicity, we have added a projection to only return the brand, the model (make), and the year. The following output is what we got:

```
{ "brand" : "Fiat", "make" : "Panda", "year" : 2015, "price" :
4199 }
{"brand": "Škoda", "make" : "Fabia", "year" : 2015, "price" :
4200 }
{"brand": "Fiat", "make" : "Grande Punto", "year" : 2015,
"price" : 4200 }
{"brand": "Fiat", "make" : "Panda", "year" : 2015, "price" :
4300 }
{"brand": "Opel", "make" : "Corsa", "year" : 2015, "price" :
4499 }
```

Finally, we will take a look at the MongoDB aggregation framework – an extremely useful tool that enables us, the developers, to offload some (or most) of the computing burden of making calculations and aggregations of varying complexity to the MongoDB server and spare our client-side, as well as our (Python-based) backend, some workload. The aggregation framework will prove itself especially valuable when we try to build some analytic charts showcasing prices, years, brands, and models.

## Aggregation framework

In the following pages, we will try to provide a brief introduction to the MongoDB aggregation framework, what it is, what benefits it offers, and why it is regarded as one of the strongest selling points of the MongoDB ecosystem.

Centered around the concept of a **pipeline** (something that you might be familiar with if you have done some analytics or if you have ever connected a few commands in Linux), the aggregation framework is, at its simplest, an alternative way to retrieve sets of documents from a collection; it is similar to the find method that we already used extensively but with the additional benefit of the possibility of data processing in different stages or steps.

With the aggregation pipeline, we basically pull documents from a MongoDB collection and feed them sequentially to various stages of the pipeline where each stage output is fed to the next stage's input until the final set of documents is returned. Each stage performs some data-processing operations on the currently selected documents, which include modifying documents, so the output documents often have a completely different structure.

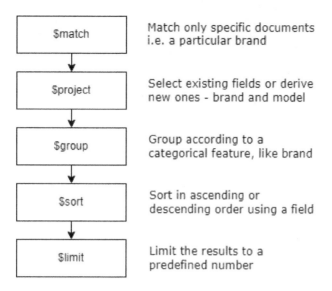

Figure 2.21 – Example of an aggregation pipeline

The operations that can be included in the stages are, for example, **match**, which is used to include only a subset of the entire collection, sorting, grouping, and projections. The MongoDB documentation site is the best place to start if you want to get acquainted with all the possibilities, but we want to start with a couple of simple examples.

The syntax for the aggregation is similar to other methods – we use the aggregate method, which takes a list of stages as a parameter.

Probably the best aggregation, to begin with, would be to mimic the find method. Let's try to get all the Fiat cars in our collection as follows:

```
db.cars.aggregate([{$match: {brand:"Fiat"}}])
```

This is probably the simplest possible aggregation and it consists of just one stage, the $match stage, which tells MongoDB that we only want the Fiats, so the output of the first stage is exactly that.

Let's say that in the second stage we want to group our Fiat cars by model and then check the average price for every model. The second stage is a bit more complicated, but bear with us, it is not that hard. Run the following lines of code:

```
db.cars.aggregate([
{$match: {brand:"Fiat"}},
{$group:{_id:{model:"$make"},avgPrice: { $avg: "$price"} }}
])
```

The second stage uses the $group directive, which tells MongoDB that we want our inputs (in our case, all the Fiat cars available) grouped, and the _id key corresponds to the document key that we want to use as the grouping key. The part {model: "$make"} is a bit counterintuitive, but it just gives MongoDB the following two important pieces of information:

- model: Without quotes or the dollar sign, it is the key that will be used for the grouping, and in our case, it makes sense that it is called *model*. We can call it any way we want; it is the key that will indicate the field that we are doing the grouping by.

- $make: It is actually required to be one of the fields present in the documents. In our case, it is called *make* and the dollar sign means that it is a *field in the document*. Other possibilities would be the year, the gearbox, and really any document field that has a categorical or ordinal meaning. The price wouldn't make much sense.

The second argument in the group stage is the actual aggregation, as follows:

- avgPrice: This is the chosen name for the quantity that we wish to map. In our case, it makes sense to call it avgPrice, but we can choose this variable's name as we please.

- $avg: This is one of the available aggregation functions in MongoDB, called accumulator operators, and they include functions such as average, count, sum, maximum, minimum, and so on. In this example, we could have used the minimum function instead of the average function in order to get the cheapest Fiat for every model.

- $price – like $make in the preceding part of the expression, this is a field belonging to the documents and it should be numeric, since calculating the average or the minimum of a string doesn't make much sense.

The following diagram illustrates this particular aggregation pipeline, with an emphasis on the group stage since we found it the most challenging for newcomers. Once the data is grouped and aggregated the way we wanted it, we can apply other simpler operations, such as sorting, ordering, and limiting.

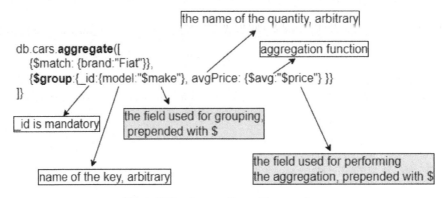

Figure 2.22 – Aggregation with grouping

Pipelines can also include data processing through the project operator – a handy tool for creating entirely new fields, derived from existing document fields, that are then carried into the next stages.

We will provide just another example to showcase the power of **project** in a pipeline stage. Let's consider the following aggregation:

```
db.cars.aggregate([
   {$match:{brand:"Opel"}},
   {$project:{_id:0,price:1,year:1,fullName:
     {$concat:["$make"," ","$brand"]}}},
     {$group:{_id:{make:"$fullName"},avgPrice:{$avg:
"$price"} }},
   {$sort: {avgPrice: -1}},
   {$limit: 10}
]).pretty()
```

This might look intimidating at first, but it is mostly composed of elements that we have already seen. There is the $match stage (we select only the Opel cars), and there is sorting by the price in descending order and cutting off at the 10 priciest cars at the end. But the projection in the middle? It is just a way to craft new variables in a stage using existing ones. In fact, the following part of code is a projection:

```
{$project:{_id:0,price:1,year:1,fullName:
     {$concat:["$make"," ","$brand"]}}},
```

In the preceding code, which is similar to what we have seen when using the plain old find() method, we use zeroes and ones to show or suppress existing fields in the document, but what about this fullName part? It is just MongoDB's way of creating new fields by using existing ones. In this case, we use the concatenate function to create a new field, called fullName, that is put together by using the existing make and brand fields. So, the output is the following:

```
{ "_id" : { "make" : "Movano Opel" }, "avgPrice" : 19999 }
{ "_id" : { "make" : "Crossland X Opel" }, "avgPrice" : 15900 }
{ "_id" : { "make" : "GT Opel" }, "avgPrice" : 15500 }
{ "_id" : { "make" : "Mokka Opel" }, "avgPrice" :
10504.833333333334 }
{ "_id" : { "make" : "Insignia Opel" }, "avgPrice" :
9406.068965517241 }
{ "_id" : { "make" : "Adam Opel" }, "avgPrice" : 7899.75 }
{ "_id" : { "make" : "Antara Opel" }, "avgPrice" :
7304.083333333333 }
{ "_id" : { "make" : "Vivaro Opel" }, "avgPrice" : 6156.5 }
```

```
{ "_id" : { "make" : "Signum Opel" }, "avgPrice" : 4000 }
{ "_id" : { "make" : "Astra Opel" }, "avgPrice" :
3858.7214285714285 }
```

We were able to take a quick look at the MongoDB aggregation framework and we have seen a couple of examples that illustrate the capabilities of the framework. We believe that the syntax and the logic for the grouping stage are the least intuitive parts, whereas the rest is similar to the simple, find-based queries. You are now equipped with a powerful tool that will help you whenever you need to summarize, analyze, or otherwise group and scrutinize your data in an app.

## Summary

Trying to condense and reduce the key information about an ecosystem as vast and as feature rich as MongoDB is not an easy task, and we admit that this chapter is heavily influenced by a personal view of what the key takeaways and potential traps are. We learned the basic building blocks that define MongoDB and its structure, and we have seen how to set up a local system as well as an online Atlas account.

You are now able to begin experimenting, importing your own data (in CSV or JSON), and playing with it. You know the basics of creating, updating, and deleting documents and you have a few simple but powerful tools in your developer's toolbox, such as the find method with its peculiar, yet powerful, filter object syntax, and the aggregation pipelines framework – a strong analytic tool in its own right. You are now able to set up a MongoDB shop anytime, anywhere; start with a free Atlas instance and begin coding, without thinking too much about the infrastructure and with the peace of mind that if, or rather when, the time comes to scale up and accommodate millions of users, your database layer will be ready and won't let you down.

In the next chapter, we are going to dive into the process of creating APIs – application programming interfaces with FastAPI – an exciting and new Python framework. We will try to provide a minimal, yet complete guide of the main concepts and features that should hopefully convince you that building APIs can be fast, efficient, and fun. Since learning how to build REST APIs with a framework is much easier through practice, we will create a very simple, yet comprehensive API that will allow us to put our freshly created database to good use. We will be able to create new (used) car entries, delete them, update them, and learn how FastAPI solves most typical development problems along the way.

# 3
# Getting Started with FastAPI

Arguably the most important part of our FARM stack is going to be the **application programming interface (API)**. The API is the brain of our system – it implements the business logic (how the data flows in and out of the system, but more importantly how it relates to the business requirements inside our system).

I believe that frameworks such as FastAPI are much easier to showcase through simple examples. So, in this chapter, we will go through some simple endpoints that are minimal self-contained REST APIs. We will use them to get acquainted with how this powerful framework handles requests and responses – the cardiovascular system of the web.

This chapter is meant to be a quick start introduction to the framework – here we will focus on standard REST API practices and how they are implemented in FastAPI. I will show how to send requests and modify them according to our needs, and I will explain how to retrieve all the data from HTTP requests – parameters and the body. We will see how easy it is to work with the response and how intuitive FastAPI is when it comes to setting cookies, headers, and other standard web-related topics.

In this chapter, we will cover the following topics:

- An overview of the FastAPI framework's main features
- Setup and requirements for a simple FastAPI app
- Specific Python features used in FastAPI (type hinting, annotations, and the async await syntax)
- How FastAPI handles typical REST API tasks – path and query parameters, the request and response body, headers, and cookies
- How to work with form data
- Anatomy of a FastAPI project and routers

# Technical requirements

For this chapter, you will need the following:

1. Python setup
2. Virtual environments
3. Code editor and plugins
4. Terminal
5. REST clients

Let's take a look at them in more detail.

## Python setup

If you do not have Python installed, now is a good time to do so. Head over to the Python download site (`https://www.python.org/downloads/`) and download the installer for your operating system. The Python website contains excellent documentation for all the major operating systems. In this book, I will be using the latest, version, which, at the time of writing, is 3.10.1. Make sure that you install or upgrade to one of the latest Python versions. FastAPI relies heavily on Python hints and annotations, so any version later than 3.6 should work. Another important thing to check is that the Python version that you have installed is reachable or, even better, the default version. You can check this by typing `python` in your terminal of choice and checking the version.

I will not describe how to install Python on your platform since there are numerous guides online that certainly cover your setup. You can also install a data science-friendly environment such as Anaconda (`https://www.anaconda.com/products/distribution`) if that is something you are already using or are comfortable with.

## Virtual environments

We must create an application directory called FARM. Inside it, we will create a virtual environment. A virtual environment is an isolated Python environment that includes a copy of the Python interpreter, which we can use to install the desired packages and *only* the needed packages – in our case, FastAPI, the Uvicorn web server, and additional packages that we will use later, as well as FastAPI dependencies such as Pydantic.

You can think of a virtual environment as a directory tree of Python executable files and packages that allow us to have different versions of Python and the various third-party packages together on a single machine, without them interfering with each other.

There are several excellent yet opinionated approaches to creating virtual environments such as **pipenv** (`https://pipenv.pypa.io/en/latest/`), **pyenv** (`https://github.com/pyenv/pyenv`), and others. I will stick to the simplest. After installing Python, you should head to your `apps` directory and, in a command prompt of your choice, run the following command:

```
python -m venv venv
```

This command should download a new Python executable and create a new directory named `venv` – it is the second argument in the command, so this can get a bit confusing. You can name it differently, but like many other things, this is a useful convention (readymade `.gitignore` files, for instance, often include `venv` to help you avoid putting the virtual environment folder under version control). Now, we should check that we can activate the newly created environment. In the `venv` folder, navigate to the `Scripts` folder and type `activate`. The prompt should change and be prepended with the name of the active environment in parenthesis – that is, `$ (venv)`.

You should also have Git installed. Head over to `https://git-scm.com/downloads` and just follow the instructions for your operating system.

Apart from a Python environment and *Git*, you should have installed a shell program – if you are working on Linux or Mac, you should be fine. On Windows, you can use Windows PowerShell or something such as Commander (`https://cmder.app`), a console emulator for Windows that has some nice features baked in.

## Code Editors

While there are many great code editors and **integrated development environments** (**IDEs**) for Python, I strongly recommend *Visual Studio Code* from Microsoft. Since its release in 2015, it has quickly become the most popular code editor, it is cross-platform, it provides a lot of integrated tools – such as an integrated terminal in which we can run our development server – it is pretty lightweight, and it provides hundreds of plugins suitable for virtually any programming task that you may have to perform.

Since we will be working with JavaScript, Python, React, and a bit of CSS for styling and running a couple of command-line processes along the way, I believe this is the easiest way to go.

## REST Clients

Finally, to be able to test our REST API, we need a REST client. Postman (`https://www.postman.com/`) is arguably the most sophisticated and customizable program for testing APIs, but there are several very viable alternatives. I prefer the simplicity of *Insomnia* (`https://insomnia.rest/`), a GUI REST client with a very clean and simple interface, and *HTTPie* (`https://httpie.io/`), a command-line REST API client that allows us to quickly test our endpoints without leaving the shell. *HTTPie* provides other nice features such as an expressive and simple syntax, handling of forms and uploads, sessions, and so on. Moreover, HTTPie is probably the easiest REST client when it comes to installation – you can install the Python version just like any other Python package, using *pip* or some other option, such as choco, apt (for Linux), brew, and so on.

For our purposes, the easiest way to install *HTTPie* is to activate the virtual environment that we will be using (`cd` into the `venv` directory, navigate to `Lib/activate`, and then activate it) and then install *HTTPie* with `pip`, as follows:

```
pip install httpie
```

Once it's been installed, you can test *HTTPie* with the following command:

```
(venv) λ http GET "https://jsonplaceholder.typicode.com/
todos/1"
```

If everything went well, you should have a pretty long output that starts with an HTTP/1.1 200 OK. In the previous command that we issued, you may be wondering what (`venv`) and the Greek letter *Lambda* (λ) mean. *venv* is just the name of our virtual environment and it means that it has been activated for the shell that we are using (if you named it some other way, you would see a different name in parenthesis), while Lambda is the shell symbol used by Commander, my shell emulator. On Linux, Mac, or Windows PowerShell, you'll get the standard > symbol. *HTTPie* makes it very easy to issue HTTP requests by simply adding POST for POST requests, payloads, form values, and so on.

## Installing the necessary packages

After setting up the virtual environment, you should activate it and install the Python libraries required for our first simple application: FastAPI itself and Uvicorn.

FastAPI needs a server to run – by a server, I mean a piece of software specifically designed to serve web applications (or REST APIs!). FastAPI exposes an **asynchronous server gateway interface** (**ASGI** – `https://asgi.readthedocs.io/`)-compatible web application but doesn't provide us with a built-in server, so a compatible Python solution is necessary.

I will not get into the specifics of the ASGI specification, but the main takeaway is that it is an asynchronous interface that enables async non-blocking applications, something that we want to make full use of our FastAPI capabilities. At the time of writing, the FastAPI documentation site lists three compatible Python ASGI-compatible servers – Uvicorn, Hypercorn, and Daphne – but we will stick to the first one as it is the most widely used and is the recommended way to work with FastAPI. You can find lots of documentation online in case you get stuck, and it offers very high performance.

To install our first two dependencies, make sure you are in your working directory with the desired virtual environment activated and install FastAPI and Uvicorn:

```
pip install fastapi uvicorn
```

Phew! This was a bit long, but now we have a decent Python coding environment that contains a shell, one or two REST clients, a great editor, and the coolest and hippest REST framework ready to rock. On the other hand, if you have ever developed a Django or Flask application, this should all be familiar ground.

Finally, let's pick a folder or clone this book's GitHub repository and activate a virtual environment (it is customary to create the environment in a folder named `venv` inside the working directory, but feel free to improvise and structure the code as you see fit). Later in this chapter, we will briefly discuss some options when it comes to structuring your FastAPI code, but for now, just make sure that you are in a folder and that your newly created virtual environment is activated.

# FastAPI in a nutshell

In *Chapter 1, Web Development and the FARM Stack*, I already mentioned why FastAPI is our REST framework of choice in the FARM stack. What sets FastAPI apart from other solutions is its speed of coding and clean code, which enables developers to spot bugs fast and early. The author of the framework himself, *Sebastian Ramirez*, often modestly emphasizes that FastAPI is just a mix of Starlette and Pydantic, while heavily relying on modern Python features, especially *type hinting*. Before diving into an example and building a FastAPI app, I believe that it is useful to quickly just go over the concepts that FastAPI is based on so that you know what to expect.

## Starlette

**Starlette** (`www.starlette.io`) is an ASGI framework that routinely places at the top in various web framework speed contests and provides numerous features that are available in FastAPI as well – WebSocket support, events on startup and shutdown, session and cookie support, background tasks, middleware implementations, templates, and many more. We will not be coding directly in Starlette, but it is very useful to know how FastAPI works under the hood and what its origins are.

## Python type hinting

**Type hinting** is a feature introduced in Python version 3.5 in an attempt to provide developers with the opportunity to check the types of the variables before runtime. By using type annotations, developers can annotate variables, functions, and classes and give indications of the types that are expected. It is important to note that these annotations are completely optional and do not make Python a statically typed language! The annotations are ignored by the Python interpreter, but they are picked up by static type checkers that will validate the code and check if it is consistent with the annotations. Code editors and IDEs, such as Visual Studio Code, will be able to provide autocomplete features, thus speeding up coding, while tools such as Mypy will provide helpful error warnings. The syntax for type hinting is as follows:

**chapter3_types.py**

```
def annotated_function(name: str, age: int) -> str:
    return f"Your name is {name.upper()} and you are {age}
        years old!"
print(annotated_function(name="marko", age=99))
```

Adding the type for the variables is done with a colon, :, while the return type is annotated with an arrow, ->. This simply means that the function takes two parameters – a string (name) and an integer (age) – that is supposed to return a string, denoted by the arrow. Note that if you try this function with a string argument for the age variable, you will still get a valid result.

Types can be the most basic Python types, such as strings or integers, but the Typing module hosts numerous data structures that can be used when we want to specify that we need a dictionary or a list or something more complex, such as a list of dictionaries.

## Pydantic

**Pydantic** is a Python library for data validation – it enforces type hints at runtime and provides user-friendly errors, allowing us to catch invalid data as soon as possible – that is, before they make it deep into the system and cause havoc. Although it is a parsing library and not a validation tool, it achieves validation by catching invalid data.

If you are working within a virtual environment that already has FastAPI installed, Pydantic will already be there since FastAPI depends on it. If you just want to play with Pydantic in a newly created virtual environment, you can install Pydantic with pip, just make sure that you are in your activated virtual environment and type:

```
pip install pydantic
```

Pydantic enables us to create data models or schemas (not to be confused with MongoDB schemas!), which are essentially a specification of how your data must be structured: what fields should be present, what their types are, which are strings, which are integers, Booleans, whether any of them are required, whether they should have default values in case no value is provided, and so on.

If you have done a bit of web development, you may have run into the painful issues that arise from the fact that the client of your web application – the user – can send essentially any data that it wants, not only what you wanted the system to ingest and process. Take, for instance, the request body – we will see that FastAPI makes it easy to extract all the data that's sent through the body, but we want to be able to differentiate various bits of data and only consider what we want and what we allow.

Furthermore, we ultimately want to have that data validated. If we require an integer value, we cannot let 5 (a string) or 3.4 (a float) pass. Pydantic allows us to explicitly define the expected type and not only on the receiving end – we can use Pydantic to validate and parse output data as well, making sure the response body is exactly how we want it to be, including some pretty complex validations.

Let's say that we want to create a simple model for inserting used cars into our database. The model should contain the following fields: brand (a string), model (string), year of production (integer), fuel – that is, if it is petrol, diesel, or LPG powered (enumeration) – and a list of countries in which it has been registered (list of strings)

Pydantic is based on Python *hints*, and we can derive our model from Pydantic's `BaseModel` class – a class that we will be using to kickstart all of our schemas. Pydantic contains numerous classes for handling and accommodating different kinds of data, but in the beginning, when defining your models, you will probably start with a `BaseModel` class – all the models are inherited from this class, so this is the class that you will want to import:

## chapter3_pydantic.py

```python
from enum import Enum
from typing import List
from pydantic import BaseModel, ValidationError

class Fuel(str, Enum):
    PETROL = 'PETROL'
    DIESEL = 'DIESEL'
    LPG = 'LPG'
class Car(BaseModel):
    brand: str
    model: str
    year: int
    fuel: Fuel
    countries: List[str]
    note:str="No note"
```

The code may look complicated at first, but it is quite straightforward. First, we imported the `Enum` class, which enables us to create an *enumeration type* for the admissible types of fuel. From the typing module, we import `List` as we will need it to validate our list of countries. `brand` and `model` are declared as string variables, while `year` is an integer.

Now that we have a model in place, we can explore its capabilities. First, let's test it out by passing some valid data and using the `json()` method, one of many methods that Pydantic provides:

## chapter3_pydantic.py (continued)

```python
car = Car(
    brand="Lancia",
    model="Musa",
    fuel="PETROL",
    year="2006",
```

```
        countries=["Italy","France"]
)
print(car.json())
```

The output will be a nicely formatted JSON file, ready to be used in a web app (note that this file is not a FastAPI app, but just a regular Python script!):

```
(venv) λ python pydantic-examples.py
{"brand": "Lancia", "model": "Musa", "year": 2006, "fuel":
"PETROL", "countries": ["Italy", "France"], "note": "No note"}
```

As you can see, the data is perfectly valid JSON – the countries list is populated (since we haven't provided any content for the note, it is populated by default) and the year is correctly cast to an integer! This is very good and very useful. Let's try and pass some invalid data. Let's omit `model` and make `year` a string that cannot be cast to an integer:

---

### chapter3_pydantic.py (continued)

```
invalid_car = Car(
    brand="Lancia",
    fuel="PETROL",
    year="something",
    countries=["Italy","France"]
)
print(invalid_car.json())
```

To get a nice error message, all we have to do is make use of Pydantic's `ValidationError` class and wrap it all in a `try-catch` block:

```
try:
    invalid_car = Car(
        brand="Lancia",
        fuel="PETROL",
        year="something",
        countries=["Italy","France"]
    )
except ValidationError as e:
    print(e)
```

After making this code modification, the command prompt will be gentle to us and pinpoint where it found errors:

```
2 validation errors for Car
model
  field required (type=value_error.missing)
year
  value is not a valid integer (type=type_error.integer)
```

You could play around with other potential errors and try various Pydantic error messages. It is important to point out that in this example, I only used the `json()` method, but many more are available: `dict()` for returning a Python dictionary, `copy()` for creating a deep copy of the model, and so on.

Finally, Pydantic offers individual field validations and with some additional packages installed, we can perform email validations, URL validations, and anything else that comes to mind. Validation is available at the field level, but also at the object level – when you need to combine different field values into a single condition – for example, to check that two passwords have been entered in two fields on a registration page match.

A pattern that is pretty common when working with Pydantic is the model's inheritance. You may, for instance, define a basic car model with just the bare minimum fields and then derive, via inheritance, different car models for editing, for showcasing in an endpoint that will feed an image gallery, and so on, similar to what we did with projections in MongoDB. We will implement this later when we start building our basic app. Another strength of Pydantic is the ability to build complex, nested models by defining schemas (or models) that rely on other or previously defined models, not unlike nesting in MongoDB.

With that, we've seen what Pydantic is and how it helps us parse and validate data, as well as complex data structures. However, we've only just scratched the surface of what is possible. We haven't examined the validator decorator or the additional external packages for special validations, but by understanding the basic mechanism of Pydantic, we can see how it makes FastAPI's data flow *safe*.

## Asynchronous I/O

If you have ever made a web app using Node.js, you may have encountered the *asynchronous programming paradigm*. The idea is to make operations that are slow compared to others – such as hefty network calls, reading files from a disk, and similar – run, but at the same time allow the system to respond to other calls and then return the appropriate response of the long-running process, while not blocking the other, less time-consuming responses. This is achieved by using an event loop – a manager of asynchronous tasks that receives requests and can move to the next one, even though the previous one hasn't finished and yielded a response.

The simplest real-life example would be baking a cake – you could do all the operations sequentially: put the dough in the oven and then grab a chair and sit for 40 minutes staring at the oven until it is finished. *After* these 40 minutes, you wait for 10 minutes for the dough to cool off; after that, you make the cream and let it rest for another 20 minutes, and then spend another 10 minutes putting it all together. That would take you 70 minutes. In the async version of our cake, we would put the dough in the oven and start working on the cream right away so that it's ready by the time the dough is ready and cool, saving 20 minutes of total preparation time. Include some other meals to prepare simultaneously, and the time gains will be much more impressive, but you get the idea.

Python has added support for asynchronous I/O programming in version 3.4 and added the `async/await` keywords in version 3.6. ASGI was introduced soon after `async` made its way into the Python world and the specification outlines how applications should be structured and called. It also defines the events that can be sent and received. FastAPI relies on ASGI and *returns an ASGI-compatible app,* which is why it is so performant.

I will prefix all the endpoint functions in this book with the `async` keyword, even before we get to the part where they are necessary. All you need to know at this point is that functions with the `async` keyword prepended are coroutines – that is, they run on the event loop. While the simple examples examined in this chapter will work even without the `async` keyword, the real power of asynchronous programming in FastAPI will be visible when we connect to our MongoDB server through an async driver – *Motor*.

## Standard REST API stuff

I listed the features that make FastAPI our REST API framework of choice in *Chapter 1, Web Development and the FARM Stack*. So, in this section, I just want to go over some of the terminologies that are pretty common in the realm of developing APIs.

Our communication will occur via the HTTP protocol, through HTTP requests and responses. In this chapter, I will provide an overview of how FastAPI handles both and how it leverages some additional libraries, such as Pydantic, to help us write faster and with fewer bugs. The server that I will be using in all the examples will be Uvicorn, although, in a more general way, the whole FastAPI and Uvicorn part of the code could be considered the server.

The basis of any REST API communication is the relevant URLs and paths. The *URL* for our local web development server will be `http://localhost:8000` since `8000` is the default port that Uvicorn uses. The *path* part (optional) of an endpoint could be `/cars`, while `http` is the *scheme.* We will see how FastAPI handles paths, why the order when defining endpoint functions in our code matters, and how we can extract variables from dynamic portions of the path in a simple way.

Every path or address – the URL and the path – provides a list of approved actions that can be performed on it – *HTTP verbs.* For example, there might be a page or a URL that lists all the cars on sale, but you cannot issue a POST request to it since this is not allowed.

In FastAPI, these verbs are implemented as Python decorators. To put it better, they are *exposed* as decorators, and they are implemented *only* if you, the developer, implement them.

FastAPI encourages the proper use of HTTP verbs concerning the data-resource operations that they perform, so you should always use POST (or the @post decorator) when creating new resources.

Finally, HTTP messages consist of a request/status line, headers, and, optionally, body data. Again, FastAPI offers us tools to easily create and modify headers, set response codes, and do pretty much anything that we please with the request and response body. It does so in a very clean and intuitive way, as we will see shortly.

In this section, we have tried to pinpoint the programming concepts and specific Python features that FastAPI is built on and enable it to be so performant and produce maintainable code. In the next section, we will go over some standard REST API operations and see how they are achieved with FastAPI.

## How does FastAPI speak REST?

Let's create a minimal FastAPI application – a classic Hello World example – and start examining how FastAPI structures the endpoints. I use the term *endpoint* to specify a unique combination of an URL (which will always be the same – in our case, our development server – that is, localhost:8000), a path (the part after the slash), and an HTTP method. In a new folder named Chapter3, for example, create a new Python file using Visual Studio Code:

### chapter3_first_endpoint.py

```
from fastapi import FastAPI
app = FastAPI()
@app.get("/")
async def root():
    return {"message": "Hello FastAPI"}
```

In just a few lines of code, we were able to accomplish several things. So, let's break down what each part does.

In the first line of chapter3_first_endpoint.py, we imported the FastAPI class from the fastapi package. Then, we instantiated an application object (we called it app since that is considered a good practice, but we could have chosen any name). This is just a Python class that provides all the functionality of our API and exposes an ASGI-compatible application – this is the application that we have to pass to our server of choice (Uvicorn).

The application is now ready and instantiated, but without endpoints, it isn't able to do or say very much. FastAPI, similar to Flask – another popular Python web framework – exposes *decorators* for HTTP methods to enable the application to respond. However, we have to implement them.

After that, we used the `@get` decorator, which corresponds to the GET method, and we passed a URL – in our case, we used `/`, which is the root path.

The decorated function is called `root`, another convention, but it could be called whatever we wanted (any valid Python function name). It is responsible for accepting any arguments (in our case, there aren't any) and responding. The value that's returned by the function, which in our case is a simple Python dictionary, will then be transformed into a JSON response and returned by the ASGI server as an HTTP response. This may seem obvious, but I believe that it is useful to break things down into the tiniest bits in the beginning.

The preceding code defines a basic fully functional application with a single endpoint. To be able to test it, we need a server – enter Uvicorn.

Now, go ahead and run the live server with Uvicorn in your command line:

```
uvicorn chapter3_first_endpoint:app --reload
```

The previous line is something that you will be using quite a lot when developing with FastAPI, so let's break it down.

> **Important Information**
>
> *Uvicorn* is our ASGI-compatible web server, and we call it directly by passing it the combination of the executable Python file (without the extension!) and the instantiated app (the FastAPI instance), separated by a colon (`:`). The `--reload` flag tells Uvicorn to reload the server each time we save our code, similar to *Nodemon* if you have worked with Node.js. You can run all the examples in this book that contain FastAPI apps by using this syntax, except where something else is suggested.

This is the output that you will get if you test our only endpoint with *HTTPie* (note that when we omit the keyword, it defaults to GET):

```
(venv) λ http "http://localhost:8000/"
HTTP/1.1 200 OK
content-length: 27
content-type: application/json
date: Fri, 01 Apr 2022 17:35:48 GMT
server: uvicorn
{
    "message": "Hello FastAPI"
}
```

*HTTPie* informs us that our simple endpoint is running; we got a nice 200 OK status code, `content-type` is correctly set to `application/json`, and the response is a JSON document that contains the desired message.

The same endpoint tests can be executed with Insomnia, a GUI REST API testing tool. The user interface is quite intuitive. This is what the same test looks like on my machine:

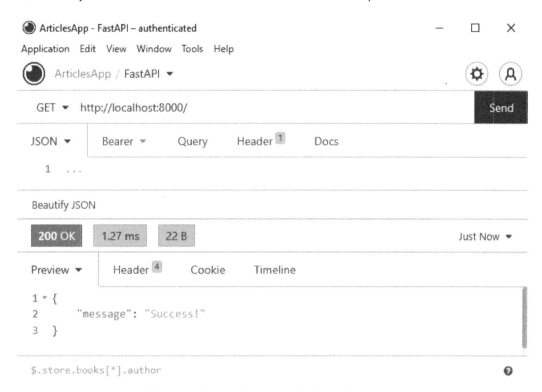

Figure 3.1 – Testing the root endpoint with Insomnia

Here, we populate the URL field, specify the HTTP method in the dropdown menu, and add every other piece of information to the request in the menu below. Having prepared the request, we can hit the **Send** button and wait for the result to appear.

I am aware that every REST API guide begins with similar silly hello-world examples, but I feel that with FastAPI, this is useful: in just a couple of lines of code, we can see the anatomy of a simple endpoint. This endpoint only *covers* the GET method directed toward the root URL (`/`), so if you try to test this app with a POST request, you should get a `405 Method Not Allowed` error (or any method other than GET).

If we wanted to create an endpoint that responds with the same message but for POST requests, we would just have to change the decorator:

## chapter3_first_endpoint.py (continued)

```python
@app.post("/")
async def post_root():
    return {"message": "Post request success"}
```

HTTPie will respond accordingly in the terminal:

```
(venv) λ http POST http://localhost:8000
HTTP/1.1 200 OK
content-length: 35
content-type: application/json
date: Sat, 26 Mar 2022 12:49:25 GMT
server: uvicorn
{
    "message": "Post request success!"
}
```

Now that we've created a couple of endpoints, this is a good time to head over to http://localhost:8000/docs and see what FastAPI has prepared for us.

## Automatic documentation

One of the first really useful features present in FastAPI is its automatically generated documentation. It is interactive in the sense that we can use it to test our API as it is being developed! FastAPI automatically lists all the endpoints that we define and provides information about the expected inputs and responses. The documentation is based on the *OpenAPI* specification and relies heavily on Python hints and the parsing and validation library Pydantic. It is an incredibly useful tool that will make you wish you had it in every framework. In the following sections, however, I will rely more on standard REST clients as I feel that they provide a more transferrable experience and enable us to compare different APIs that may not be Python-based, such as Next.js API routes.

We have created a minimal yet fully functional API with a single endpoint and we were able to see the *syntax* and structure of an app. In the next section, I am going to cover the basic elements of a REST API request-response cycle and how we can control every single aspect of the process.

# Let's build a showcase API!

REST APIs are all about cycles of HTTP requests and responses – it is the engine that powers the web and is implemented in every web framework, speaking the language of the web – the HTTP protocol. I feel that the best way to showcase FastAPI's capabilities is to dive right in and create simple endpoints and focus on specific parts of code that achieve the desired functionalities. Rather than the usual CRUD operations that we will implement in the forthcoming chapters, I want to focus on the process of retrieving and setting request and response elements.

## Retrieving path and query parameters

The first endpoint will be for retrieving a car by its unique ID:

### chapter3_path.py

```
from fastapi import FastAPI
app = FastAPI()
@app.get("/car/{id}")
async def root(id):
    return {"car_id":id}
```

The first line of the preceding snippet defines a dynamic path: the static part is defined with `car/`, while `{id}` is a standard Python string-formatted dynamic parameter in the sense that it can be anything – a string or a number.

Let's try it out and test the endpoint with an ID equal to 1:

```
(venv) λ http "http://localhost:8000/car/1"
HTTP/1.1 200 OK
content-length: 14
content-type: application/json
date: Mon, 28 Mar 2022 20:31:58 GMT
server: uvicorn
{
    "car_id": "1"
}
```

We got our JSON response back, but here, 1 in the response is a *string* (hint: quotes). You can try this same route with an ID equal to a string:

```
(venv) λ http http://localhost:8000/car/billy
HTTP/1.1 200 OK
{
    "car_id": "billy"
}
```

FastAPI doesn't complain and returns our string, which was provided as part of the dynamic parameter, but this is where Python's newer features come into play. Enter type hinting.

Returning to our FastAPI route (or endpoint), to make the car ID become an integer, it is enough to *hint at* the type of the variable parameter. The endpoint will look like this:

```
@app.get("/carh/{id}")
async def hinted_car_id(id:int):
    return {"car_id":id}
```

I have given it a new path: /carh/{id} (the h after car means hint). Apart from the name of the function (hinted_car_id), the only difference is in the argument: the semicolon followed by int means that we expect an integer, but FastAPI takes this very seriously.

If we take a look at the interactive documentation at http:localhost:8000/docs and try to insert a string in the id field for the /carh/ endpoint, we will get an error and will not be able to proceed.

If we try it out in our REST client and test the /carh/ route by passing it a string, we will see that FastAPI is yelling at us, but this is for our own good! We got several useful messages. First, FastAPI set the status code for us correctly – that is, 422 Unprocessable Entity – and in the body of the response, it pointed out what the problem was – the value is not a valid integer. It also gives us the location where the error occurred: in the path – that is, the id part. This is a trivial example, but imagine that you are sending a complex request with a complicated path, several query strings, and maybe additional information in the header. Using type hinting quickly solves these problems.

If you try to access the endpoint without specifying any ID, you will get yet another error:

```
(venv) λ http http://localhost:8000/carh/
HTTP/1.1 404 Not Found
{
    "detail": "Not Found"
}
```

FastAPI has, again, correctly set the status code, giving us a nice 404 Not Found error, and repeated this message in the body. The endpoint that we hit does not exist – we need to specify a value after the slash.

Situations may arise where you have similar paths, but one of them is dynamic, while the other one is static. A typical case could be an application that has numerous users – hitting the API at the URL defined by /users/id would give you some information about the user with the selected ID, while /users/me would typically be an endpoint that displays your information and allows you to modify it in some way.

In these situations, it is important to remember that, like in other web frameworks, order matters.

The following piece of code will *not* yield the desired results:

## chapter3_wrong_path_order.py

```
@app.get("/user/{id}")
async def user(id:int):
    return {"User_id":id}
@app.get("/user/me")
async def user():
    return {"User_id":"This is me!"}
```

By testing the /user/me endpoint, we get an *Unprocessable Entity* error, much like when we tried the same thing previously – passing a string in the URL. This is quite logical once you remember that order matters – FastAPI finds the first matching URL, checks the types, and throws an error. If the first match is the one with the fixed path, everything works as intended.

Another powerful feature of FastAPI's path treatment is how it limits the path to a specific set of values and a path function, imported from FastAPI, which enables us to perform additional validation on the path.

I will not delve into the details here, but let's just say that we want to have a URL path that should accept two values and allow the following:

- account_type: This can be free or pro
- months: This must be an integer between 3 and 12

FastAPI allows us to solve this at the path level by letting us create a class based on Enum for the account type. This class defines all the possible values for the account variable. In our case, there are just two – free and pro:

---

### chapter3_restrict_path.py

```
from enum import Enum
from fastapi import FastAPI, Path
app = FastAPI()
class AccountType(str, Enum):
    FREE = "free"
    PRO = "pro"
```

Finally, in the actual endpoint, we combine this class with the utilities from the Path function (do not forget to import it along with FastAPI from fastapi!):

```
@app.get("/account/{acc_type}/{months}")
async def account( acc_type:AccountType, months:int = Path(...,
ge=3,le=12)):
    return {
            "message":"Account created",
            "account_type":acc_type,
            "months":months
            }
```

FastAPI was able to pack a lot of punch in the preceding code: by setting the type of the acc_type part of the path to our previously defined class, we ensured that only the free or pro value can be passed. The months variable, however, is handled by the Path utility function.

As for other topics in this part, I strongly advise you to head over to the excellent documentation site and see what other options are available – in this case, the Path function received three parameters. The three dots mean that the value is required and that no default value has been provided, ge=3 means that the value can be greater or equal to 3, while le=12 means that it can be smaller or equal to 12.

With that, we've learned how to validate, restrict, and order our path parameters. Now, let's look at the **query parameters**. Query parameters are added at the end of the URL by using the *?min_price=2000&max_price=4000* format.

The question mark in the previous expression is a separator that tells us where the query string begins, while the ampersands, &, allow us to add more than one assignment (the equals signs, =).

Query parameters are usually used to apply filters, sort, order, or limit query sets, apply paginations to a long list of results, and similar tasks. FastAPI treats them similarly to path parameters. They will be, so to say, automatically picked up by FastAPI and available for processing in our endpoint functions.

Let's create a simple endpoint that accepts two query parameters for the minimum and the maximum prices of the car:

## chapter3_query_string.py

```
@app.get("/cars/price")
async def cars_by_price(min_price: int=0, max_price:
int=100000):
    return{"Message":f"Listing cars with prices between {min_
        price} and {max_price}"}
```

Let's test this endpoint with HTTPie:

```
(venv) λ http "http://localhost:8000/cars/price?min_
price=2000&max_price=4000"
HTTP/1.1 200 OK
content-length: 60
content-type: application/json
date: Mon, 28 Mar 2022 21:20:24 GMT
server: uvicorn
{
    "Message": "Listing cars with prices between 2000 and 4000"
}
```

Of course, this particular solution is not very good – we do not ensure the basic condition that the minimum price should be lower than the maximum price, but that can easily be handled by Pydantic object-level validation.

FastAPI picked up our query parameters and performed the same parsing and validation checks it did previously. It is worth mentioning that FastAPI provides the `Query` function, which is very similar to the `Path` function that we used previously – we can use the greater than, less than, or equal conditions, as well as set default values.

With that, we've seen how FastAPI enables us to work with data that is passed through the path and query parameters, as well as the tools it uses under the hood to perform parsing and validation as soon as possible. Now, let's examine the main data vehicle of REST APIs: the request body.

## The request body – the bulk of the data

REST APIs enable two-way communication between a client – usually a web browser or similar device and an API server. The bulk of this data is carried over in the request and response body. A request body consists of the data that's sent from the client to our API, if there is such data, while the response body is the data sent from the API server to our client(s). This data can be encoded in various ways (XML was quite popular 15 years ago, for example) but in this book, we will consider exclusively **JavaScript Object Notation (JSON)** since it is used everywhere and it plays exceptionally nicely with our database solution of choice, MongoDB.

When sending data, we should always use POST requests to create new resources, PUT and PATCH to update resources, and the DELETE method to delete. Since the body of a request can and will contain raw data – in our case, MongoDB documents or arrays of documents – we will see how we can leverage the power of Pydantic models to our benefit. But first, let's see how the mechanism works, without any validation or modeling.

In the following snippet for a hypothetical endpoint that would be used to insert new cars in our future database, we pass just the generic request body as the data. We expect it to be a dictionary:

```
@app.post("/cars")
async def new_car(data: Dict=Body(...)):
    print(data)
    return {
        "message":data
    }
```

Intuitively, you may have guessed that the `Body` function is somewhat similar to the previously introduced `Path` and `Query` functions, yet there is a difference – when working with the request body, this function is *mandatory*.

The three dots indicate that the body is required (you must send something), but this is the only requirement. Let's try to insert a car (a Fiat 500, made in 2015):

```
(venv) λ http POST "http://localhost:8000/cars" brand="FIAT"
model="500" year=2015
HTTP/1.1 200 OK
content-length: 56
content-type: application/json
date: Mon, 28 Mar 2022 21:27:31 GMT
server: uvicorn
{
    "message": {
        "brand": "FIAT",
        "model": "500",
        "year": "2015"
    }
}
```

Again, FastAPI functions do the heavy lifting for us – we were able to retrieve all the data that was passed to the request body and make it available to our function for further processing – database insertion, optional preprocessing, and so on. On the other hand, we could have passed just about any key-value pairs to the body. For example, we could set the number of legs to 4 (cars do not have legs, yet), and it would make its way into the request body, disregarding modern car engineering.

Keen observers may have noticed that while all went well, FastAPI sent us a 200 response status again, even though a `201 Resource Created` error may have been more appropriate and, well, exact. We could have had some MongoDB insertion at the end of the function, after all. Do not worry – we will see how easy it is to modify the response body as well, but for now, let's see why Pydantic shines when it comes to request bodies.

Let's say that we want to enforce a certain structure for our request body. After all, we cannot allow users to send arbitrary fields and data and bomb our precious POST endpoint. To create new car entries, we *only* want the `brand`, `model`, and production `year` fields.

We will create a simple Pydantic model with the desired types:

## chapter3_body2.py

```
from fastapi import FastAPI, Body
from pydantic import BaseModel
```

```
class InsertCar(BaseModel):
    brand: str
    model: str
    year: int



app = FastAPI()


@app.post("/cars")
async def new_car(data: Dict=Body(...)):
    print(data)
    return {
        "message":data
    }
```

By now, you already know that the first two parameters are expected to be strings, while the year must be an integer; all of them are required.

Now, if we try to post the same data that we did previously but with additional fields, we will only get these three fields back. Also, these fields will go through Pydantic parsing and validation and throw meaningful error messages if something does not conform to the data specification.

I encourage you to play with this endpoint and try different post-data combinations. The following is an example:

```
(venv) λ http POST "http://localhost:8000/carsmodel"
brand="Fiat" model="500" breed="Dobermann" year=2018
HTTP/1.1 200 OK
{
    "message": {
        "brand": "Fiat",
        "model": "500",
        "year": 2018
    }
}
```

This combination of Pydantic model validation and the Body function provides all the necessary flexibility when working with request data. This is because you can combine them and pass different pieces of information using the same request bus ride, so to speak.

If we wanted to pass a user with a promo code along with the new car data, we could try to define a Pydantic model for the user and extract the promo code with the Body function. First, let's define a minimal user model:

```
class InsertUser(BaseModel):
    username: str
    name: str
```

Now, we can create a more complex function that will process two Pydantic models and an optional user promo code – we have set the default value to None:

## chapter3_body2.py

```
@app.post("/car/user")
async def new_car_model(
    car: InsertCar,
    user: InsertUser,
    code: int=Body(None) ):
    return {
        "car":car,
        "user":user,
        "code":code
    }
```

For this request, which contains a full-fledged JSON object with two nested objects and some code, I opted to use Insomnia since I find it easier than typing JSON in the command prompt or resorting to piping. I guess it is a matter of preference, but I believe that when developing and testing REST APIs, it is useful to have a GUI tool such as Insomnia or Postman and a command-line client (such as cURL or httpie). This is what Insomnia looks like when testing this particular endpoint:

Figure 3.2 – Insomnia REST client interface for testing the endpoint

After playing around with the combination of request bodies and Pydantic models, we have seen that we can control the inflow of the data and be confident that the data that's available to our API endpoint will be what we want it and expect it to be. Sometimes, however, we may want to go to the bare metal and work with the raw request object. FastAPI covers that case too.

## The request object

I have mentioned several times that FastAPI is built on the Starlette web framework and that it uses numerous Starlette features. The raw request object in FastAPI is Starlette's request object and it can be accessed in our functions once it's been imported from FastAPI directly. Bear in mind that by using the request object directly, you are missing out on FastAPI's most important features: Pydantic parsing and validation, as well as self-documentation! However, there might be situations in which you need to have the raw request.

Let's look at an example:

**chapter3_raw_request.py**

```
from fastapi import FastAPI, Request
app = FastAPI()
@app.get("/cars")
async def raw_request(request:Request):
    return {
        "message":request.base_url,
        "all":dir(request)
    }
```

In the preceding code, we created a minimal FastAPI app, imported the `Request` class, and used it in the (only) endpoint. If you test this endpoint with your REST client, you will only get the base URL as the message, while the `all` part lists all the methods and properties of the `Request` object so that you have an idea of what is available.

All of these methods and properties are available for you to use in your application.

With that, we've seen how FastAPI facilitates our work with the main HTTP transport mechanisms – request bodies, query strings, and paths. Now, we will cover other, equally important aspects of any web framework solution.

## Cookies and headers, form data, and files

When speaking of the ways our web framework ingests data, any discussion would be incomplete without including topics such as handling form data, handling files, and manipulating cookies and headers. This section will provide simple examples of how FastAPI handles these tasks.

## Headers

Header parameters are handled in a similar way to query and path parameters and, as we will see later, cookies. We can collect them, so to speak, using the `Header` function. Headers are essential in topics such as authentication and authorization as they often carry **JSON Web Tokens (JWTs)**, which are used for identifying users and their permissions.

Let's try to read the user agent by using the `Header` function:

```
from fastapi import FastAPI, Header
app = FastAPI()
@app.get("/headers")
async def read_headers(user_agent: str | None = Header(None)):
    return {"User-Agent": user_agent}
```

Depending on the software you use to execute the test for the endpoint, you will get different results. When using HTTPie, I got this:

```
(venv) λ http GET "http://localhost:8000/headers"
HTTP/1.1 200 OK
content-length: 29
content-type: application/json
date: Sun, 27 Mar 2022 09:26:49 GMT
server: uvicorn
{
    "User-Agent": "HTTPie/3.1.0"
}
```

On the other hand, Insomnia correctly outputs the version:

```
{
    "User-Agent": "insomnia/2021.7.2"
}
```

You can extract all the headers in this way and FastAPI is nice enough to provide further assistance: it will convert names into lowercase, convert the keys into snake case, and so on.

## Cookies

Cookies work in a very similar way and although they can be extracted manually from the `Cookies` header, the framework offers a utility function, conveniently named `Cookie`, that does all the work in a way similar to `Query`, `Path`, and `Header`.

## Forms (and files)

So far, we have only dealt with JSON data and that is alright – after all, it is the ubiquitous language of the web and our main vehicle for moving data back and forth. There are cases, however, that require a different data encoding – forms might be processed directly by your API, with data encoded as `multipart/form-data` or `form-urlencoded`.

> **Important Note**
>
> Notice that although we can have multiple `Form` parameters in a path operation, we cannot declare Body fields that we expect to be in JSON. The HTTP request will have the body encoded using only `application/x-www-form-urlencoded` instead of `application/json`. This limitation is part of the HTTP protocol and has nothing to do with FastAPI itself.

The simplest way to cover both form cases – with and without including files for upload – is to start by installing `python-multipart`, a streaming multipart parser for Python. Stop your server and use `pip` to install it:

```
pip install python-multipart
```

The `Form` function works similarly to the previously examined utility functions, but with the difference that it looks for form-encoded parameters. Let's look at a simple example in which we wish to upload a (car!) image and a couple of form fields, such as the brand and the model. I will use a photo that I found on Pexels (photo by *Yogesh Yadav*: `https://www.pexels.com/photo/white-vintage-car-parked-on-green-grass-8746027/`):

```
from fastapi import FastAPI, Form, File, UploadFile
app = FastAPI()
@app.post("/upload")
async def upload(file:UploadFile=File(...),
brand:str=Form(...), model:str=Form(...)):
    return {
        "brand": brand,
        "model": model,
        "file_name":file.filename}
```

The preceding code handles the form parameters via the `Form` function and the uploaded file by using the `UploadFile` utility class.

The photo, however, isn't saved on the disk – its presence is merely acknowledged, and the filename is returned. Testing this endpoint in Insomnia looks like this:

Figure 3.3 – Testing file uploads and form fields with the Insomnia REST client

To save the image to a disk, we need to copy the buffer to an actual file on the disk. The following code achieves this:

```
import shutil
from fastapi import FastAPI, Form, File, UploadFile
app = FastAPI()
@app.post("/upload")
async def upload(picture:UploadFile=File(...),
brand:str=Form(...), model:str=Form(...)):
    with open("saved_file.png", "wb") as buffer:
        shutil.copyfileobj(picture.file, buffer)
    return {
        "brand": brand,
        "model": model,
        "file_name":picture.filename
        }
```

The open block opens a file on the disk using a specified filename and copies the FastAPI file that's sent through the form. I have hardcoded the filename, so any new upload will simply overwrite the existing file, but you could use some randomly generated filename while using the UUID library, for example.

File uploading is an operation that you probably won't be doing this way – file uploads can be handled by the Python async file library known as *aiofiles* or as a background task, which is another feature of FastAPI. However, I wanted to provide a rather complete picture of how you can handle everyday web tasks with the framework.

## FastAPI response customization

In the previous sections, we looked at numerous small examples of FastAPI requests, saw how we can reach every corner of the request – the path, the query string, the request body, headers, and cookies – and saw how to work with form-encoded requests. Now, let's take a closer look at FastAPI's response objects. In all the cases that we have seen so far, we returned a Python dictionary that was then serialized into JSON correctly by FastAPI. The framework enables us, the developers, to customize the response in a very granular way, as we will see in the next few sections.

The first thing that you may want to change in an HTTP response is going to be the status code. You may also want to provide some meaningful errors when things do not go as planned. FastAPI conveniently raises classic Python exceptions when HTTP errors are present. FastAPI puts a lot of emphasis on using standard-compliant meaningful response codes that minimize the need to create custom payload messages. For instance, you don't want to send a *200 OK* status code for everything and then notify users of errors by using the payload – FastAPI encourages good practices.

### Setting status codes

HTTP status codes indicate if an operation was successful or if there was an error. These codes also provide information about the type of operation, and they can be divided into several groups: informational, successful, client errors, server errors, and so on. It isn't necessary to memorize the status codes, although you probably know what a 404 or a 500 code is, unfortunately.

FastAPI makes it incredibly easy to set a status code – it is enough to just pass the desired `status_code` variable to the decorator. Here, we are using the 208 status code for a simple endpoint:

```
from fastapi import FastAPI, status
app = FastAPI()
@app.get("/", status_code=status.HTTP_208_ALREADY_REPORTED)
async def raw_fa_response():
    return {
        "message":"fastapi response"
    }
```

Testing the root route in *HTTPie* yields the following output:

```
(venv) λ http GET "http://localhost:8000"
HTTP/1.1 208 Already Reported
content-length: 30
content-type: application/json
date: Sun, 27 Mar 2022 20:14:25 GMT
server: uvicorn
{
    "message": "fastapi response"
}
```

Similarly, we can set status codes for the delete, update, or create operations.

FastAPI sets the 200 status by default if it doesn't encounter exceptions, so it is up to us to set the correct codes for the various API operations, such as 204 No Content for deleting, 201 for creating, and so on. It is a good practice that is particularly encouraged.

Pydantic can be used for response modeling as well – we can limit or otherwise modify the fields that should appear in the response and perform similar checks that it does for the request body by using the `response_model` argument.

I will not get into all the capabilities of FastAPI when it comes to customizing the response, but I will mention that modifying and setting headers and cookies is as simple as reading them from the HTTP request and the framework has us covered!

### HTTP errors

Errors are bound to happen, no matter how meticulously you design your backend – for example, users somehow find a way to send the wrong parameters to a query, the frontend sends the wrong request body, or the database goes offline (although that shouldn't happen since we will be using MongoDB!) – anything can happen. It is of paramount importance to detect these errors as soon as possible (this is a *leitmotiv* in FastAPI) and send clear and complete messages to the frontend, as well as the user. We can do this by raising exceptions.

FastAPI heavily relies on web standards and tries to enforce good practices in every facet of the development process, so it puts a lot of emphasis on using HTTP status codes. These codes provide a clear indication of the type of problem that has arisen, while the payload can be used to further clarify the cause of the problem.

FastAPI uses a Python exception, aptly called `HTTPExeption`, to raise HTTP errors. This class allows us to set a status code and set an error message.

Returning to our example of inserting new cars into the database, we could set a custom exception like this:

```
@app.post("/carsmodel")
async def new_car_model(car:InsertCar):
    if car.year>2022:
        raise HTTPException(
        status.HTTP_406_NOT_ACCEPTABLE,
        detail="The car doesn't exist yet!"
    )
    return {
        "message":car
    }
```

When trying to insert a car that hasn't been built yet, the response is as follows:

```
(venv) λ http POST http://localhost:8000/carsmodel brand="fiat"
model="500L" year=2023
HTTP/1.1 406 Not Acceptable
content-length: 39
content-type: application/json
date: Tue, 29 Mar 2022 18:37:42 GMT
server: uvicorn
{
    "detail": "The car doesn't exist yet!"
}
```

This is a pretty contrived example as I do not expect you to make custom exceptions for any possible problem that might arise, but I believe that this gives a good idea of what is possible and the flexibility that FastAPI gives you.

We just had a pretty fast ride through the main features of FastAPI, with particular emphasis on ways to get data out of the request and how to set the response according to our needs. Now, let's summarize this chapter.

## Summary

It is not easy to cover the basics of such a rich web framework in a relatively short number of pages. Rather than diving deep into specific topics, we covered very simple examples of how FastAPI achieves the most common REST API tasks and the way it can help you, as a developer, by leveraging modern Python features and libraries such as Pydantic.

In this chapter, you learned how FastAPI enables you to perform requests and responses through HTTP and how you can tap into it, at any point, and customize and access the elements of the request, as well as the response. We briefly addressed headers and cookies, query strings and paths, forms and files, and the main part of the cycle: the request and the response bodies.

Finally, you learned how to split your API into routers and how to organize your app into logical resource-based units.

There are many features of the framework that we haven't mentioned and that you are highly likely to encounter in even the simplest web applications. In *Chapter 5, Building the Backend for Our Application*, when we begin developing our simple application with FastAPI and MongoDB, we will learn how to connect the API to a MongoDB database and when to use an asynchronous driver. There, we will learn how to split our API into logical units using routers and make extensive use of the FastAPI dependency injection system.

In the next chapter, we will provide a quick introduction to React – our user interface library of choice. We will try to cover the absolute minimum necessary so that we can start using and discovering its incredibly powerful features and simplicity.

# 4

# Setting Up a
# React Workflow

This title might be a bit awkward, but really, I am going to go over a bit of React since it is a vast topic that deserves a separate book, and there are plenty of very good ones on the market. I listed the reasons for choosing React in the first place, back when we were analyzing our stack in *Chapter 1, Web Development and the FARM Stack*, so we will not go over it again. Instead, I will try to make a concise and short introduction to React, while pinpointing what I feel are the most important topics and features that you should be aware of in order to be proficient as soon as possible.

In this chapter, we're going to create a very simple React app, or better – the frontend of an app – through which we will showcase the main features and the most salient concepts that will make working with React worth your while. We will begin with the prerequisites and tools (such as Node.js, some Visual Studio Code extensions, and more). We will also learn how to use the standard command-line tool **Create React App** for quick-starting new applications, and then I will go over the concept of components and the role of JSX – the essence of React.

We will design a simple application in terms of components, and we will see how decoupling helps us write modular and maintainable code. We will briefly glance over two of the most important hooks and see how they solve some web development problems that are as ancient as the web itself. Finally, we will deploy our shell app and briefly discuss the deployment possibilities.

In this chapter, we will cover the following main topics:

- The basic ideas behind React
- Creating React apps and the resulting starter files
- Styling with Tailwind CSS
- Functional components and JSX – the language of React
- Managing state with the `useState` hook and communicating with APIs using the `useEffect` hook
- Exploring React Router and other goodies

By the end of the chapter, you will have created a minimal, yet fully functional React web app, and you will become part of an army of frontend developers who value simple tools to be able to achieve complex functionalities, without being confined within a strict framework.

## Technical requirements

Starting a React project involves less setup, although the structure of the project will be more complicated than the Python one, as you will soon be able to see. Creating a React-based application used to involve several steps, such as setting up a build system, a transpiler, creating a directory structure, and more. Fortunately for us, a script, which is conveniently called **Create-React-App**, is there to do all the heavy lifting for us! The only requirement is to have a working and updated Node.js installation on your local machine.

If you do not have Node.js on your machine, head over to `https://nodejs.org/en/download/`, grab the version for your operating system, and then follow the instructions. I am currently using version 14, but feel free to use a newer version. When installing, check all the boxes – you want *npm* (Node.js' package manager) and optional additional command-line tools if you are on a Windows machine.

Since you already have Visual Studio Code installed (haven't you?), this is a good moment to install a great React extension called ES7+ React/Redux/React-Native snippets – it will allow you to speed up the creation of components – the building blocks of a React app. Finally, if you are developing and testing your apps in Google Chrome, there is a neat extension called **React Developer Tools** that will enable you to debug your react apps quicker and spot potential problems easier.

## Let's Create (a) React App

As I mentioned earlier, `create-react-app` takes away much of the heavy work when starting a project, and we will be using it throughout this book. However, bear in mind that there are other ways to set up React; for instance, you can include it through a CDN just like plain old jQuery if you want to go old-school!

Let's create a simple app that we will be building upon in this introduction. Grab a folder, mine is called `chapter4`, cd into it, and from your Terminal of choice type in the following:

```
npx create-react-app cars
```

Now watch the magic happen before your eyes! Npx is a tool that is included with the latest versions of *npm*, and it allows us to run executable scripts without the need to install them on your machine. Please allow the process to finish. This can take a while and the output might be cryptic, but eventually, we will have a properly initiated React project ready to be developed.

The Terminal will inform you that you can run several commands, but at this point, we will follow the suggestion and change the directory into the newly created `cars` directory (because that is what we called our project when we ran `create-react-app`) and run the following command:

```
npm start
```

You will be greeted by a gray screen with a slowly rotating blue React logo. Success! However, behind this dead-simple page, there is tons of code, and we can examine this generated code by looking inside the `cars` folder that the good `create-react-app` robot (I always imagined it as a robot) built for us.

The is a `node_modules` directory that, like in all Node.js projects, contains all the project dependencies, and there are lots of them! You will not need to touch this folder except in extreme debugging operations, so let's move on to the next one. In the `Public` folder, there are a couple of generic files that we will soon remove, such as the PNG logos and the `favicon.ico` file, but there is also an extremely important HTML file – the `index.html`. This bare-bones file contains a `div`, with the `id` of the root and this `div` is the place where React will put our whole application.

Moving on to the `src` directory, this is where we will be doing all of our work. The `App.js` file that represents our entire application – all the components, menus, headers and footers, lists, and controls – will be hosted on this file, which, in turn, will be rendered in our single `div` with the `id` of the root in the HTML file. This monstrous complexity is necessary for the flexibility and capabilities that React will be able to provide us while developing, in just a few more steps.

Since I will not delve much into the styling of our React apps in this book, I want to get it out of the way as quickly as possible and in the easiest way possible in my opinion. React enables us to style applications in a myriad of ways – you can use classic CSS style sheets or SASS, you can opt for JavaScript-style objects, and there are very modern and weird but efficient solutions such as **Styled Components**. Additionally, all of the major visual frameworks have a React version – Material UI, Bootstrap, and Semantic UI – you name it. I will be using Tailwind CSS, which has an atypical approach that I like, and I feel that it doesn't get in the way too much. I found Tailwind CSS excellent for defining basic, simple styles that make the page look simple and clean, while it is perfectly good for achieving pixel-perfect designs from Figma or Adobe XD files if needed.

## Tailwind CSS and Installation

Essentially, **Tailwind CSS** is a utility-first framework that translates CSS into a bunch of classes that can be used directly in the markup and enable us to achieve complex designs. Just by adding classes to our HTML elements, we will be able to create completely styled documents. Check it out on their excellent website at `https://tailwindcss.com/` and get acquainted with it, as we will be using it for all our React-styling needs.

To install the Tailwind CSS framework in our *cars* project, we will follow the procedure from `https://tailwindcss.com/docs/guides/create-react-app`. Follow these steps:

1.  First, we need to install the packages using npm. Stop your server with *Ctrl + C* and run the following:

    ```
    npm install -D tailwindcss postcss autoprefixer
    ```

    The preceding command installs Tailwind and two other dependencies as development dependencies.

2.  Next, we will automatically create the necessary config files with the following command:

    ```
    npx tailwindcss init -p
    ```

3.  Now, we need to tell Tailwind where to look for files. Open the `tailwind.config.js` file and make sure it contains the following:

    ```
    module.exports = {
      content: [
        "./src/**/*.{js,jsx,ts,tsx}",
      ],
      theme: {
        extend: {},
      },
      plugins: [],
    }
    ```

4.  Finally, edit the `index.css` file in your `src` folder, delete everything – the styles that powered our rotating logo page – and just leave the following:

    ```
    @tailwind base;
    @tailwind components;
    @tailwind utilities;
    ```

5.  This is kind of embarrassing, but important. As it turns out, as of 2022, you *need* to run the following:

    ```
    npm install postcss@latest
    ```

    This is in order to update the `postcss` package to its latest version and make Tailwind work as expected. Do not forget to run `npm start` again – it will start our development server, which reloads every time we save our changes!

6.  Finally, edit the App.js file – clear everything and just leave the following:

```
function App() {
  return (
    <div className="App">
      <h1 className="bg-slate-500 text-white text-
        center">This is a Tailwind styled site!</h1>
    </div>
  );
}
export default App;
```

Don't worry about the weird className stuff – this is JSX, React's language for creating HTML – but take a look at the classes (they are classes, despite the naming). The first one tells Tailwind to apply a background of slate-500 (it's a color) and the text-white and text-center classes are pretty self-explanatory. You will notice that Visual Studio Code does some nice autocompletion stuff as soon as you type in the first quote. Phew! We have a basic React + Tailwind setup. Now let's move on and see whether it was worth it. If you want to practice Tailwind CSS a bit, try creating a full-height page with some creepy dashed borders! Next, we will tackle the most fundamental parts of React: JSX. This is the language that React uses to create the HTML and the components – the building blocks that will eventually compose our application.

## JSX and the Components – the building blocks

We might safely say that JSX is the glue that holds the whole React concept together. The smallest building blocks of a React page or app are so-called **React elements**. A simple element might be as follows:

```
const title = <h1>The Car Sales App</h1>
```

This is an interesting concept – it looks like an H1 HTML element, but it also definitely looks like JavaScript, too. And you would be right – JSX enables us to create React elements that can be inserted into React's virtual DOM tree that is different from the actual HTML. React takes care of the tedious job of updating the DOM to match the virtual DOM and compiles the JSX elements (through something called Babel) into actual HTML elements. Why JSX, you wonder? Well, first, it is a full-fledged programming language – JavaScript in all its glory and power. React elements are immutable – once we create them, we cannot change them, and as the React site states, they are like single frames in a movie. However, they can be replaced with new elements.

It is important to note that every React component, including our App file, which is currently the only component that we have, must return *one and only one* element – a div or a fragment (essentially, an empty tag, <>) and all the React elements enclosed in it. Let's try and write some simple elements and modify our App.js file to look like this:

```
function App() {
  let data = ["Fiat", "Peugeot","Ford","Renault","Citroen"]
  return (
    <div className="App max-w-3xl mx-auto h-full">
      <h1 className="bg-slate-500 text-white text-center
        ">This is a Tailwind styled site!</h1>
      <div>
        {data.map(
          (el)=>{
            return <div>Cars listed as <span className=
              "font-bold">{el.toUpperCase()}</span></div>
          }
        )}
      </div>
    </div>
  );
}
export default App;
```

Our simple page should look like the following:

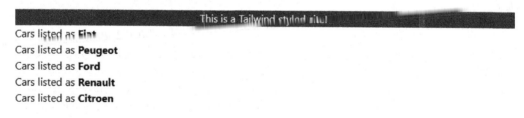

Figure 4.1 – Our nearly blank Tailwind CSS – the React page

Let's take a look at what we just did, or better yet, what JSX was able to provide us. First, we have declared some data – a simple list of car brands in an array. For now, we will pretend that we got this data from an external API. After all, it's all JavaScript. Then, in the return statement, we were able to map over this array using the JavaScript map function – we called the elements of the el array. Finally, we return these elements – in this case, they are strings, and we wrap them in template literals (another ES6 feature) and, just to be fancy, transform them to uppercase. The whole function returns exactly one `div` element. Since `class` is a reserved name in JavaScript, React uses the `className` keyword, and we can see that we used it quite a bit since Tailwind is very verbose.

Finally, let's add a little something to our `App.js` file, so React doesn't complain in the console. Change the `return` statement by adding a `key` property:

```
return <div key={el}>Cars listed as <span className="font-
bold">{el.toUpperCase()}</span></div>
```

The key is a unique identifier that React needs anytime it creates arrays of DOM elements, so it knows which one to replace, keep, or remove. This is a rather simplistic example, but it shows the basics of the power of React's handwriting – JSX. The important thing to remember is that we have to return exactly one element – be it a `div` element, a title, or a React fragment.

To sum it up, and for those of you who might be coming from a different UI framework or library (such as Vue.js, Svelte, or Angular), React does not have a proper templating language with a dedicated syntax for looping over arrays of objects or `if-else` constructs. Instead, you can rely on the full power of JavaScript and use the standard language features such as `map` for iterating through arrays, `filter` for filtering data, ternary operators for `if-else` constructs, template literals for string interpolations, and more. Coming from classical templating languages such as Jinja2 and Handlebars, I must admit it can take some time to adjust. But after a while, it becomes very natural, and you don't really have to think much about rules and what can and cannot be done (almost anything can!).

Now we will speak about arguably React's most important feature – components.

## Components

The whole idea or paradigm of modern web development (we're talking 2020s modern) is built around the concept of breaking complex UIs into smaller, more manageable units – components. In React since its beginning, components could be created by extending a JavaScript component class, using the render method, and defining functions. With the introduction of hooks, which are special functions that allow us to interact with the state and life cycle of the components directly, React development became much more flexible and concise – at least in my humble opinion. But let's talk about components.

Components are reusable pieces of the UI, and we can think of them as functions returning JSX – pieces or units of UI. One of the first stages of planning the development of a react site is the identification of areas, that is, pieces that could be abstracted into components and reused in some way or, at the very least, abstracted into separate units.

Let's try to create a minimal component for displaying the header on a page. The component should have an easy task: just to display the header, in our case, the title of the page, and maybe some simple navigation links.

Functional components in React.js are defined as files with .jsx or .js extensions, and like our App.js file (which is also a component – the root component), they must return a single JSX element. The filenames should be capitalized. This is a great moment in which to use our previously installed React extension for Visual Studio Code as it provides useful snippets for creating standard components. Follow these steps:

1.  Let's create a folder called components in our src folder along with a new file called Header.js in it.

2.  Now, open the newly created file and type in rafce. The editor should suggest something cryptically to you, called reactArrowFunctionExportComponent.

3.  Select it and you will see your file filled with a typical ES6 arrow function component exported:

```
const Header = () => {
  return (
    <div>Header</div>
  )
}
export default Header
```

This file defines a single JSX topmost element – called Header – and exports it at the bottom.

4.  Let's make some edits to this file, making use of our Tailwind CSS framework classes: we will make a div element on the left-hand side containing the title and a couple of links on the right-hand side. At this point, we will not worry about responsiveness or fancy coloring. I just want to create some contrast so that we can see what we have made:

```
const Header = () => {
  return (
    <div className="flex flex-row bg-orange-600 text-
        white align-middle justify-center p-5">
      <h1>Cars Sales App</h1>
    </div>
  )
}
export default Header
```

5.  After these edits, which we will explain in a bit and which are purely Tailwind-related, go ahead and import the first component to our App.js file. Imports are handled in terms of the relative path – just remember that the dot denotes the current directory of the file (src, in our case), while /components is the folder in which we are keeping our components. The App.js file should now look like this:

```
import Header from "./components/Header";
function App() {
  let data = [
    {brand:"Fiat", color:"green", model:"500L",
      price:7000, "year":2020,"id":1},
    {brand:"Peugeot", color:"red", model:"5008",
      price:8000, "year":2018,"id":2},
    {brand:"Volkswagen", color:"white", model:"Golf
      7", price:8500, "year":2019,"id":3},
    {brand:"Fiat", color:"green", model:"Tipo",
      price:10000, "year":2019,"id":4},
    {brand:"Kia", color:"black", model:"Ceed",
      price:6000, "year":2010,"id":5},
    {brand:"Volkswagen", color:"white", model:"Golf
      7", price:8500, "year":2019,"id":15},
    {brand:"Fiat", color:"gray", model:"Ritmo",
      price:300, "year":1990,"id":21}
  ]
  return (
    <div className="App max-w-3xl mx-auto h-full">
      <Header/>
      <div>
        {data.map(
          (el)=>{
            return (
              <div key={el.id}>
                <span className="font-bold">
                {el.brand.toUpperCase()}</span>
              </div>
            )
          }
```

```
        )}
      </div>
    </div>
  );
}
export default App;
```

If you reload our app… I'm just kidding, React should be doing that job for you if you haven't stopped the npm run start process. You will see that our simple web page now has a simple header component. It is an H1 element and has some basic formatting – it is orange and centered. We imported the component as a self-closing tag.

So, you just made your first, very simple, React functional component. In this way, we can break down the functionality of our entire website: we can add a footer, maybe some navigation, and more. In fact, the process of breaking an app down into components and deciding what should constitute a single component is so important that the React documentation has an excellent page dedicated to the process: https://reactjs.org/docs/thinking-in-react.html.

In the following diagram, you can see a simple example of breaking an application user interface into separate components. Each rectangle represents an independent component that is imported into the main app component. Some might be repeated several times, while others – such as the header and the footer – might be present with only one instance:

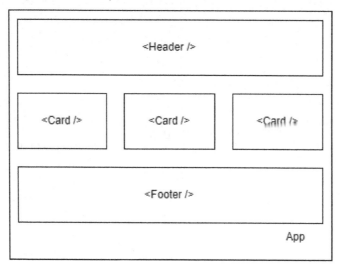

Figure 4.2 – Breaking an app into components

Crafting components like this is nice and quick, but it can become boring if the output is… fixed, so to speak. Fortunately, React components are functions, and functions can take arguments, and usually, they are able to do something useful with those arguments. Let's say that we want to create a component that will replace our rather ugly-looking list of car brands and display the information in a more eye-pleasing and informative way. We can then pass the data for each car in our data array (an object) and have it formatted the way we want.

Let's redo our procedure for building components. Follow these steps:

1.  Create a new file in the `components` folder, name it `Card.js`, and type `rafce` in order to get the VSC extension to fire. You will then see something like this:

    ```
    const Card = () => {
      return (
        <div>Card</div>
      )
    }
    export default Card
    ```

2.  Now, let us import the `Card` component into our `App.js` file in the same way as we did with the `Header`:

    ```
    import Header from "./components/Header";
    import Card from "./components/Card";

    function App() {
      let data = [
      ]

      return (
        <div className="App max-w-3xl mx-auto h-full">
          <Header/>
          <div>
            {data.map(
              (el)=>{
                return (
                  <Card key={el.id} car = {el} />
                )
              }
    ```

```
      )}
    </div>
  </div>
  );
}
export default App;
```

Now, instead of returning the `divs` when mapping through our data – we are returning our `Card` component and passing it the key (that is, the ID of the car object; note that it just has to be unique or React will yell at us!). Additionally, we are passing it something that we called `car` and set to the element – the `car` object.

If you take a look at our page, you will not be impressed – it's just a bunch of Tailwind-bland *Card* texts. However, we did achieve something – we passed data through props (short for properties) to each `Card`. We just have to "accept" it in the component.

3.  Let's call this function argument `props` and log it to the console. In the `Card.js` file, modify the first two lines:

```
const Card = (props) => {
    console.log(props)
    return (
    <div>Card</div>
  )
}
export default Card
```

The app will not change, but if you take a look at the console output in Google Chrome, you will see that we are getting back all of the `car` objects inside our `Card` components

4.  Now we can go on and populate the `Card` with the data:

```
const Card = (props) => {
    return (
    <div>
        {props.car.brand}
        {props.car.model}
        {props.car.year}
        {props.car.price}
        {props.car.color}
    </div>
```

```
    )
  }
  export default Card
```

We've got something that will not win any design awards but will get all of our data back into the component.

5.  Now you can get creative: dive into some Tailwind CSS documentation and come up with a card style that you like. I am going to make something really simple, and I am going to get rid of this props.car repetition by using some JavaScript ES6 destructuring:

```
const Card = ({car}) => {
    let {brand, price, model, year, color} = car
    return (
    <div className="shadow-md p-5 flex flex-col">
        <div className="font-extrabold text-center
            border-b-2">{brand} {model}</div>
        <div>Year: {year}</div>
        <div>Price: <span className="font-semibold
            text- orange-600">{price}</span></div>
        <div>Color: {color}</div>
    </div>
    )
  }
  export default Card
```

In the App.js file, I have just added a couple of classes to the wrapper div: grid grid-cols-3 my-3 gap-3. Once you get the hang of Tailwind CSS, you will be able to read them very easily. We make the div to a grid with three columns, and we add some y-padding and a grid-gap.

We have seen how easy it is to pass props to components, and once we can do that, the sky is the limit! Well, not quite. Props provide one-way communication, but in the majority of apps, you will have to deal with the state.

I will not delve into some of the very technical definitions of state. Since React's job is to keep the UI in sync with the current situation of our app, we can stick to a more descriptive definition.

A state can be thought of as a set of data that represents the **user interface** (**UI**) at any given moment. In our case, the state could be a set of selected cars, which we would like to inquire about and save them for later by giving them stars or some follow icon. Forms can have different states depending on the types of inputs: text fields can be empty (waiting to be filled) or populated, checkboxes can be checked, or unchecked, and drop-down menus can be selected or not. You get the idea. The state is such an important topic in React (and, to be honest, in other UI frameworks and libraries) that entire books and conferences are dedicated to it. In this chapter, we will barely scratch the surface of how React Hooks help us to define and maintain state throughout our component's life cycle, that is, while the component is alive.

In the early days of yore, you had to create React components by extending the JavaScript classes and maintain the state through a series of `this` calls that made working with the state a bit verbose and cumbersome. With the introduction of React Hooks, we have at our disposal several easy mechanisms for dealing with the state, from very simple ones to more complex ones. In the next section, we are going to take a look at a couple of React Hooks and learn how they can help us to write concise and maintainable code.

# React Hooks, events, and state

A great definition of React or its components is that it is, essentially, a *function that converts a state to a user interface* – a React component is literally a function, as we have seen, and it takes props as arguments. The output of the function (the component, really!) is a JSX element. Essentially, React hooks are functional constructs that enable us to tap into the life cycle of a component and mess with its state.

## Creating stateful variables with useState

The first, and probably the most fundamental hook, is the `useState` hook, which enables us to maintain a certain state throughout our component. Let's say that we want to maintain some kind of state in our one-page app – we want to set a budget limit and how much money we are willing to spend, so the website doesn't try to lure us into even looking at those cars that are just too expensive. We will make a simple textbox, set it to display just numeric values, and hook it up with a state variable that we will aptly name `budget`. I have made quite a few changes to the App.js file, but we will go over it line by line:

```
import Header from "./components/Header";
import Card from "./components/Card";
import {useState} from 'react'
function App() {
    let data = [ ]
    let [budget, setBudget] = useState(4000)
```

```
    const onChangeHandler = (event)=>{
    setBudget(event.target.value)
}


  return (
    <div className="App max-w-3xl mx-auto h-full">
      <Header/>
      <div className="border-2 border-yellow-500 my-5 p-
        3">Your current budget is:
      <span className="">{budget}</span></div>
      <div className="grid grid-cols-3 my-3 gap-3">
        {data.map(
          (el)=>{
            return (
              <Card key={el.id} car = {el} />
              )
          }
        )}
      </div>
      <div className="bg-gray-300 rounded-md p-3">
        <label htmlFor="budget">Budget:</label>
        <input type="number" onChange={onChangeHandler}
            id="budget" name="budget" min="300" max="10000"
            step="100" value={budget}></input>
      </div>
    </div>
  );
}
export default App;
```

Let's see what we did here. First, we imported the useState hook from React. The useState hook, probably the simplest of them all, returns two values – a variable (which can be anything we want – an array or an object) and a function that sets the value for this state variable. Although you can use any legal JavaScript name, it is a good convention to use the name of the variable – in our case, budget – and the same name, prepended with set: setBudget. That's all there is to it! With this simple line of code, we have told React to set up a state unit called budget and to set up a setter. The argument of the useState() call is the initial value. In our case, we have set it to be 4,000 Euros:

Figure 4.3 – Our minimal React Tailwind page

Now we are free to use this state variable across the page. Note that we placed the `useState` call inside the `App` functional component – if you try to place it elsewhere, it will not work: hooks tap into the life cycle of components from the inside of the bodies of the functions defining the components themselves.

Moving down to the bottom of the component, we can see that we added a simple textbox. We set it to only display numeric values with HTML, and we added an `onchange` handler.

This is a good moment to mention that React uses the so-called `SyntheticEvent` – a wrapper around the browser's native events that enables React to achieve cross-browser compatibility. The documentation is very straightforward, and you can find it on the React website: `https://reactjs.org/docs/events.html`. Once you have remembered a couple of differences (the events are using camelCase, rather than lowercase, and you must pass them a function in JSX), you will be writing event handlers in no time.

Back to our `App.js` file. We added an `onChange` event to the textbox and set it to be handled by a function – we called it `onChangeHandler`.

This `onChangeHandler` could hardly get any simpler: it just takes the current value of the textbox (`target.value`, just like the original DOM events; remember, it's just a wrapper) and sets our budget state to this value using our `useState` call defined just above the function. Finally, we added a `div` element just below the `Header` component that uses this `budget` value and displays it. That's it – we added a state variable to our app – the root component. We can set it and get it, and we are displaying it on the page!

Now let us try another thing. We have the user entering their budget and displaying it on the page. Wouldn't it be nice if we could somehow differentiate between cars that fit said budget and those that do not? To get this to work, we will need to set our small data sample that is currently hardcoded to be a state variable itself, and then we could just filter it and display only those within our price range.

I will not go through the code for this, but you can find it in this book's GitHub repository. The procedure would be to set a new state variable that holds an array of cars satisfying the condition that their price is less than or equal to our budget (hint: JavaScript filtering arrays) and then just add `setDisplayedCars` to the budget event handler.

At this point, I must encourage you to dive into the excellent React.js documentation and learn more about the `useState` hook and its big brother, the `useReducer` hook. This is a hook that might be thought of as a generalization of the `useState` hook and that is best suited when you have to deal with numerous pieces of state that are *interconnected,* so managing them with many simple `useState` hooks could end up being tedious and difficult to maintain.

Now I am going to delete the contents of our `App.js` file, leaving only the empty Tailwind-styled canvas and the header:

```
import Header from "./components/Header";
function App() {
  return (
    <div className="App max-w-3xl mx-auto h-full">
     <Header/>
    </div>
  );
}
export default App;
```

You have seen how the `useState` hook enables you to add a `stateful` variable in a very simple and straightforward way and how to manipulate the state through regular events.

Now it is time to see how we can get our data from our efficient FastAPI backend into our beautiful React.js frontend. We will get to know another hook: `useEffect`.

# Communicate with APIs using useEffect

We have already seen how React and its components transform the state and the data into a user interface. We will do all the fun stuff of connecting our MongoDB layer to FastAPI and then powering a React frontend in the following chapter. Here, we will use a free mock rest API. However, we do need to address the problem of accessing external data and the management of external events in general. "External" with regards to *what,* you might wonder?

Well, we have seen that React and its mighty hooks are centered around the task of synchronizing the UI to the state and the data. Components can contain other components, and together, they form what is known as a component tree, which is then constantly compared to the current state. React does all of this coordination work – what should be rendered, updated, and more.

Events that are outside the flow of the React data flow process are called **side effects**. Some side effects might be setting or getting data values in local storage or session storage (maybe we want to save the data of logged-in users' until the next session), measuring the dimensions of some DOM element (for instance, we want to display different layouts for different browser sizes), and most notably, getting or fetching data from an external system, maybe in the form of a REST API call.

When working with React, one thing to always bear in mind is that it works in a continuous data flow, with an underlying system constantly scanning for updates and ready to re-render components that it deems in need of an update. We will illustrate this with a simple example. We are working on our *Cars Sales* application, and we need to list all the users that were kind (and smart enough!) and registered an account.

The task at hand is a simple and common one. We have a dedicated page – it will probably live in a URL called /users or something similar, and it should be populated with the data (think of a JavaScript array of objects) from an external API. This API will be powered by FastAPI, but for now, we will use a readymade mock solution called **Regres**.

The GET call we need to make should be directed toward the URL, https://reqres.in/api/users.

We already understand how to make components, provide them props, and set their state, so that shouldn't be a problem. But what are we going to do about loading data from an external API? We'll just use something such as Fetch or Axios, right? Like we were using a normal plain JavaScript app. Let's give it a try:

1.  Modify the App.js in a way that includes a standard fetch call to the API, including the json method to get the data to a console.

```
import Header from "./components/Header";
function App() {

  fetch('https://reqres.in/api/users')
    .then(response=>response.json())
    .then(json=>console.log(json))
  return (
    <div className="App max-w-3xl mx-auto h-full">
     <Header/>
    </div>
```

```
    );
  }
  export default App;
```

Our app will continue to be blank with an orange header, but if you take a look at the console in Chrome, you will see that we are actually getting our users back, six of them. So, we just need to put them in a state variable, and we should be good to go, right?

2.  Let's add a state variable and a corresponding set method by using our old friend, the useState hook (warning: the following code is wrong, and it will bomb your browser and, potentially, get you into trouble with your API provider!):

```
  import {useState} from 'react'
  import Header from "./components/Header";
  function App() {
    let [users, setUsers] = useState([])
    fetch('https://reqres.in/api/users')
      .then(response=>response.json())
      .then(json=>setUsers(json['data']))

    return (
      <div className="App max-w-3xl mx-auto h-full">
        <Header/>
        <ul>
          {users.map(
            (el)=>{
              return (
                <li>{el.email}</li>
                )
            }
          )}
        </ul>
      </div>
    );
  }
  export default App;
```

The preceding code just won't run, or it will run but not in the way that you might expect. If you manage to open the developer's console in Chrome, you will see that the page is constantly making requests to our poor API server, flooding it in the process. Why is that?

I found this problem very illustrative of the way React works, and once you get the hang of it, it will begin to make sense. The problem is located at the top of the App function. We declared a state variable with useState, and then we naively proceeded to set its value after a fetch call to our external API. After firing the setUsers method, React noticed that there is a change of a state variable, so a re-render is in order. Then, React just calls the function again, re-encounters the fetch call, sets the value of a state variable, and… you get it. We are in an infinite loop.

The useEffect hook is meant for cases like this – interacting with the world outside of our React app in a safe and controlled way.

3.  The syntax of the hook is quite simple, import it directly from React, and then call it inside our component with the following form:

```
useEffect(()=>{
    console.log("This just happened!")
}, [])
```

Note that useEffect takes in two arguments – the first is a function that will execute after every render, and the second one is an array of dependencies in which we list all the values that we want to monitor for a change. If any of these values change, the function declared as the first argument will run (again).

4.  Armed with this knowledge, we can turn to our App component and try something like this:

```
import {useState, useEffect} from 'react'
import Header from "./components/Header";
function App() {
  let [users, setUsers] = useState([])
  useEffect(()=>{
    fetch('https://regres.in/apl/users')
    .then(response=>response.json())
    .then(json=>setUsers(json['data']))
  }, [])
  return (
    <div className="App max-w-3xl mx-auto h-full">
      <Header/>
      <ul>
        {users.map(
          (el)=>{
            return (
              <li key={el.id}>{el.email}</li>
              )
```

```
            }
        )}
      </ul>
    </div>
  );
}
export default App;
```

Like some kind of magic, the page seems to display our data just the way we wanted it – a list of user emails, for a total of six (our API will not give us more than that, but it is more than enough for our purposes). Add after this:

You might be wondering why we passed an empty array to our `useEffect` function. Simply put, this array - also known as a dependency array - allows us to control when the `useEffect` will fire. In our case, we provided an empty dependency array so the `useEffect` hook function will fire off only once, after the initial render. If we provided a state variable, controlled via a `useState` hook to the array, `useEffect` would fire every time that provided state variable changed.

The React documentation on the subject is a very useful read: `https://reactjs.org/docs/hooks-reference.html#conditionally-firing-an-effect`

Now, since we want to showcase our dependency array, we can make use of the fact that our REST API of choice offers us two pages of users: `https://reqres.in/api/users?page=2`.

5.  We can make another state variable, an integer, to monitor the page we are currently viewing, and we can make a simple button with a state handler. The handler function will make use of ES6's ternary operator – if the state is equal to `1` set it to `0` and vice versa:

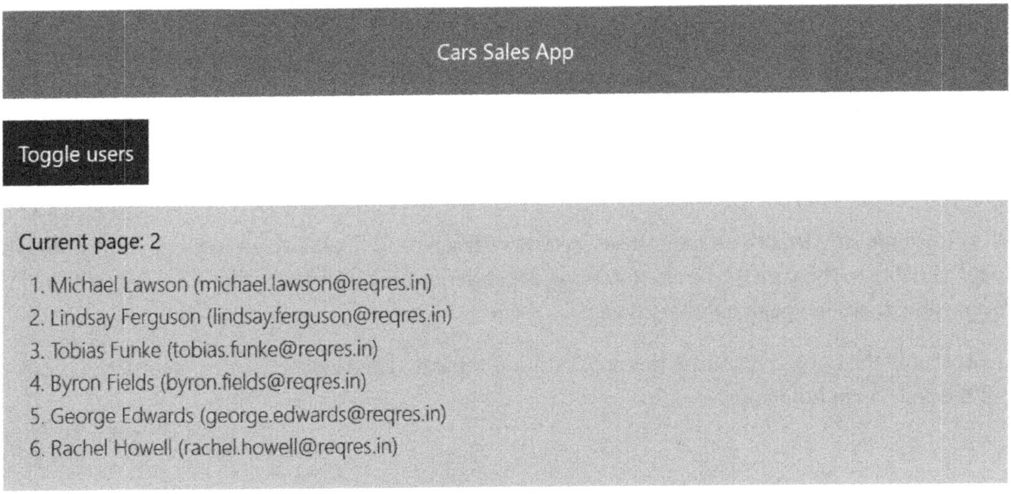

Figure 4.4 – Displaying users from an external API

The code for adding the toggle – logic is straightforward:

```
import Header from "./components/Header";
import {useState, useEffect} from 'react'
function App() {
  let [users, setUsers] = useState([])
  let [page, setPage] = useState(1)
    useEffect((()=>{
    fetch(`https://reqres.in/api/users?page=${page}`)
    .then(response=>response.json())
    .then(json=>setUsers(json['data']))
    }, [page])
  return (
    <div className="App max-w-3xl mx-auto h-full">
     <Header/>
     <button className="border border-gray-500 rounded-md
       p-2 m-5" onClick={()=>{page===1?setPage(2):
         setPage(1)}}>Toggle users</button>
      <ul>
        {users&&users.map(el=>{
        return (
          <li key={el.id}>{el.email}</li>
          )
        })}
   </ul>
     </div>
    );
}
export default App;
```

We also made sure to short-circuit the users' array variable and the JSX mapping logic, and added the page variable to the useEffect function's dependency array – this way the function will execute every time there is a page number change, or toggle.

Note that in the book's repository this application is separated and called Users, in order to preserve all the code form both apps.

Finally, `useEffect` only fires when the contents of the dependency array change, and in our case, that is the page variable. Now, clicking on the button fetches us the first or second page of the users, and no API calls are made in between, except for the initial fetch that follows immediately after the first component render.

Like with `useState`, there are much more subtleties involved. For example, we can provide a cleanup function at the bottom of the `useEffect` body to make sure that any long-lasting effects are removed and so on, but this should give you a basic idea of how to handle actions that reach out to an external API.

There are several other hooks that you will want to use in your projects – the `useMemo` hook for **memoizing** values of a function helps us to avoid unnecessary repeated costly function calls. Additionally, `useContext` allows React to cover an entire area of components and pass values directly without having to pass them through several components that might not actually need it (prop drilling). We can even create our own hooks and abstract functionality that can be reused in several places of the app, ensuring better maintainability and less repetition. In the upcoming chapters, we will use a couple of hooks in order to achieve the desired functionality elegantly and simply.

In conclusion, a personal note – I tried to learn React while there were no hooks around, and I must be honest, I *did not* like it. The state management with class components and life cycle methods just did not sit well with me, and I admit that, probably, my background and lack of classical Computer Science training played a role in that. With the entrance of hooks, the whole ecosystem just became much clearer and cleaner, and the mapping of business logic to UIs is much more streamlined and, well, logical. I can only suggest that you take some time and dive into the hooks system, it will be worth it, I promise!

You now have the knowledge that is necessary to set and get states in your components or apps and to communicate with external API services in a predictable and controllable way, while crafting clean and simple code. Just using React and its hooks can give you web developer superpowers, but there is a whole world of packages and modules built around React that is just as important as the core libraries.

## Exploring React Router and other goodies

So far, we have only created a couple of single-page apps that are really single pages – we haven't touched some advanced functionalities, and they do not even qualify as apps. However, single-page apps are not limited to a single URL – if you navigate to your Gmail account, you will see that the URL does, in fact, change with every action that you might take. While there are several solutions that enable us to achieve routing in **Single-Page Applications (SPAs)**, **React Router** is the de facto standard solution, and it is a well-tested, mature package that has recently had a major update (version 6).

The underlying idea of a frontend page router is that it enables us to render different components on the same page depending on the route that is loaded. For instance, the `/about` route would cause the app to load a component called `About.js` in the main App component, removing other, previously loaded components and so on. In its latest version, React Router has made some breaking changes, but the logic is unaltered. The package provides us with a basic structure – `BrowserRouter` – which is used to wrap our entire root App component. We will create a basic router for our *cars* application in the next chapter, but here, I just want to convey the idea and the principles that lie underneath.

React itself is so popular and omnipresent that it has created an impressive ecosystem around itself. I have already mentioned that, besides Tailwind, you can use virtually any UI or CSS framework either directly or through some optimized React version, such as Bootstrap, or more *reacty* such as Ant design. We can enhance our user experience with subtle animations through *React Motion*, and we can speed up the development of forms with some excellent form libraries such as *Formik* or *React Hook Form*. For complex state problems, *Redux* is the most popular and widely adopted industry standard, but there are many smaller or specialized libraries for local and global state management.

In this book, in our *cars* application, we will make a couple of charts, and we will see why data visualization specialists are turning to React. For instance, the combination of React Hooks and D3.js enables us to make virtually everything achievable with D3.js (and that's *a lot*), while making data management easier through React. Bear in mind that we have barely scratched the surface of what is possible to achieve with React, and this chapter is really meant just to get you started and whet your appetite.

## Summary

We made it through a short and atypical introduction to the world's most popular user interface library – React.js. I tried to cover the absolute basics and point the reader in a certain direction, rather than trying to elaborate on topics that require separate chapters or entire books. I have covered the topics that I believe are enough to get started.

We have seen what **JSX** is and why it is so convenient for developers. We introduced the basic building blocks of React, **functional components**, and the basic rules that must be followed when designing them. I have introduced two fundamental **React Hooks** that, when combined, allow you to begin building basic user interfaces, maintain and change state in the components and interact with external APIs.

Finally, I mentioned some of the **React libraries** that will make your life easier when developing custom applications – they all have excellent documentation and are updated frequently, so covering them in depth would defy the purpose of this chapter.

In the next chapter, we will use some of this basic knowledge and use React to create a simple but fully functional and dynamic for our application.

# Part 2 – Parts of the Stack Working Together

In this part, we start building a simple, yet realistic full-stack application and explore the JWT authentication flow with the FARM stack.

This part includes the following chapters:

- *Chapter 5, Building the Backend for Our Application*
- *Chapter 6, Building the Frontend of the Application*
- *Chapter 7, Authentication and Authorization*

# 5

# Building the Backend for Our Application

In the previous chapter, you learned just enough React to be able to think in components and JSX and to express your UI interactivity in terms of Hooks and handlers. It is time to put this new creativity to good use and build something!

In this chapter, we will take a simple yet concrete application specification and try to create a simple backend. We will do the following:

- Connect to an instance of MongoDB and learn about Python drivers
- Connect asynchronously to our database
- Create Pydantic models for our data
- Make a more manageable application structure with APIRouter
- Define path operations for our CRUD functionality
- Introduce FastAPI middleware and use it to enable our backend to connect to our frontend
- Deploy our backend to Heroku – a platform-as-a-service

In this chapter, we will cover the following main topics:

- Introducing our app
- Creating a MongoDB instance for our app
- Creating our FastAPI backend
- Deployment to Heroku

The goal of this chapter is to build a complete FastAPI backend with CRUD functionality. It will be a very simple application with a very basic data model, and in this phase, there will be no users defined – just pure and simple create, read, update, and delete operations on a set of entities: cars. By the end of the chapter, you should have a solid foundation for the process of backend development, with MongoDB as the database layer and FastAPI as the framework of choice, and be able to apply a similar process to any data that you might wish to model and serve through a modern API.

## Technical requirements

The technical requirements for this chapter are identical to those in *Chapter 3, Getting Started with FastAPI* – we will create a brand-new Python environment and install all of our dependencies in it. In addition, you should already have a MongoDB (free) account and a cluster – you can refer to *Chapter 2, Setting Up the Document Store with MongoDB* for the detailed procedure of setting up the account, the credentials needed for connecting to the instance of the database, and the connection of Compass (the MongoDB desktop client). If you prefer, you could also use a local MongoDB instance – just replace the connection string (database URL, database name, and collection name) with the ones on your local MongoDB installation.

You should be able to run all the code from this chapter on a relatively modest machine (with at least 8 GB of RAM, but, hey, the more the merrier!) and you should have a relatively recent Python version (at least 3.6).

## Introducing our app

It is time to put all of our knowledge to work and create our first FARM stack app! Our employer, a company that sells used cars, has decided to create an application that will be used *internally* for the management of car ads. The specification at this point is quite simple – the app should be able to store and provide data about the cars (brand, make, year of production, kilometers, and so on) and offer *basic CRUD functionality*. The user interface should be simple so that employees can get working right away – cars are inserted into the database, they can be listed, the price can be updated, and they can be deleted.

I am going to start with the database layer – we will begin by working on an Atlas MongoDB instance right away since we need to be able to create fast deployments of the app and obtain fast and frequent feedback from the stakeholders – the car sales company owner (although, in this case, that shouldn't be an issue, right?). After creating a database (I have already created an online account in *Chapter 2, Setting Up the Document Store with MongoDB*), we will work on the FastAPI backend: I will show you how we can break our app into routes with the FastAPI router and handle multiple groups of URLs – for now, just for car instances. After crafting the pydantic models for cars, we will create the routes for all of the basic operations: creating cars, updating them, deleting them, and reading them, all together or individually. Finally, in the following chapter, I am going to create a very simple React-based user interface for displaying and managing cars, and I will be using Tailwind CSS since it gives me a type of designer's flexibility that other frameworks struggle to provide.

A note to everyone who has had to start from such a simple specification – this is often what the stakeholder *thinks* will be needed, but it is almost always not the product that they will end up with. I have deliberately made this initial specification oversimplified to simulate how, in my experience, 80% of projects without a proper and dedicated web development department begin.

After having defined our brief app specification, it is time to dive into the fun stuff: let's begin by setting up the database layer and building our data models and the API!

## Creating a MongoDB instance for our app

We have already seen how to start with the MongoDB setup in *Chapter 2, Setting Up the Document Store with MongoDB*. Now, I will just say that we need to create a new database – I will call mine `carsApp` – and, inside of it, a collection, which I will aptly name `cars1`. I assume that you have followed the procedure outlined in *Chapter 2, Setting Up the Document Store with MongoDB*, you have defined a database user with a username and password, and you have allowed all possible IP addresses to connect to it. This is **not** the most secure way of working with MongoDB, nor is it recommended, but for our purposes it will simplify the workflow. The next step is getting our connection string information and keeping it somewhere safe. For now, I will keep them in a handy text file in the following format:

```
DB_URL = "mongodb+srv://<dbName>:<dbPassword>@cluster0.fkm24.
mongodb.net/?retryWrites=true&w=majority"
DB_NAME = "carsApp"
COLLECTION_NAME = "cars1"
```

Later on, we will make sure to import these constants, as well as other API keys for authentication or external services in the format of environment variables, and be careful not to commit them to our GitHub repositories, as we do not want to allow the world to use our accounts. I will show later how various platforms such as Netlify, Vercel, Heroku, and Deta handle these keys, but for now let's just keep them in a plain text file, out of reach of the version control system. This is all we need for now, and later on, I will connect MongoDB Compass for a direct view of our data.

Once our database is ready and we have all the data needed to make connections, it is time to begin crafting our backend – the brain of our application.

## Creating our FastAPI backend

I will now begin with the creation of the FastAPI-powered backend. I like to start with a folder that bears the project name, so in this case, I will go with `Ch5`, as in *Chapter 5 , Building the Backend for Our Application*. A more natural name would be `CarsApp` or something similar. Next, I am going to create a folder inside called **backend** and create a fresh Python environment inside of it. These are the steps:

1.   Create a folder named `Ch5`, or name it whatever you please.

2.  cd into it and create a folder named backend.

3.  cd into the /backend folder and create a Python environment with the following command:

    ```
    python -m venv venv
    ```

4.  The command will create a folder called venv. Activate the environment by typing the following command:

    ```
    venv\Scripts\activate.bat
    ```

5.  The Python environment should be now activated – you should have your command prompt prepended with venv. Now, it is time to install our Python dependencies. While in the same activated environment, issue the following:

    ```
    pip install fastapi motor dnspython pydantic uvicorn
    ```

    We now should have a pristine Python environment and we can begin creating our backend. If you are wondering what **motor** and **dnspython** are, the former is our asynchronous MongoDB driver for Python, while the latter is a package needed for Python to be able to resolve the DNS of our MongoDB and point the driver and the whole application to the correct instance of MongoDB.

I like to begin with a bottom-up approach, or back to front, if you will. That essentially means that I like to have all of my data types and data flows defined upfront, modeled into the database, and with validation rules implemented. The model in our case is very simple – we have only cars as our entities and I will deliberately use a very limited subset of car features. It might seem silly but predicting the prices of used cars, with all their features, such as engine type, kilometers, vehicle type, safety standards, country of origin, and many more, is an interesting topic in its own right and several very interesting scientific papers have been published with various machine learning models and techniques proposed. I repeat, here and now, we are only going to use the following features:

- Brand – the car brand (Fiat, Opel, BMW), a string

- Make – or model (Meriva, C5, Laguna), also a string

- Year – the year of production (like 2015), an integer

- Cm3 – the engine displacement, proportional to the power of the engine, integers in the range of 1,000-4,000

- Km – the mileage of the car, expressed in Km, integer in the range of a couple of hundred thousand

- Price – the price of the car in euros, an integer, usually in the range of 1,000-10,000

Besides these features, there could be at least 20 or so more, while other data related to the management app could and probably should include a couple of date/time fields (when the car was listed, when it was sold), some Booleans (sold or not, displayed or not, and so on), maybe a location, some relations… But I repeat, we are *only given the task of building the simplest possible CRUD application* and, for now, we will stick with this. So, let's create our pydantic models.

### Creating the Pydantic models and the problem of ObjectId

While the fields are simple and we are not going to perform some fine-tuned validation, you will immediately face a problem that should be tackled upfront. We have seen that MongoDB uses something called `ObjectId`, assigns every document a property `_id`, and stores documents as **BSON (binary JSON)**. FastAPI, or Python really, encodes and decodes data as *JSON strings* and that is also what will be expected in our frontend. As I have seen, there are basically *two* possibilities: to preserve the `ObjectId` field in MongoDB or to transform it into a `string` representation that will ensure uniqueness. While both options are viable, I will opt for the latter as it is simpler to set up and it will require us to write less code for serializing objects. See the example here:

```
from bson import ObjectId
class PyObjectId(ObjectId):
    @classmethod
    def __get_validators__(cls):
        yield cls.validate
    @classmethod
    def validate(cls, v):
        if not ObjectId.is_valid(v):
            raise ValueError("Invalid objectid")
        return ObjectId(v)
    @classmethod
    def __modify_schema__(cls, field_schema):
        field_schema.update(type="string")
```

The preceding code basically just defines our own implementation of `ObjectId` functionality, along with some validation and the update of the schema in order to output `strings`. Now, we just have to extend Pydantic's `BaseModel` with the `PyObjectId` that we just created and use it as the basis for all of our models:

```
class MongoBaseModel(BaseModel):
    id: PyObjectId = Field(default_factory=PyObjectId, alias="_
        id")
    class Config:
        json_encoders = {ObjectId: str}
```

It is important to note that we have used the *alias* option in order to be able to use the field in our Pydantic model. Having our version of the BaseModel (called MongoBaseModel) ready, we can now proceed and define our other fields:

```
class CarBase(MongoBaseModel):
    brand: str = Field(..., min_length=3)
    make: str = Field(..., min_length=3)
    year: int = Field(...)
    price: int = Field(...)
    km: int = Field(...)
    cm3: int = Field(...)
```

While we're at it, let's define the model for our update route – we want to be able to provide just a single field and update only that field in the model. We have seen how pydantic manages to achieve this:

```
class CarUpdate(MongoBaseModel):
    price: Optional[int] = None
class CarDB(CarBase):
    pass
```

As you can see, all the fields are optional and set to None by default, while the CarDB model for now just mimics the CarBase model – we made it just to be consistent with the convention of having a model that represents the instance in the database. In this case, they just happen to be identical, but they will not always be. The final ingredient of our model will, however, reside elsewhere – in the API functions. Since we have decided to treat our IDs as strings, we need a way to serialize them – enter jsonable_encoder, a utility function that lives in the fastapi.encoders module. If you want to play around with the code and see how it all fits together, I suggest you open a Python session within our environment, import CarDB from the models.py file, and import the jsonable_encoder.

You may test the Pydantic model with the following lines:

```
car = {'brand':'Fiat', 'make':'500', 'km':4000,'cm3':2000,'pr
ice':3000, 'year':1998}
cdb = CarDB(**car)
jsonable_encoder(cdb)
```

You should then get the following output:

```
{'_id': '62702c8dd7269d7b7970190b', 'brand': 'Fiat', 'make':
'500', 'year': 1998, 'price': 3000, 'km': 4000, 'cm3': 2000}
```

This is precisely what we need – a nice JSON representation and a plain text string for our ID.

## Connecting FastAPI to MongoDB

Now, I want to set up our FastAPI application and connect it to the MongoDB database. I will use a Python package for managing environment variables – **python-decouple**, very similar to the Node.js version of environment management. Another popular Python package with similar functionality is *dotenv*. But **python-decouple** seems to play nicer with our preferred deployment solutions. You can install it by entering the following command into your activated virtual environment:

```
$ pip install python-decouple
```

We will copy our MongoDB connection `string` and database and collection names into a `.env` file using the simple `dotenv` syntax (basically no hyphens). Your `.env` file should look something like this:

```
DB_URL=mongodb+srv://username:password@cluster0.fkm24.mongodb.
net/?retryWrites=true&w=majority
DB_NAME=carsApp
```

We can now start with our `main.py` file. Let's begin by importing the `decouple` module and reading its contents into a variable called `config`. The `cast` option means simply that the values that `decouple` is reading from our `.env` file should be `string` values, like so:

```
from decouple import config
DB_URL = config('DB_URL', cast=str)
DB_NAME = config('DB_NAME', cast=str)
```

We now have our sensitive data available for development, yet it shouldn't make it to the version control system. Make sure that you have a valid `.gitignore` file that includes the following:

```
venv/
__pycache__/
.env
```

This is just the way I like to start things off; you might find a more suitable workflow. After having the MongoDB credentials in place, I want to kickstart our application, so I begin with the following:

```
from fastapi import FastAPI
from motor.motor_asyncio import AsyncIOMotorClient


app = FastAPI()


@app.on_event("startup")
```

```
async def startup_db_client():
    app.mongodb_client = AsyncIOMotorClient(DB_URL)
    app.mongodb = app.mongodb_client[DB_NAME]

@app.on_event("shutdown")
async def shutdown_db_client():
    app.mongodb_client.close()
```

Apart from the loading of environment variables, the only really interesting thing here is that we were able to attach the MongoDB connection to the event startup of FastAPI and to close the connection to a similar FastAPI event, shutdown (`https://fastapi.tiangolo.com/advanced/events/`). There are other possibilities of handling the connection, but I feel that this is the most natural and simplest way. OK, we have instantiated our FastAPI app and we have hooked our MongoDB, but what is **Motor** and all this async stuff? Let's take a pause from our app and talk a bit about drivers.

MongoDB, like other relational or NoSQL databases, needs a *driver* in order to be able to communicate with a programming language – in our case, Python. MongoDB provides us with several options. For instance, **MongoEngine** is an **object-relational mapper (ORM)** that provides functionality that would be a bit redundant since we are using Pydantic for our model schemas and validation, and **PyMongo** is the official Python driver that provides all the needed functionality at a low level. However, PyMongo does not support asynchronous operations. Enter Motor (`https://motor.readthedocs.io/`), which dubs itself a coroutine-based asynchronous API for MongoDB. Initially developed for **Tornado**, Motor is now widely used together with FastAPI, as its syntax is very similar to PyMongo's (PyMongo is a dependency) and it is quite straightforward. We will go over the typical async parts of the Motor-related code. It should be said that, for our application in this chapter, we could have settled for PyMongo and achieved practically identical performance, but this is an oversimplified and trivial example that is meant to be instructive, so it is better if we see how Motor works right away.

In our `main.py` file, we imported the Motor async client and fed it our `connection string`. That is all that we need to do in order to obtain a connection to our server, while the following line specifies the database that we are going to use. The collection name isn't specified – we will insert and read from it in the API functions (maybe we'll have more collections down the line, who knows?).

Finally, instead of calling **Uvicorn** – our ASGI-compatible server – from the command line, we could have wrapped the call in a typical pythonic `if-name-main` loop so that we could run the server by just typing `python main.py` in the command prompt. In that case, we would just have added the following at the end of the `main.py` file:

```
if __name__ == "__main__":
    uvicorn.run(
        "main:app",
        reload=True
    )
```

## Structuring FastAPI applications with routers

Putting all of our request-response logic in one file is perfectly possible, but as you start building even slightly larger projects, you will see that it is not a good solution. FastAPI, like Express.js or Flask (with *blueprints*), provides *APIRouter* – a module designed to handle *a group of path operations related to a single type of object*. Using this approach, it could make sense to assign an APIRouter to handle cars at the /cars path, maybe later, another one for users at /users, and so on. The FastAPI proposes a type of project structure that is simple enough yet able to accommodate most of the use cases that you might encounter. I will jumpstart this structure by simply adding another folder in our /backend project folder and call it routers. Inside, we will add an empty __init__.py file, making the folder a Python package, and our first APIRouter called cars.py. Modify the /routers/ cars.py file to match the following:

```
from fastapi import APIRouter
router = APIRouter()
@router.get("/", response_description="List all cars")
async def list_cars():
    return {"data":"All cars will go here."}
```

Routers in FastAPI are pleasantly simple to work with: we import the APIRouter on top, then we instantiate it, and after that, we just treat it as a partial FastAPI app, if you will, defining routes with the familiar decorators, response descriptions, and all the stuff that we have seen so far. This is just a simple test route that should return a single JSON response, but in order to be able to use it, we have to hook it up to main.py, our instance of FastAPI.

First, we need to import the router, and since they will reside in separate folders but have the same name (router.py), in order to be able to distinguish one from another, we will rename it, at the top of the main.py file:

```
from routers.cars import router as cars_router
```

In the same main.py file, add the following lines (after the line where you instantiated the FastAPI app):

```
app.include_router(cars_router, prefix="/cars", tags=["cars"])
```

This line tells our FastAPI application to attach the router that we just defined and to assign it the /cars prefix , which means that it will respond to requests whose path begins with /cars. Finally, we added the tags property in order to have it displayed and nicely grouped in the **OpenAPI** documentation. If you navigate now to the documentation, you should indeed find just one route defined at /cars and responding only to GET requests. It is intuitive that this procedure can have us building "parallel" or same-level routers in no time, but one of the biggest benefits of using APIRouters is that they support *nesting*, which enables us to manage quite complex hierarchies of endpoints effortlessly!

It is now time to create our first endpoint, and that for me is usually a /POST route when I do not have any previous data inserted or imported into the database. I will explain in detail what is going on with the first endpoint and the remaining endpoints should be much clearer. I will leave our dummy GET endpoint for now and just add some imports at the top of the file. You should, of course, be adhering to the Python imports order convention (standard library imports, third-party imports, local application/library specific imports)! This is what we're going to need for now in main.py:

```
from fastapi import APIRouter, Request, Body, status
from fastapi.encoders import jsonable_encoder
from fastapi.responses import JSONResponse
from models import CarBase
```

In the same file, after our dummy test GET route, add the following endpoint:

```
@router.post("/", response_description="Add new car")
async def create_car(request: Request, car: CarBase =
Body(...)):
    car = jsonable_encoder(car)
    new_car = await      request.app.mongodb["cars1"].insert_
        one(car)
    created_car = await request.app.mongodb["cars1"].find_one(
        {"_id": new_car.inserted_id}
    )
    return JSONResponse(status_code=status.HTTP_201_CREATED,
        content=created_car)
```

There is really nothing particularly new to you here: we have seen how to create async endpoints, we are annotating the request and the car arguments, and we are setting the car to be of type CarBase, our Pydantic model that we defined previously. In the first line inside the function, we are using the jsonable_encoder helper in order to steamroll our ObjectId and cast it to a string. Finally, we define a new_car variable and we assign it an async operation – a MongoDB insertion.

Here, things get interesting: you will remember that in main.py we were able to "attach" a MongoDB client to our application instance. Well, this client is still here and we can find it in the routers as well, so we only need to provide the following:

```
request.app.mongodb["cars1"]
```

After this, we can use all the PyMongo/Motor operations for querying MongoDB. I will not get into every aspect of the syntax, but the tutorial on PyMongo (https://pymongo.readthedocs.io/en/stable/tutorial.html) is very useful and I wholeheartedly recommend that you take a look. Insert_one means exactly that: insert one instance into the database. The analogy with the native MongoDB syntax is fully present.

Finally, we want to return the inserted object through the response, and it is an excellent opportunity to see how our first query is working. The `created_car` is a `find_one` MongoDB query result, translated into the Motor/Python language: we still have to define the collection and bring over our `request.app.mongodb` client that is omnipresent in our app, and then we simply supply the ID of the freshly inserted car. Try it out in the interactive documentation or fire up **Insomnia** or **HTTPie**. If you installed HTTPie in our new virtual environment, you could play with this endpoint and insert some dummy data:

```
(venv) λ http POST "http://localhost:8000/cars/" brand="aaa"
make="500" year=2015 cm3=1222 price=2000 km=100000
```

At the same time, you can monitor the database in Compass and see that it is indeed getting populated! This is exciting. If we try to pass some faulty data, pydantic will be our fierce guardian and will notify us of any data that does not belong in the database.

Let us now try to retrieve a car by its ID. The following code should be understandable. In the `routers/car.py` file, after our `/POST` handling route, add the following code:

```
@router.get("/{id}", response_description="Get a single car")
async def show_car(id: str, request: Request):
    if (car := await request.app.mongodb
        ["cars1"].find_one({"_id": id})) is not None:
            return CarDB(**car)
    raise HTTPException(status_code=404, detail=f"Car with
    {id} not found")
```

This path has just a couple of specific points that I want to tackle: as the argument, we are expecting an ID (`id`), which is of type `string` and we take the request. The `if` line includes some Python syntactical sugar – we are using the controversial walrus operator, `:=` (a colon followed with an equals sign). It simply enables us to do an assignment (the result of the awaited MongoDB operation) and return it, while checking that it actually exists. After that, we simply pass our `car` instance from the database to the Pydantic model `CarDB` and return it. If the car is not to be found, we raise an HTTP exception with a meaningful message and the appropriate status code.

We are now ready to replace our dummy *GET* route with a fairly more complex path operation. In the file `cars/router.py` replace the dummy route with the following:

```
@router.get("/", response_description="List all cars")
async def list_all_cars(
    request: Request,
    min_price: int=0,
    max_price:int=100000,
```

```
    brand:Optional[str]=None
    ) -> List[CarDB]:
    query = {"price":{"$lt":max_price, "$gt":min_price}}
    if brand:
        query["brand"] = brand
    full_query = request.app.mongodb['cars1'].find(query).
sort("_id",1)
    results = [CarDB(**raw_car) async for raw_car in
      full_query]
    return results
```

Again, nothing is really new in this path – we are setting some default values for our query parameters – the minimum and maximum price and we add the *brand* into the mix, enabling us to query by brand. We could of course make this much more complex, but I believe that this is more than enough in order to showcase the main ideas.

I built a dictionary for the query and simply named it *query*. Since it is a Python dictionary that we pass to MongoDB, it is very easy to update or modify according to our needs. In this case, we just check for the existence of a *brand* parameter. If such a parameter is provided, we simply add it to our query dictionary before passing it to MongoDB. Finally, in the query, we added a sorting function.

The results are returned in the form of an *async generator* with the *async-for* construct. There are other viable options here – we could use something like the following:

```
 results = await full_query().to_list(1000)
```

There is one more thing that needs to be fixed at this point – this query is returning just too many cars all at once – all of them in fact! At this point, it might not seem like a problem but try importing a couple of thousand cars into our database and watch as things become tricky. While there are ways to limit the query on the client (React) side, it is much more efficient to use the database layer to perform the pagination and return to the client only a limited set of results. Before leaving the GET route, let's add some simple pagination functionality. Pagination is basically defined with a query string denoting the page that we want to get, while the variable parameter is the number of items (cars) that we want to get on every "page." I will just make a simple hardcoded solution for now with a fixed number of results (25, to be precise), but later we will see how this simple functionality can be parameterized.

Modify the cars/router.py and add the following parts:

```
@router.get("/", response_description="List all cars")
async def list_all_cars(
    request: Request,
    min_price: int=0,
```

```
    max_price:int=100000,
    brand: Optional[str] = None,
    page:int=1,
) -> List[CarDB]:

    RESULTS_PER_PAGE = 25
    skip = (page-1)*RESULTS_PER_PAGE
    query = {"price":{"$lt":max_price, "$gt":min_price}}
    if brand:
        query["brand"] = brand

    full_query = request.app.mongodb
        ['cars1'].find(query).sort("_id",-
        1).skip(skip).limit(RESULTS_PER_PAGE)
    results = [CarDB(**raw_car) async for raw_car in
        full_query]
    return results
```

We have two more routes in order to complete our CRUD job – the U(pdate) and D(elete). They should be pretty simple compared to what we have seen, as it is only a matter of implementing what we have done with the previous paths. A further simplification is to allow *only* the price to be updated, as the remaining data shouldn't really change (although a periodic mileage-decreasing function could come in handy!). Let's add these path operations to our `cars/router.py` file:

```
@router.patch("/{id}", response_description="Update car")
async def update_task(id: str, request: Request, car:
CarUpdate = Body(...)):
    await request.app.mongodb['cars1'].update_one(
        {"_id": id}, {"$set": car.dict(exclude_unset=True)}
    )
    if (car := await request.app.mongodbm
        ['cars1'].find_one({"_id": id})) is not None:
    return CarDB(**car)
    raise HTTPException(status_code=404, detail=f"Car with
        {id} not found")


@router.delete("/{id}", response_description="Delete car")
async def delete_task(id: str, request: Request):
```

```
delete_result = await request.app.mongodb
   ['cars1'].delete_one({"_id": id})
if delete_result.deleted_count == 1:
    return JSONResponse(status_code=status.
       HTTP_204_NO_CONTENT)
raise HTTPException(status_code=404, detail=f"Car with
   {id} not found")
```

These routes are very similar to the others – we use the PATCH method to update and the DELETE method to delete. The interesting thing in this code is the set operation in the update route: we took advantage of the exclude_unset flag in order to enable MongoDB to update only the fields that are provided in the request, leaving the rest unaltered.

Congratulations! You now have your first fully functional REST API with CRUD functionality and some fancy filtering baked in when it comes to reading data. There are still a couple of things to do in order to enable our app to be usable from within a frontend framework, React, for instance.

### CORS – Cross Origin Resource Sharing

**Cross origin resource sharing** (CORS) refers to the policy that is applied when we incur into situations where our backend (FastAPI) has to communicate with the frontend (React) and they reside on different origins. An origin is simply a combination of a **protocol** (http, for instance) a **domain** (like localhost or farmstack.net), and a **port** (80, or 8000, or 3000). The default action is to *block* all unauthorized CORS requests, so if you try to run a React project on port 3000 and try to access our fresh cars API, you will fail. In order to make it work, frameworks provide a way of specifying which origins are allowed to make requests to our API, and FastAPI is no different – it makes it ridiculously easy in fact.

FastAPI implements the concept of **middleware** – something that you might have encountered in Django or Express.js – two popular frameworks that make extensive use of the concept. Middleware is simply a set of functions that run on every request and tap into the request/response cycle, intercepting the request, manipulating it in some desired way, then taking the response before it is sent to the browser or client, performing additional manipulation if needed, and finally, returning the final response.

Middleware is really based on the ASGI specification, and it is implemented in Starlette, so FastAPI enables us to use it in all our routes and optionally tie it to a part of an application (via APIRouter) or the entire app. Let's see how we can implement them in order to allow our API to accept incoming requests from our React frontend, which will run (for now) on port 3000, React's default:

1.  Fire up your main.py file where our main app resides and add the following import at the beginning:

    ```
    from fastapi.middleware.cors import CORSMiddleware
    ```

2. After all the imports, let's define some origins for which we want to allow communication:

```
origins = [
    "http://localhost",
    "http://localhost:8080",
    "http://localhost:3000",
    "http://localhost:8000",
]
```

3. Finally, we have to add this middleware to our application in order to make use of it. The FastAPI recommended way of doing so is to just use the addMiddleware method on the app itself, right after instantiating the app:

```
app = FastAPI()
app.add_middleware(
    CORSMiddleware,
    allow_origins=origins,
    allow_credentials=True,
    allow_methods=["*"],
    allow_headers=["*"],
)
```

4. While, another viable option is to import the middleware directly from Starlette and include it in the instantiation call:

```
from starlette.middleware import Middleware
from starlette.middleware.cors import CORSMiddleware


middleware = [
    Middleware(
        CORSMiddleware,
        allow_origins=["*"],
        allow_credentials=True,
        allow_methods=["*"],
        allow_headers=["*"],
    )
]
app = FastAPI(middleware=middleware)
```

5.   In this case, the complete `main.py` file will look like this:

```python
from decouple import config
from fastapi import FastAPI
from fastapi.middleware.cors import CORSMiddleware
from motor.motor_asyncio import AsyncIOMotorClient
from routers.cars import router as cars_router

DB_URL = config("DB_URL", cast=str)
DB_NAME = config("DB_NAME", cast=str)
origins = ["*"]

app = FastAPI()
app.add_middleware(
    CORSMiddleware,
    allow_origins=origins,
    allow_credentials=True,
    allow_methods=["*"],
    allow_headers=["*"],
)

@app.on_event("startup")
async def startup_db_client():
    app.mongodb_client = AsyncIOMotorClient(DB_URL)
    app.mongodb = app.mongodb_client[DB_NAME]


@app.on_event("shutdown")
async def shutdown_db_client():
    app.mongodb_client.close()
app.include_router(cars_router, prefix="/cars",
tags=["cars"])
```

Finally, in the GitHub repository of the book, I have provided a real, albeit a bit crippled, dataset of cars in a convenient CSV format and a simple script for importing them into MongoDB. They could be imported directly in Compass as a CSV file, but that would bypass our pydantic model, which treats IDs as strings, so we wouldn't be able to query our data relying on `ObjectId`. The script uses a plain synchronous PyMongo driver and a CSV reader, along with some validation logic. You are more than welcome to take it for a test drive and import as many cars as you want. I know that I always wanted to have some data to play around with, so I just wanted to provide it. By the way, the data is real, and it was scraped two years ago.

# Deployment to Heroku

If you have been able to play with our backend a bit and test it with HTTPie or Insomnia, you will certainly be satisfied with your work, as you will be able to see how your API responds to all the CRUD operations. After all, we were able to complete our first task! Wouldn't it be great if we could deploy our backend for the world to see?

We will examine deployment options for a FastAPI project later, but I feel that this is a good moment to quickly show how easy the deployment of a FastAPI app to a **platform-as-a-service** (**PaaS**) can be. I get motivated and excited like a little kid every time I put something online, so I want to quickly show you how you can deploy this simple API to Heroku.

Heroku is one of the leading container-based platforms for the deployment and management of applications; it has been on the market for quite some time now and it has a free tier (albeit with some limitations that will not be a deal-breaker for our purposes).

The main concept of Heroku is the use of Dynos – virtualized containers for applications that are scalable and run Linux in isolated environments. You can get acquainted with the infrastructure and principles on their site: `https://www.heroku.com/dynos`. Heroku is a versatile and powerful tool to have under your belt, so it seems right to make our first deployment using it, using the following steps:

1. The first step is to create a Heroku account – it is free and all you need is a valid email address. Go to `https://signup.heroku.com/`, fill in the form, and validate your email address.

2. The second step is to download the Heroku CLI – the magic tool that will enable us to easily deploy our FastAPI interface. Navigate to `https://devcenter.heroku.com/articles/heroku-cli` or simply google `download Heroku CLI` and follow the instructions relative to your operating system.

   Remember that you should have Git already installed and your backend folder under version control. It is a good moment to double-check our `.gitignore` file. It should contain (at least) the following:

   ```
   venv/
   __pycache__/
   .env
   .vscode/settings.json
   ```

3.  Fire up the Heroku CLI (you might need to restart the shell if you just installed Heroku CLI in order to make it available!) and log in. In the shell, ideally the one hosting your virtual environment, type the following:

```
heroku login
```

4.  If you are not already logged in, and chances are you aren't since you just started, you will be prompted to open a browser and insert your credentials. Do so and close the tab.

5.  Heroku needs a GitHub repository to work, so now is a good moment to save our precious work and commit our changes. In your shell, type the following commands:

```
git add .
```

6.  Then, think of a meaningful message and type the following:

```
git commit -m "first API version - CRUD working"
```

7.  Now that we have our application under (version) control, we are ready to deploy to Heroku! First, we need to create something called a *Procfile* – it is really what we are going to name it, no extensions. It is simply a way of telling Heroku what process(es) it should run for the deployment. Create the file in the /backend directory and make sure it contains only the following line:

```
web: uvicorn main:app -host 0.0.0.0 -port=$PORT
```

8.  The last step in this preparation is to tell Heroku which Python libraries are needed for our project in order to collect them and run them. In the past, I often had to play a bit of a trial-and-error game with various versions of packages since the Python versions might differ on Heroku's dyno and the local machine. The safest way of solving this is to list the bare minimum in the requirements.txt file and let the cloud Python interpreter figure out the dependencies – in case you are not bound to a specific version of a package. In this case, my requirements.txt file is as follows:

```
dnspython
fastapi
motor
PythonDNS
uvicorn
python-decouple
```

9.  Now, we are ready to create a new Heroku app – in the terminal, type the following:

```
heroku create
```

The previous command generated a new app for us and it also created a remote Git repository on Heroku itself. When we push our code to this remote repo, the deployment will automatically begin. If you are curious, you can issue `git remote -v` and verify that the remote is indeed on Heroku (`git.heroku.com/your-random-app-name.git`).

You will be greeted with the URL of your Heroku app, so it might be a good idea to keep it somewhere copy-pasted.

10. The last thing that should be done before pushing our code to Heroku is to set the environment variables, since they are not in the repository. Although this can be done from the Heroku web interface (`config` – reveal variables) it is easier to do from the shell, the syntax is the following:

```
heroku config:set DB_URL="mongodb+srv://yourdata"
```

Repeat this for the DB_NAME and other variables if needed.

11. It was a bit of work, I'll admit, but now you finally get to type the following (drumroll!):

```
git push heroku master
```

You will be able to follow the process in the shell output: building the stack, detecting the Python environment, installing dependencies, discovering process types from the Procfile... Finally, it should output that the Deployment is done. You can type `heroku open` and you should be able to see your app with a blunt Not Found page. If, however, test the URL with `/cars` appended, you should see your FastAPI backend in all its glory!

## Summary

In this chapter, we have created a fully functional CRUD backend application for our cars – MongoDB is connected at each startup of the app and disconnected on each shutdown, and we have this connection available in every request. We implemented simple yet functional, and, I hope, illustrative models and opted for strings as IDs in our database. It is time to create our frontend while trying to keep it equally simple.

There are many improvements and not-so-advanced features that should be implemented in this API, but I have omitted them for the sake of brevity. Pagination of results – with the use of the limit and skip operators in MongoDB implemented as query strings in FastAPI – is probably the first thing that comes to mind. FastAPI and its way of handling query strings, combined with the Motor/PyMongo way of constructing MongoDB queries as Python dictionaries, offers almost unlimited flexibility and extensibility. If you feel inclined to try things out, I suggest that you try to implement a couple more endpoints with the use of the MongoDB aggregation framework.

Finally, you have learned a valuable skill: you have successfully deployed your API to Heroku, a popular platform for the development, management, and deployment of all kinds of apps, and now you can show your work to a friend that loves a good API!

With our backend in place and with the initial specification ready, I want to move on to the front end – in the next chapter, we will create a simple React and implement all of the FastAPI endpoints that we just built.

# 6
# Building the Frontend of the Application

In the previous chapter, you learned how to build a simple yet complete FastAPI backend – an API for car management with the complete set of CRUD operations and some filtering and pagination. Now, we will create an equally simple frontend with our knowledge of React, JSX, and a couple of Hooks. In this chapter, we will be creating a very bare-bones React frontend for our API. I will start by creating the React app using the create-react-app tool and then set up Tailwind CSS for styling. After that, I will give a very brief introduction to an essential React package, React Router, and I will define the virtual pages that our app will need. Finally, we are going to add the basic functionality and interactivity needed in order to be able to perform CRUD operations on our MongoDB instance, using the FastAPI backend that we created. This application is not going to be very realistic – there will be no security implemented and we will rely only on the backend validation rules from FastAPI. The idea is to showcase the flow of data between MongoDB and the React web page through FastAPI.

In this chapter, we will cover the following topics:

- Sketching the application pages and components
- Setting up Tailwind CSS and React Router 6
- Scaffolding the needed components
- Creating the virtual pages and their functionalities

By the end of the chapter, you will be able to implement simple but essential CRUD operations and you will be able to apply the same logic to any type of data that you might need. Limiting ourselves to just two essential React Hooks is not really an important factor here – you will see that we can achieve the desired functionality and later extend this approach as new requirements are imposed.

# Technical requirements

The technical requirements for this chapter are the same as the ones described in *Chapter 4, Setting Up a React Workflow*: you will need Node.js (version 14 or later) in order to be able to develop your React application. Along with Node.js, you should have Visual Studio Code, which is probably one of the best tools when working with such a broad range of technologies (MongoDB, Python, React, JavaScript, shell).

Besides these installed tools, you should keep FastAPI running in a separate shell in order to be able to connect it to our frontend.

# Creating our Frontend with React

With our backend ready and eager to respond to requests, we can now prepare our React environment. First, I want to give you a brief overview of what we are going to build.

With the help of our friend, `create-react-app`, we will create an app called frontend in our project folder. Then, we will set up *Tailwind CSS*, our UI library of choice in the same way that we did in the previous chapter, so I will not waste your time repeating the same steps.

I will then give a very brief introduction to React Router, a package that allows us to monitor the URL of our frontend and display different pages accordingly. Finally, I am going to tackle the pages needed for the application that roughly correspond to the path operations: a page for inserting a new car, one for listing and querying them, and one for modifying the price of the car or deleting it. I will make use of the basics that we saw in *Chapter 4, Setting Up a React Workflow*: create-react-app, Tailwind, some Hooks, and some very simple components. After that, we will be adding basic CRUD functionality to our frontend.

## Setting up React and Tailwind

We have already been through this, but just keep in mind that you should be at the root of our project (`CLI3`) and type the following:

```
npx create-react-app frontend
```

After this process has been completed, follow the procedure from *Chapter 4, Setting Up a React Workflow*, and install and set up Tailwind CSS. The procedure is exactly the same and we should end up with the same starter React project with Tailwind CSS enabled. As denoted in *Chapter 4, Setting Up a React Workflow*, you can examine the generated page and test it with some simple classes, such as `bg-red-500`. If everything is working, the page should turn red, and you are ready to continue.

## Installing and setting up React Router 6

Now, we need to start thinking about all of the possible pages that our application should have, and this is maybe a moment to take out a notebook or a piece of paper and start doing some drawings. This is a trivial application, so let's just say that we want these basic "pages" (I put quotes because they're not really pages – they are routes within the same page):

- A home page, at the route /.

- A cars page for displaying all cars or according to some filter: /cars.

- A new car page, with a form for inserting new cars: /cars/new.

- A single car page, for viewing a single car by ID: /cars/:id – this page will also be responsible for updating prices and deleting cars, as I want to keep things as simple as possible.

Let's start setting up the router: first, we have to install it. Follow these steps:

1.  Stop the process if it is still running and type the following:

    ```
    npm install react-router-dom@6
    ```

    Now, I do not know if you have already worked with the router, but it used to be installed in the App.jsx component and we enabled routing from there, application-wide. The latest version, 6, instructs us to use the index and, since I really do not want to enter into the intricacies of this powerful React package, I will just show you how to set up a few basic routes and leave you to the excellent documentation online. React Router has evolved a lot since the last versions and version 6 has seen numerous improvements and changes, as well as the ability to handle nested routes differently than in the previous versions. The basic ideas, however, remain the same: the router passes properties (for example, the location) to the components it renders. In the following chapter, we will gradually introduce a couple of other features of the router, but for now, this will suffice.

    React Router basically provides us with a set of components and Hooks that allow us to implement declarative routing.

2.  In the src/index.js file, the document into which React injects all of its magic, import after React on ReactDOM the following packages:

    ```
    import {BrowserRouter,Routes,Route,
    } from "react-router-dom";
    ```

3.   Now comes the tedious part: we should create empty components for each route in our router, so remember the React Visual Studio Code plugin shortcut (hint: **rafce**) and create a folder inside your source directory. Inside this folder, which I named /pages, I will scaffold the following components: Car, NewCar, and Cars; they all have the same plain structure. This, for instance, is what the Cars component looks like:

```
const Cars = () => {
  return (
    <div>Cars</div>
  )
}
export default Cars
```

4.   Now that we have our components/pages laid out, we can import them all into the index.js file and hook the router up. Edit the src/index.js file:

```
import React from 'react';
import ReactDOM from 'react-dom/client';
import {
  BrowserRouter,
  Routes,
  Route,
} from "react-router-dom";
import Car from './pages/Car';
import Cars from './pages/Cars';
import NewCar from './pages/NewCar';
import './index.css';
import App from './App';

const root = ReactDOM.createRoot(document.
getElementById('root'));
root.render(
    <React.StrictMode>
      <BrowserRouter>
      <Routes>
        <Route path="/" element={<App />} />
        <Route path="cars" element={<Cars />} />
        <Route path="cars/new" element={<NewCar />} />
        <Route path="cars/:id" element={<Car />} />
```

```
            <Route path="about" element={<About />} />
        </Routes>
      </BrowserRouter>
      </React.StrictMode>
    );
```

This is a bit long, I know, but I prefer to show you the whole file so that you can see what is going on. Essentially, every path (`/car`, `/cars`, and so on) is wrapped inside a Route component, and they all have an element or component (that we kept in the `/pages` folder) that will render when their number (route) is called. React Router 6 enables nested routing so that all of our car-related CRUD routes can be laid down in a more elegant way, but I just want to go with the simplest solution for now. If you start the server with `npm start` and try out a couple of routes manually (navigating to `http://localhost:3000/cars`, for instance), you should see our boring white components responding to the routes.

Notice that, with this setup of the React Router, `App.jsx` has lost some significance: it is just a page like all of the others, as the router contents get loaded directly into the `index.js` file, effectively bypassing the App component – we could have loaded the router into the `App.js` file instead.

With our virtual pages ready to be coded, we can proceed and create a basic structure for our app – the reusable components and the layout.

## Layout and components

Single-page React-based applications may have numerous virtual pages, but the chance is that they will share some, if not the vast majority of, elements: a header with navigation, a footer, and maybe even more. Since we are planning our application and we have correctly identified the header and the footer as reusable components that will be shared across all pages, we need a way to ensure that we do not have to import them into every page. Enter the `layout` component. It is simply a React component that will wrap the content provided via props and include all the shared components across the app. Without further ado, let's make a folder called `components` in the `src` folder and create generic components called `Header.jsx` and `Footer.jsx`. Finally, let's create a component called `Layout.jsx` and edit it a bit:

```
import Header from "./Header";
import Footer from "./Footer";
const Layout = ({children}) => {
  return (
    <div className="flex flex-col h-screen bg-orange-400">
        <Header />
        <div className="flex-1">{children}</div>
```

```
            <Footer/>
        </div>
    )
}
export default Layout
```

Now, in order to be able to use our beautiful orange layout (I am kidding, it's ugly but it's visible), we have to wrap our pages (App, Car, Cars, and so on) like the App.js file, for instance:

```
import Layout from "./components/Layout";
function App() {
  return (
    <Layout>
      <div>
        This is the App
      </div>
    </Layout>
  );
}
export default App;
```

If you inspect the root page, which displays the App component, you will see that I have made the page a *flexbox* display, with the content able to grow and fill the page, while the header and footer take up only their own height. Believe it or not, achieving this layout just a decade ago required some fiddling. I will not get into the Tailwind CSS classes, but they are made to be intuitive: flex means display:flex, flex-col translates to flex-direction:column, h-screen means height:100vh, and so on.

More manual labor ahead: you should wrap all the remaining pages in the layout component, so let's do it... Done? Great! On to some more interesting things.

Let's just create some navigation in our Header.jsx component first:

```
import {NavLink} from "react-router-dom";
const Header = () => {
  return (
    <nav className="flex justify-between relative items-center
        font-mono h-16">
      <Link to="/" className="pl-8 text-xl font-bold">Cars
          FARM</Link>
      <div className="pr-8 font-semibold">
```

```
                <NavLink className={({ isActive }) =>
                    isActive ? "active-link" : "p-4"
                } to="/">Home</NavLink>
                <NavLink className={({ isActive }) =>
                    isActive ? "active-link" : "p-4"
                } to="/cars">Cars</NavLink>
                <NavLink className={({ isActive }) =>
                    isActive ? "active-link" : "p-4"
                } to="/new">New Car</NavLink>
            </div>
        </nav>
    )
}
export default Header
```

I strongly encourage you to get acquainted with the Tailwind way of doing things – it looks kind of weird at the beginning, but after a while, you just catch yourself styling apps and web pages through classes incredibly quickly. In the preceding code, Tailwind does everything for us: we have a single nav element and the classes applied make it a flex container, set the direction to row (the default), justify the items between, center them vertically, and apply a height of 4 rem (h-16), while the font-mono class sets the display font to be Monospace. For the links, I used React Router's components *NavLink* and *Link*, which provide navigation to our app. The difference is that *NavLink* is aware of the current page and is thus able to provide a different class according to the *isActive* flag.

Finally, the .active-link class is *not* something provided by Tailwind: I made it up. I then went to my index.css file and edited it in order to apply existing Tailwind classes to my custom active-link class (the text is white, the background is yellowish, and it has some padding and shadow):

```
@tailwind base;
@tailwind components;
@tailwind utilities;
@layer utilities{
    .active-link{
    @apply bg-yellow-500 p-4 shadow-md text-white
    }
}
```

The @apply directive is a handy way to apply multiple Tailwind classes (and respective styles) to an element without polluting the HTML/JSX markup too much.

After having scaffolded our components, we can now add a bit of style, using our Tailwind CSS utility framework. I will not put the code here, but you can find it in the repository and, since Tailwind is really just CSS classes, you should be able to see exactly what each class does.

## Creating the pages functionalities

It is finally time for our beautiful React frontend to meet our speedy FastAPI! I am now going to connect our React shell with the API in order to enable the CRUD functionality that is our main (and for now, only) task. I want to begin with the /cars page, which should display all the cars and maybe provide some filters – a dropdown with the most frequent car brands, for example. We will later see how we can leverage MongoDB's distinct method in order to populate such a field.

We will need a simple card component, and in order to keep things really simple, I will just use image placeholders instead of real pictures of cars. Let's put our humble knowledge of React Hooks to good use and create a new Cars.jsx component (or page):

```
import Layout from "../components/Layout"
import Card from "../components/Card"
import {useState, useEffect} from 'react'

const Cars = () => {
    const [cars, setCars] = useState([])
    const [brand, setBrand] = useState('')
    const [isPending, setIsPending] = useState(true)

    useEffect(()=>{
        fetch(`http://localhost:8000/cars?brand=${brand}`)
            .then(response=>response.json())
            .then(json=>setCars(json))
            setIsPending(false)
    }, [brand])
```

This is a chunk of code that shouldn't present any concern, so let's take a look at it from top to bottom. First, we import our components – the Layout and the Card component, which will be used to display the individual cars. After that, we import our two Hooks – useState and useEffect. The Cars function uses three state variables: cars, for the array of cars to be displayed (initially an empty array), brand (initially we set it to an empty string), and a flag – isPending. This flag will be set to true while the frontend is fetching the JSON response from our API and will be reverted to false when the data is loaded.

The `useEffect` function, as we saw in the previous chapter, takes two arguments – a function that will be executed for external effects and an array of dependencies. In our case, the function to be executed is very simple: a simple `fetch` request to our API, using a single query parameter – the string, initially set to an empty string, thus returning all the cars. We could have added the price range selectors, and I suggest that you try adding them yourself, maybe with two numeric text inputs. The array dependency is simple in this case – we want to run the `fetch` only when the brand state changes, so that it goes into the array. If you were to implement other filters, this is the place to put them. Notice that I have used the old-school JavaScript promise syntax with `then()`. We cannot use async/await functions in `useEffect`, although we can declare them and then call them when needed. Since we are performing a very simple `fetch` request, this will do the job. Now, what do we do with the selector for the car brands?

The following arrow function is the handler of the brand selector:

```
const handleChangeBrand = (event) => {
    setCars([])
    setBrand(event.target.value)
    setIsPending(true)
}
```

Again, I have kept the code very simple: this function will be passed as the handler of the `brand` select input and, when triggered, it will carry out a couple of operations: first, we set the `cars` array to be empty, then we set the brand to the value of the selected option, and finally, we set the pending flag to `true`.

Let's take a look at the `return` statement of the components, the JSX. I have removed all the numerous Tailwind classes in order to make the file more readable:

```
return (
    <Layout>
        <h2>Cars - {brand?brand:"all brands"}</h2>
        <div>
        <label htmlFor="cars">Choose a brand: </label>
            <select name="cars" id="cars"
              onChange={handleChangeBrand}>
                <option value="">All cars</option>
                <option value="Fiat">Fiat</option>
                … more options here
            </select>
        </div>
        <div>
```

```
{isPending && <div>
    <h2>Loading cars, brand:{brand}...</h2>
</div>}
<div>
    {cars && cars.map(
        (el)=>{
            return (<Card key={el._id} car =
            {el} />)
        }
    )}
</div>
</div>
</Layout>
)
```

The JSX that eventually outputs our /cars page begins with an h2 element that displays the brand of the selected cars if selected. Immediately after that, we are greeted with our brand selector that has our previously defined onChange handler attached. Finally, we have a loading div that is usually represented by a spinner image and that will be visible only while the API is being read – chances are you will not be able to see it on your local machine.

The cars are displayed in standard React cars&&cars.map() fashion: if the cars array is populated, then map over the array and put each car into a card. I will not display the code for the card since it is practically identical to the code from *Chapter 4, Setting Up a React Workflow*.

The following screenshot shows what our **single-page app** (**SPA**) should look like – it is very simple, with a header containing the navigation, the main body, and a simple dark footer.

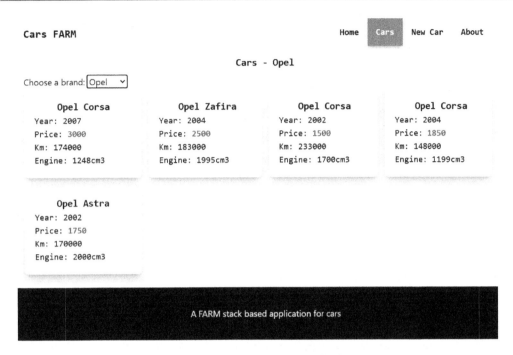

Figure 6.1 – The Cars FARM application displaying cars

The page will not win any awards, but it does what it was supposed to do – it displays cars from our FastAPI service, and it even has some filtering capabilities!

Let's tackle the creation part of CRUD, the page that we assigned the /new route in the React Router setting. I want to point out that in a real-world setting, you probably wouldn't want to create the following page same way that I did. I want, however, to display some basic React features and how the communication with the FastAPI server can be as transparent as possible. Let's break the code down – first, we are going to need a form input component. Again, in a real setting, you will probably want to use something like *Formik* or the *React Form Hook*, but I just want to show how React enables us to deal with the data flow in a much easier way compared to vanilla JavaScript or older solutions such as jQuery.

The form helper component will really have a simple task: it just needs to display a form element, set its type (numeric or text in our case), the label, name, and an onChange event handler:

```
const FormInput = (props) => {
    const { label, placeholder, type, onChange, name } = props
    return (
      <div>
          <label>{label}</label>
          <input
```

```
                    placeholder={placeholder}
                    type={type}
                    name={name}
                    onChange={onChange}
                     />
        </div>
      )
    }
    export default FormInput
```

I have omitted the Tailwind classes again in order to preserve some space. The input field takes a total of five props and the component structure is very simple.

Now, on to the NewCar.js component. First, I want to import our Hooks, the Layout component and the FormInput component:

```
import {useState} from 'react'
import {useNavigate} from "react-router-dom"
import Layout from "../components/Layout"
import FormInput from '../components/FormInput';
```

After the usual imports, we have a newcomer – useNavigate from the React Router – which is simply a function that will allow me to programmatically navigate to another React page. Alongside our Layout component that wraps every single page, I imported the FormInput component. The logic here is simple – we abstracted the form input because we want to be able to reuse it, so we can fit all the inputs into an array. Bear in mind that here we are playing with only five car features, while most car sales sites have at least 30 or even 50!

At the beginning of the NewCar arrow function component, I want to initialize an empty car object and then gradually populate it with the form. I defined an object at the beginning – the emptyCar, which is basically a car object with all of its features set to empty or null. This object will be used to initialize our state variable, which I called newCar – the car that, if everything goes according to plan, will have the honor of being inserted in our MongoDB:

```
const NewCar = () => {
    const emptyCar = {
        "brand":"",
        "make":"",
        "year":null,
        "cm3":null,
        "price":null
```

```
}
const inputs = [
    {
        id:"brand",
        name:"brand",
        type:"text",
        placeholder:"Brand",
        label:"Brand"
    },
    {
        id:"make",
        name:"make",
        type:"text",
        placeholder:"Make",
        label:"Make"
    },
    {
        id:"year",
        name:"year",
        type:"number",
        placeholder:"Year",
        label:"Year"
    },
    {
        id:"price",
        name:"price",
        type:"number",
        placeholder:"Price",
        label:"Price"
    },
    {
        id:"cm3",
        name:"cm3",
        type:"number",
        placeholder:"Cm3",
        label:"Cm3"
```

```
        },
        {
            id:"km",
            name:"km",
            type:"number",
            placeholder:"km",
            label:"km"
        },

    ]
```

Next, I defined an array of inputs that correspond to the features of our car, which, in turn, is defined in our pydantic model. The name is important, so it has to be lowercase since these will be the keys to our JSON objects! Returning to real-life car sales sites, you would probably want to put the inputs in a separate file if the number is too big, or resort to an external library.

The next part is about making use of the state variables:

```
const [newCar, setNewCar] = useState(emptyCar)
const [error, setError] = useState([])
const navigate = useNavigate();
```

As I mentioned earlier, we have one crucial state – the newCar object. I initialize it with the emptyCar object, setting all the properties to empty strings and nulls. I have added another state variable called error and set it to an empty array – here, I will put all the errors that come directly from our backend. I will not implement client-side validation because I want to show the bare-bones communication between FastAPI and its pydantic responses and React. In a real-world environment, you would use some client-side validation and not even try to send incomplete or invalid data to the server! The last line just instantiates the navigation for React Router. Here, we move on to the event handlers:

```
const handleSubmit = (e) =>{
    e.preventDefault()
    addCar(newCar)
}
const onChange = (e) => {
    setNewCar({...newCar, [e.target.name]: e.target.value})
}
const handleReset = (e) => {
    setNewCar(emptyCar)
}
```

handleSubmit simply prevents the default submitting of the form, a React classic, and then uses the spread operator (three dots) to update the initially "empty" newCar object with the property that is passed to the handler. This is why it was important to set the names of the inputs correctly, as the field brand, for instance, in the handler function becomes { "brand" : " Ford" } and part of the newCar object. Since I passed this same handler (onChange) to every input in my inputs array, that simply means that every time you change the value of any input, the newCar state object will be updated.

The handleReset simply resets the form (no preventDefault here because we want that to happen) and resets our newCar to the initial (empty) values. Let's now see the main function of the component, the addCar:

```
const addCar = async (newCar)=>{
    const response = await fetch("http://localhost:8000/cars/",{
     method:"POST",
     headers:{
         'Content-Type':'application/json'
     },
     body:JSON.stringify(newCar)
    })
    const data = await response.json()


    if(!response.ok) {
        let errArray = data.detail.map(el=>{
            return `${el.loc[1]} -${el.msg}`
        })
        setError(errArray)
        } else {
        setError([])
            navigate('/cars')
        }
    }
```

There is a lot going on here – first, I try to send a fetch request to our API using the appropriate method (POST), header (content-type set to application/json), and the body as a JSON object. I repeat: you would *not* want to do it this way without proper validation! This is for demonstration purposes because I find it useful to see the data flow through both the backend and the frontend.

The FastAPI backend will send some response, and that response might be valid or not. If the response is OK, which is just a concise way of telling us that the status code of the response is in the 200-299 range (so, 200 OK or 201 CREATED – the good stuff), we set the error to an empty array and navigate, with the help of React Router, happily to a new location – in my case, /cars. If, however, the response is not OK, I gladly take the FastAPI error messages (because there are several – for every field, for every invalid or required but missing value) and map them into the errors array. I did a bit of parsing, but you can figure it out easily if you analyze any error response from FastAPI's POST requests: the errors are under the details key, and they have a location (in this case, it is always the body and the field) and a message. I constructed this array on purpose because I wanted to display it on the page, but it is not something that you would do like this: you would want to mark the form fields containing errors with the color red or something similar and display the messages beside the corresponding fields.

Let's see the output of the component now:

```
return (
    <Layout>
        <div>
            <h1>Insert a New Car</h1>
        </div>
        <div>New car status:{JSON.stringify(newCar)}</div>
        {error && <ul>
        {error && error.map(
            (el, index)=>(<li key={index}>{el}</li>)
                )
            }
        </ul>}
        <div>
            <form onSubmit={handleSubmit}>
                {inputs.map((input) => (
                    <FormInput
                        key={input.id}
                        name={input.name}
                        {...input}
                        value={newCar[input.name]}
                        onChange={onChange}
                        required />
                ))}
```

```
            <button type="submit"
                onClick={handleSubmit}>Insert</button>
        <button type="reset"
          onClick={handleReset}>Reset</button>
            </form>
            </div>
            </Layout>
    )
}
```

Again, I have removed the Tailwind classes and started the file with just a simple title. After the title, I displayed the `newCar` object in its stringified version so that we can monitor its state and how it reacts to updates. After the `newCar` object, I display the errors array – you must submit the form with some errors in order to see them.

Finally, there is a form – the only interesting part is probably the mapping over the inputs array and the destructuring of values passed to its elements. This is what the page should look like:

Figure 6.2 – The Insert a New Car page

Try to play around with the form and customize it using some prettier Tailwind class combinations.

## Creating the car details and the update/delete page

The bulk of the work is done – we are able to create new cars and list them. I will now create the *details* page, a page component that will be used to display just one vehicle. It will not be particularly content-rich, since we have only five fields in our model and they easily fit inside the card. Imagine, however, that we had dozens of fields representing car features: color, type of engine, overall state, insurance, and maybe the location. Well, all of those fields would be displayed on the *details* page. Since I want to keep this very simple, I am going to add the update and delete actions to this page – without creating a dedicated React route for an edit-car page.

This /car/:id page will thus serve three purposes: it will display the car details, covering the get/:id route, but will also host two simple buttons – one for updating the price of the car (although we could add and edit any of the fields) and one for permanently deleting the car. For simplicity's sake, I will not create a pop-up or modal window that you would typically want to have when destroying resources. The purpose of the chapter is *only* to create a CRUD application, and this is precisely what we're doing here. Let's crack open the src/pages/Car.jsx file and have a look at it. The imports are the following:

```
import {useState, useEffect} from 'react'
import {useParams, useNavigate} from "react-router-dom"
import Layout from '../components/Layout'
import FormInput from '../components/FormInput'
```

By now, you have already become a React *connoisseur*, so you know that we are using useEffect and useState to fetch the individual car data and manage its state, while the React Router imports are for catching the id of the car and for navigating away programmatically. Finally, you have already seen the Layout component and the FormInput component as I have used them in the /new route. Let's take a look at the first part of the functional component:

```
const Car = () => {
    const {id} = useParams()
    const navigate = useNavigate()
    const [car, setCar] = useState(null)
    const [price, setPrice] = useState(null)
    const [error, setError] = useState([])
    const [isPending, setIsPending] = useState(true)
    ...
```

Apart from using the `useParams()` to capture the ID of the specific car and instantiating the navigation using the `useNavigate` hook, I set up no less than four state variables: the car (we are going to get it by using the ID), the price – the only editable property of the car, and the two helper states that we have already seen – the `error` (which is really an array of errors) and the `isPending` flag, for making sure that we have finished fetching. Let's see the rest of the components:

```
(continued)
const onChange = (event)=>{
    setPrice(event.target.value)
    }
const getCar = async() => {
    const res = await fetch('http://localhost:8000/cars/'+id )
    if (!res.ok){
        setError("Error fetching car")
        } else {
        const data = await res.json()
        setCar(data)
        setPrice(data.price)
        }
        setIsPending(false)
    }
```

The onChange handler is just for setting the new price of the car when we need to adjust it, while the bulk is contained in the getCar function. The dynamic is identical to what we have already done to get all of the cars: I make a fetch request using the ID of the desired car that the router was kind enough to provide me with and then I check the response – if it is OK (in the 200-299 range), I set the car state variable to the obtained car data, and populate the price variable – the variable that is the value of the input field – to the current price. In case of errors, I populate the error with a message. At the end, I remove the isPending flag.

Now we'll move on to the delete and update handlers, which will make HTTP requests to our DELETE and PATCH FastAPI endpoints:

```
const handleDelete = async () => {
const response = await fetch(`http://localhost:8000/
cars/${id}`,{
    method:"DELETE",
    headers:{
        'Content-Type':'application/json'
    }
```

```
    })
    if(!response.ok) {
        const data  = await response.json()
        let errArray = data.detail.map(el=>{
                return `${el.loc[1]} -${el.msg}`
            })
        setError(errArray)
        } else {
        setError([])
        navigate("/cars")
        }
    }
```

By this point, all of this code should be second nature to you, although I admit that it is not very elegant: I simply issue a DELETE request to the /cars/id endpoint and check for any errors. Since it is a DELETE request, remember that we do not actually expect anything in the response, so there is really no point in trying to get it or parse it – I just want the HTTP status code. If the response code is OK, I use navigate() to go to the desired page, using the power of React Router. Updating the car is very similar:

```
const updatePrice = async () => {
        const response = await fetch(`http://localhost:8000/
cars/${id}`,{
            method:"PATCH",
            headers:{
                'Content-Type':'application/json'
                },
            body: JSON.stringify({price})
                })

    const data = await response.json()
    if(!response.ok) {
        let errArray = data.detail.map(el=>{
            return `${el.loc[1]} -${el.msg}`
            })
        setError(errArray)
    } else {
        setError([])
```

```
        getCar()
        }
    }
```

The interesting part of this chunk of code is that we send a PATCH request, knowing that our smart FastAPI backend will know to only update the provided field – the price. After the usual error checking routine, if everything is OK, then we make a new call to the getCar function – that way, the UI (our page) gets updated with the new data – the new price. The useEffect call is as follows:

```
useEffect(()=>{
    getCar()
},[])
```

The component's JSX is full of Tailwind classes, and, in this case, I want to leave them so you can get a feel for what they achieve.

The first part of the return statement is used to check whether the isPending state variable is equal to true and then to display a div with a notification. This should probably contain a spinner or something more intuitive, but a red background will do for now. If there are errors in the error array, they will be iterated over and displayed in an unordered list with minimal styling:

```
return (
    <Layout>
        {isPending && <div className="bg-red-500 w-full
            text-white h-10 text-lg">
                <h2>Loading car...</h2>
        </div>}
        {error && <ul className="flex flex-col mx-auto
            text-center">
                { error && error.map(
                    (el, index)=>(
                        <li key={index} className="my-2 p-1
                            border-2 border-red-700 max-w-md mx-
                            auto">{el}</li>
                    )
                )
            }
        </ul>}
```

The part that follows directly in the same function outputs the selected car data: the brand and make, there is an image placeholder, and there is a `div` for displaying the `Price`, `Year`, and `Km` variables:

```
{car&&<div>
    <div className="flex flex-col justify-between min-h-full
        items-center">
    <div className="font-bold text-xl text-gray-600 my-3">
        {car.brand} {car.make}
    </div>
    <div className="max-w-xl">
        <img alt="A car!" src="https://via.placeholder.com
            /960x550.png?text=IMAGINE+A+CAR!" />
    </div>
    <div className="flex flex-col items-center font-normal
        text-lg">
        <div>Price: <span className="font-semibold text-
            orange-600 text-xl">{car.price}</span></div>
            <div>Year: {car.year}</div>
            <div>Km: {car.km}</div>
        </div>
```

Finally, I just added a simple form input for updating the price and a couple of buttons – the first will update the price of the car to the value of the input and the second one will trigger a DELETE request:

```
<div className="flex flex-row">
    <FormInput label='change price'
        placeholder={price}
        type="number"
        value={price}
        onChange={onChange}
        required />
<button
    onClick={updatePrice}
    className="bg-yellow-500 text-white p-2 rounded-md m-3
        transition-opacity hover:opacity-80">
    Edit price
</button>
<button
    onClick={handleDelete}
```

```
        className="bg-red-700 text-white p-2 rounded-md m-3
            transition-opacity hover:opacity-80">
        Delete Car
    </button>
    </div>
    <p>Warning: deleting is permanent!</p>
        </div>
            </div>}
        </Layout>
    )
}
export default Car
```

Instead of describing what the JSX does, I believe that it is easier to take a look at the screenshot of the generated page:

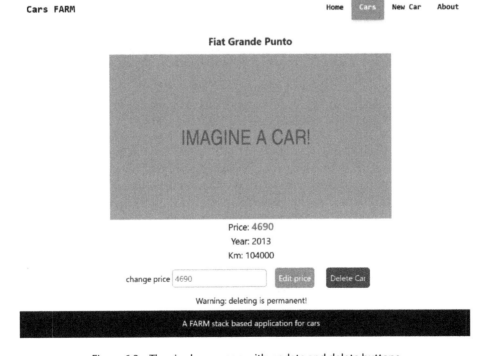

Figure 6.3 – The single car page with update and delete buttons

Apart from the Layout component that "includes" the menu and the footer, I just display the car data, along with the input for updating the price and two buttons, connected to our handlers for updating and deleting.

The application that you just created is pretty ugly, although Tailwind manages to hold it together. A person running this app locally on their laptop can insert new cars as they are arriving to be sold, can delete them, and can update their price. That is a very crude CRUD application (pun intended!) but it meets our initial goal and I hope that it sheds some light on the mechanism of connecting MongoDB, FastAPI, and React.

Once you get the hang of making HTTP requests to the backend and using Hooks to map the response data to UI elements, you will have web developer superpowers and almost unlimited flexibility at your fingertips. Meeting new requirements and implementing new features with the FARM stack is, I firmly believe, much easier than with other framework stacks.

The application that we have built together in this chapter is far from being production-ready – even for an intranet app locally run on an old laptop that is supposed to just get the job done. But hey! You made a full-stack application:

- You have defined some pydantic models and defined rules for data validation, ensuring data integrity and validity.

- You have created a MongoDB Atlas online database (for free!) and connected it in an efficient manner to your FastAPI backend using a modern async Python driver (Motor).

- You have crafted several endpoints for your application. You are able to create, read, list, update, and delete entities – in this case, cars, but this approach is very easy to generalize and apply to practically any type of data that can fit in your MongoDB database (and that's a lot!).

- You have created a React application using the CRA tool and made use of the latest features, React Router 6 and Hooks, in order to scaffold your components and pages and make sure that the data from FastAPI flows precisely the way you want it to.

The application that we have built is not going to be deployed to an online server or service, since it doesn't really meet any basic requirements, but we will tackle that in the next chapter. I want to make our app a bit more realistic and add users to it. And with users flying around, that means that we will have to talk about authentication and authorization.

## Summary

We have managed to create a very rudimentary React single-page application and we connected it to our FastAPI backend. Our app is able to display cars, edit their price, and delete cars from MongoDB, so we can safely say that we have achieved the initial goal – we have CRUD functionality.

This application is not only a kind of proof-of-concept, but it is also completely unusable for any kind of work: our API is not protected in any way and anyone with the URL of our endpoint can begin issuing requests, inserting fake cars, or editing and deleting existing ones! We could, of course, run MongoDB on our own local computer, but that would kind of defy the purpose of this book.

In the next chapter, we will introduce the basic ideas and concepts of authentication and authorization and we will explore ways in which we can make our FARM stack apps secure and usable.

# 7

# Authentication and Authorization

The concept of authentication (proving that the user is who they claim to be) and authorization (making sure that the authenticated user should or should not be able to perform certain operations on our API) is very complex, and several good (and thick) books are dedicated to it. In this chapter, we will explore the topics of authentication and authorization from a very practical standpoint and from our FARM-stack perspective.

We will begin with a very simple yet robust and extensible setup for our FastAPI backend, based on JWT – arguably the most popular authentication method in the last couple of years. Then, we will see how to integrate our JWT-based authentication methods into React, leveraging some of React's coolest and newest features – namely Hooks, Context, and React Router.

The topics we will cover in this chapter are the following:

- The user model and how it relates to our other resources
- A brief overview of the JWT authentication mechanism – the big picture
- An overview of the authentication and authorization tools that FastAPI has to offer
- How to protect our routes, routers, or the entire app
- Various solutions for authenticating with React

By the end of this chapter, you should have a solid grasp of authentication methods that both FastAPI on the backend and React on the frontend have to offer, and you will be able to authenticate users and control what they can and cannot do within your application with granularity and precision.

# Technical requirements

To run the sample application in this chapter, you should have both Node.js and Python installed on your local computer. The requirements are identical to those in the previous chapter, and the new packages that we will install will be pointed out. You should have a newer Python installation (version 3.6 or newer) and Node.js installation (version 14 or more). Your computer should be able to handle a couple of Visual Studio Code instances open at the same time, along with a couple of terminals and maybe a dozen browser tabs.

# Understanding JSON Web Token – our key to security

HTTP is a stateless protocol, and that fact alone implies several important consequences. One of them is that if we want to persist some kind of **state** between requests, we must resort to a mechanism that will be able to **remember** who the logged-in user was, what the selected cars during a previous browser session were, or what the site preferences were.

Broadly speaking, there are many strategies that we can employ when performing authentication. Credential-based authentication requires the user to enter some personal credentials, usually a username or an email and a password. A new method that has gained some traction over the last years is the concept of a passwordless login – once the user creates an account, they are emailed a magic link that is used for authenticating a session, without the need to type (and remember!) passwords. Biometric passwords use some bio-feature of the user, such as a fingerprint, while social authentications use the user's account on social networks (Google, Facebook, or LinkedIn) to associate the user with their account. In this chapter, we will consider a classic personal credentials method – when a user registers, they get to provide an email and choose a password and, optionally, a username.

While there are different ways of maintaining the identity of a user across different parts of an app, **JSON Web Token (JWT)** is arguably the most common and popular method of connecting frontend applications (React, Vue.js, and Angular) or mobile apps with an API (in our case, a REST API). JWT is nothing but a standard – a way of structuring a big string composed of seemingly random characters and numbers.

JWT contains three parts – the header, the payload, and the signature. The header hosts metadata about the token itself: the algorithm used for signing the token and the type of the token.

The payload is the most interesting part. It contains the data (claims): the ID of the user (or the username) and the **Issued at (iat)** field, the date and time of issuing the token, the expiry (the time at which the token ceases to be valid), and optionally, other fields. The *payload* is decodable and readable by everyone. There is a very useful site – `https://jwt.io` – that enables us to play with tokens and see how they look.

Finally, probably the most important part of the token is the signature – the part of the token that guarantees the claims made by the token, so to speak. The signature is reproduced (calculated) and compared with the original, thus preventing the modification of the claims. Put simply, if a JWT token which can be easily "read," claims that the username is John, we could tamper with it and modify the username to be Rita, but by doing so, we would alter the signature, which wouldn't match anymore, rendering the said token invalid. It is really a simple yet ingenious mechanism if you think about it.

The token is hence able to completely replace the authentication data – user or email and password combinations that do not need to go flying over the wire more than once.

In this section, we have learned what JWT is, what the logic behind it is, and why you might want to resort to it for your authentication and authorization system. In the forthcoming sections, we will address how to implement a JSON Web Token – based authentication flow in our app.

# FastAPI backend with users and relationships

Web applications (or mobile apps, for that matter) are not very useful if they are not secure – we keep hearing about tiny errors in the authentication implementations that ended up with hundreds of thousands or even millions of compromised accounts that might include sensitive and valuable information.

FastAPI is based on *OpenAPI* – previously known as *Swagger* – an open specification for crafting APIs. As such, OpenAPI enables us to define various security schemes, compatible with the various protocols (`apiKey`, `http`, `oauth2`, `openIdConnect`, and so on). While the FastAPI documentation website provides an excellent and detailed tutorial on creating an authentication flow, it is based on the `oauth2` protocol, which uses form data for sending the credentials (username and password).

There are literally dozens of ways you could implement some type of security for your API, but what I really want to accomplish in this chapter is just to give you an idea of what the viable options are and to create a simple authentication system based on JWT and JSON as the transport mechanism, a workflow that is easily extendable to fit your future needs, and one that provides just enough moving parts to be able to see the mechanism itself. In the following sections, we will devise a simple user model that will enable us to have an authentication flow. We will then learn how to encode the user data into a JWT token and how to require the token for accessing the protected routes.

## Creating a User model and MongoDB relationships

In order to be able to even discuss the concepts of authenticating users, we have to introduce the entity of users to our app – up until now, we have only seen how to perform CRUD operations on a single entity (cars). A real application will probably have at least a couple of models, and the user's model is certainly going to be mandatory. While you could store various data in the user's model, it really depends on your needs; for a small application, a couple of fields will suffice – an email and/or username, a password, maybe some role (regular user, admin, or editor), and so on. For a publishing platform, you would want to add a short bio, maybe an image, and so on.

Modeling data with MongoDB is inherently different from modeling relational databases, as discussed in *Chapter 2, Setting Up the Document Store with MongoDB*, and the driving idea is to think of queries upfront and model your relationships, taking into account the queries that your app is going to be making most frequently.

First of all, what are our **requirements**? Well, our stakeholders are quite happy with the previous CRUD application, and eventually, they want to turn it into a public website – the cars should be displayed for potential customers, while the pages for inserting new cars and updating or deleting the existing ones should be protected. Two types of users are envisioned for the moment: salespersons – employees that can insert new cars and edit and delete "their" own cars (that is, the company cars for which they are responsible), and admins – a couple of managers who will oversee the whole process and who should be able to perform all the operations, regardless of whose entity it is. In order to keep things as simple as possible, I will make a simple reference-based model; the car will simply have an additional field – such as a foreign key – with the ID of the user, very similar to a relational database model. We could embed a list of all the users' cars into the user model, but in this app, this will be more than enough.

Let's begin with the models of our application. We should probably apply the same structure as we did for the routers – create a /models directory and two files (users.py and cars.py) – but in order to keep the project as simple as possible, I am going to put them together in a single models.py file. This should be avoided in cases where you have more than two models!

Let's begin with main.py, the entry point of our application, which will be very similar to the one used in the previous chapter:

```
from decouple import config
from fastapi import FastAPI
from fastapi.middleware.cors import CORSMiddleware
from motor.motor_asyncio import AsyncIOMotorClient
from routers.cars import router as cars_router
from routers.users import router as users_router


DB_URL = config('DB_URL', cast=str)
DB_NAME = config('DB_NAME', cast=str)
```

I have just added a new router – the one that we will be creating right now:

```
origins = [
    "*"
]
app = FastAPI()
app.add_middleware(
    CORSMiddleware,
```

```
        allow_origins=origins,
        allow_credentials=True,
        allow_methods=["*"],
        allow_headers=["*"]
)
@app.on_event("startup")
async def startup_db_client():
        app.mongodb_client = AsyncIOMotorClient(DB_URL)
        app.mongodb = app.mongodb_client[DB_NAME]


@app.on_event("shutdown")
async def shutdown_db_client():
        app.mongodb_client.close()


app.include_router(cars_router, prefix="/cars", tags=["cars"])
app.include_router(users_router, prefix="/users",
tags=["users"])
```

The main.py file is practically unaltered, and that is one of the benefits of having a modular structure for our app. We just mounted the additional /users router, while maintaining the same logic – connect the database client on startup, disconnect on shutdown, and load the database variables using decouple.

Let's create our models.py file now. The following code is almost identical to the one we wrote for our CRUD app in *Chapter 5, Building the Backend for Our Application* – we declare the imports and create MongoBaseModel in order to flatten ObjectId into a string:

```
from enum import Enum
from bson import ObjectId
from typing import Optional
from pydantic import EmailStr, Field, BaseModel, validator
from email_validator import validate_email, EmailNotValidError
```

We imported the email_validator package that is needed for, well, email validation:

```
class PyObjectId(ObjectId):
    @classmethod
    def __get_validators__(cls):
        yield cls.validate
```

```
    @classmethod
    def validate(cls, v):
        if not ObjectId.is_valid(v):
            raise ValueError("Invalid objectid")
        return ObjectId(v)
    @classmethod
    def __modify_schema__(cls, field_schema):
        field_schema.update(type="string")

class MongoBaseModel(BaseModel):
    id: PyObjectId = Field(default_factory=PyObjectId,
        alias="_id")
    class Config:
        json_encoders = {ObjectId: str}
```

Notice that we imported the email validator package since it is not part of Pydantic – you should install it with the following:

```
pip install  email-validator
```

It is a package needed for Pydantic to validate the email addresses since we want to require a valid email address when the user registers. Although I will not implement a client-side registration flow in this chapter, I will create the user creation route, and it will require a valid email address. Who knows, maybe the owner of the company decides to introduce user accounts for customers later on?

On to the same file, models.py, and to the actual user model. We are defining two roles – a salesperson and an admin – and a very basic user model containing only the username, email, password, and role fields. Since the email field is the only one that cannot be directly validated from Pydantic, we add a simple validation method by using the email validator package. It is really simple – it just returns an error if the value provided isn't a valid email:

```
class Role(str, Enum):
    SALESPERSON = "SALESPERSON"
    ADMIN = "ADMIN"


class UserBase(MongoBaseModel):
    username: str = Field(..., min_length=3, max_length=15)
    email: str = Field(...)
```

```
    password: str = Field(...)
    role: Role

    @validator("email")
    def valid_email(cls, v):
        try:
            email = validate_email(v).email
            return email
        except EmailNotValidError as e:
            raise EmailNotValidError
```

Since we have already seen how Pydantic handles validation, this should be pretty self-explanatory. I defined two roles – a salesperson and an admin – and the users must fit into one of these two roles. We are now ready to define our user model and a couple of helper models:

```
class UserBase(MongoBaseModel):
    username: str = Field(..., min_length=3, max_length=15)
    email: str = EmailStr(...)
    password: str = Field(...)
    role: Role
    @validator("email")
    def valid_email(cls, v):
        try:
            email = validate_email(v).email
            return email
        except EmailNotValidError as e:
            raise EmailNotValidError
class LoginBase(BaseModel):
    email: str = EmailStr(...)
    password: str = Field(...)
class CurrentUser(BaseModel):
    email: str = EmailStr(...)
    username: str = Field(...)
    role: str = Field(...)
```

`UserModel` is simple enough: we require a username with a length between 3 and 15 characters, a valid email address, a password, and a role. I have added two additional models: `LoginBase` for the login route, and `CurrentUser`, which contains the data that we will extract from the model when we want to check who is currently making the requests. Moving on to the `Cars` model that I decided to put in the same `models.py` file, little has changed:

```
class CarBase(MongoBaseModel):
    brand: str = Field(..., min_length=3)
    make: str = Field(..., min_length=1)
    year: int = Field(..., gt=1975, lt=2023)
    price: int = Field(...)
    km: int = Field(...)
    cm3: int = Field(..., gt=600, lt=8000)


class CarDB(CarBase):
    owner: str = Field(...)
class CarUpdate(MongoBaseModel):
    price: Optional[int] = None
```

The base model is intact, with all the features that we had earlier (mileage, year of production, and so on). I have just added a new model, called `CarDB`, which extends the `CarBase` model and adds an owner field – that is, `id` of the user assigned to the car, and since we converted all our MongoDB `ObjectIds` to strings, it is a string as well. The `CarUpdate` model contains only the optional price update.

It is important to point out that this model is a great oversimplification of a real system. We would probably want to add a list of car IDs as a field in the User model, we would have a bunch of `DateTime` fields denoting the moment when the car was put up for sale, sold, reserved, and so on. However, in this chapter, I only want to implement a rather simple JWT-based authentication system and keep only the bare minimum functionality needed in order to have a working mechanism.

On to the authentication file, aptly called `authentication.py`. Let's quickly go over the requirements of our authentication mechanism:

- Once the user submits the registration form and sends us their password, the password should be hashed and only then inserted into the database

- We should have a function ready to compare this stored password hash with the subsequent passwords submitted during the login phase in order to verify whether they match

- We should be able to create/encode JWT tokens and decode them with a custom expiry time and with a payload containing the *user ID*

- Finally, we should have a function that accepts the request through dependency injection and returns either the ID of the user making the request or a message such as *invalid token* or *token expired*

The following mechanism is inspired and adapted from a YouTube video (`https://www.youtube.com/watch?v=xZnOoO3ImSY`), which offers an alternative and simpler approach than the one proposed in the FastAPI documentation.

Let's begin building our `authentication.py` file. First, we need to install a couple of libraries needed for the JWT authentication mechanism. `Pyjwt` is a library for encoding and decoding JWTs, while `passlib` is a library for hashing strings. Stop your FastAPI server and, in the active environment, insert the following command:

```
pip install pyjwt passlib['bcrypt']
```

Now we are ready to declare our imports in the `authentication.py` file as follows:

```
import jwt
from fastapi import HTTPException, Security
from fastapi.security import HTTPAuthorizationCredentials,
HTTPBearer
from passlib.context import CryptContext
from datetime import datetime, timedelta
```

As we said earlier, `jwt` is here to enable us to encode and decode JWTs, while FastAPI provides us with the bulk of the needed functionality. `HTTPException` is going to take care of cases in which the token is not valid – effectively turning exceptions in code into valid HTTP responses – while `Security` is used for authorization and for highlighting routes that will need a user to be authenticated in the automatic documentation. `HTTPBearer` is a FastAPI class ensuring that the HTTP request has the appropriate authentication header, while `HTTPAuthorizationCredentials` is the object type returned from the dependency injection.

`CryptContext` is used for creating a context for hashing passwords and it lives under `passlib.context`. Finally, we imported some `datetime` utilities for signing the token and giving it the desired expiry date.

After having declared our imports, it is time to create a class I will call `Authorization`, which will expose methods responsible for all the needed authentication steps:

```
class Authorization():
    security = HTTPBearer()
    pwd_context = CryptContext(schemes=["bcrypt"],
        deprecated="auto")
    secret = 'FARMSTACKsecretString'
```

We are instantiating FastAPI's simplest authentication – HTTPBearer – and creating a password context with CryptContext, using the bcrypt algorithm. We also need a secret string that could be generated automatically for increased security. Next, we will take care of hashing the password:

```
def get_password_hash(self, password):
    return self.pwd_context.hash(password)

def verify_password(self, plain_password, hashed_password):
    return self.pwd_context.verify(plain_password, hashed_
        password)
```

These rather simple functions ensure that the user's password is hashed and that it can be verified by comparing it to the plain text version. The second function returns a simple true or false value. We are now at the heart of the class – creating the JWT:

```
def encode_token(self, user_id):
    payload = {
        'exp': datetime.utcnow() + timedelta(days=0,
minutes=35),
        'iat': datetime.utcnow(),
        'sub': user_id
    }
    return jwt.encode(
        payload,
        self.secret,
        algorithm='HS256'
    )
```

The preceding function does the bulk of the work – it takes user_id as the sole parameter and puts it in the sub section of the payload. Bear in mind that we could encode more information in the JWT – the user's role or username for instance. In that case, the sub section would have a structure of a dictionary and the JWT would be considerably longer. The expiry time is set to 35 minutes, while issued at time is set to the moment of JWT creation. Finally, the function uses the jwt. encode method to encode the token. We provide the algorithm (HS256) and a secret as arguments.

The decode part of the class is very similar; we just reverse the process and provide exceptions in case they are needed:

```
def decode_token(self, token):
    try:
        payload = jwt.decode(token, self.secret,
```

```
algorithms=['HS256'])
            return payload['sub']
        except jwt.ExpiredSignatureError:
            raise HTTPException(status_code=401,
detail='Signature has expired')
        except jwt.InvalidTokenError as e:
            raise HTTPException(status_code=401,
detail='Invalid token')
```

The decode_token function returns just the sub part of the token – in our case, the user's ID – while we provide appropriate exceptions in case the token is not valid or if it has expired. Finally, we create our auth_wrapper function that will be used for dependency injection in the routes. If the function returns the user's ID, the route will be accessible; otherwise, we will get HTTPException:

```
    def auth_wrapper(self, auth: HTTPAuthorizationCredentials =
Security(security)):
        return self.decode_token(auth.credentials)
```

The authorization.py file is under 40 lines long but packs quite a punch – it enables us to protect routes by leveraging the excellent FastAPI's dependency injection mechanism.

Let's dive into the *users* router and put our authentication logic to the test. In the routers folder, create a users.py file and begin with the imports and class instantiations:

```
from fastapi import APIRouter, Request, Body, status,
HTTPException, Depends
from fastapi.encoders import jsonable_encoder
from fastapi.responses import JSONResponse
from models import UserBase, LoginBase, CurrentUser
from authentication import AuthHandler


router = APIRouter()
auth_handler = AuthHandler()
```

After the standard FastAPI imports, including jsonable_encoder and JSONResponse, we import our user models and the AuthHandler class from authorization.py. We then proceed to create the router that will be responsible for all the user's routes and an instance of AuthHandler. Let's begin with a registration route, so we can create some users and test them with a REST client:

```
@router.post("/register", response_description="Register user")
async def register(request: Request, newUser: UserBase =
```

```
Body(...)) -> UserBase:

    newUser.password = auth_handler.get_password_hash(newUser.
        password)
    newUser = jsonable_encoder(newUser)
```

The register route, which will be available at the /users/register URL, takes in a request and a newUser instance, modeled by Pydantic's UserBase class, through the body of the request. The first thing that we do is replace the password with the hashed password and convert the Pydantic model into a jsonable_encoder instance.

Now, we perform the standard registration checks – the email and the username should be available; otherwise, we throw an exception, notifying the user that the username or password has already been taken:

```
    if (
        existing_email := await request.app.mongodb["users"].
            find_one({"email": newUser["email"]}) is not None):
        raise HTTPException(
            status_code=409, detail=f"User with email
                {newUser['email']} already exists"
        )
    if (
        existing_username := await request.app.mongodb["users"]
            .find_one({"username": newUser["username"]}) is not
                None):
        raise HTTPException(
            status_code=409, detail=f"User with username
                {newUser['username']} already exists",
        )
```

The previous functions could and should be refactored to allow for further checks, but I want them to be as explicit as possible. The final part of the function is trivial; we just need to insert the user into MongoDB! You can see this in the following code:

```
    user = await request.app.mongodb["users"].insert_
        one(newUser)
    created_user = await request.app.mongodb["users"].find_one(
        {"_id": user.inserted_id}
    )
```

```
    return JSONResponse(status_code=status.HTTP_201_CREATED,
        content=created_user)
```

We return the standard 201 CREATED status code, and we are now ready to perform some basic tests using *HTTPie*, our command-line REST client. Let's try and create a user as follows:

```
(venv) λ http POST 127.0.0.1:8000/users/register
username="bill" password="bill" role="ADMIN" email="koko@gmail.
    com"
{
    "_id": "629333d7e33842d9499e6ac7",
    "email": "koko@gmail.com",
    "password": "$2b$12$HKGcr5CnxV7coSMgx41gRu34Q11Qb.
        m5XZHlX1tslH8ppqlVB2oJK",
    "role": "ADMIN",
    "username": "bill"
}
```

We get a new user with a hashed password, a role, and _id. Of course, we wouldn't want to send the password back to the user, even if it is hashed, but you already have the knowledge to create a new Pydantic model that returns all the fields except the password. Let's move on to the login route – it is very similar to what you might have already used with Flask or Express.js. We receive the email and password (we could have opted for a username) and, first, we try to find the user by email. After that, we compare the password with our hashing function:

```
@router.post("/login", response_description="Login user")
async def login(request: Request, loginUser: LoginBase =
Body(...)) -> str:
    user = await request.app.mongodb["users"].find_
        one({"email": loginUser.email})
    if (user is None) or (
        not auth_handler.verify_password(loginUser.password,
            user["password"])
    ):
        raise HTTPException(status_code=401, detail="Invalid
            email and/or password")
    token = auth_handler.encode_token(user["_id"])
    response = JSONResponse(content={"token": token})
    return response
```

If the user exists and the password passes the hash verification, we create a token and return it as a JSON response. This precious token will then be responsible for authentication all over our app and it will be the only data that needs to be sent to the server with every request. We can test the login route as well by hitting the /users/login route with the appropriate credentials:

```
λ http POST http://127.0.0.1:8000/users/login email="tanja@
gmail.com" password="tanja"
HTTP/1.1 200 OK
content-length: 184
content-type: application/json
date: Wed, 01 Jun 2022 20:13:32 GMT
server: uvicorn
{
    "token": "eyJ0eXAiOiJKV1QiLCJhbGciOiJIUzI1NiJ9.
eyJleHAiOjE2NTQxMTY1MTMsImlhdCI6MTY1NDExNDQxMywic3
ViIjoiNjI4OTQyODU3YTBjYmZlNGE2MzQwNDdkIn0.v1FTBM0wI1DKUw_
VVCJlsSItM58sDzDnwGbzyDKs_pc"
}
```

We got the token back! If you want, you can try the same route with the wrong username/password combination and check the response.

We will need one final route in the users router: the /me route. This route is not supposed to be called directly and generate a page, only to be used as a helper – a way of verifying the currently logged user making the request. The /me route should not accept any parameters except the authentication dependency – the perfect opportunity to test our authentication wrapper:

```
@router.get("/me", response_description="Logged in user data")
async def me(request: Request, userId=Depends(auth_handler.
auth_wrapper)):
    currentUser = await request.app.mongodb["users"].find_
        one({"_id": userId})
    result = CurrentUser(**currentUser).dict()
    result["id"] = userId
    return JSONResponse(status_code=status.HTTP_200_OK,
        content=result)
```

This route is pretty simple: if the provided token is valid and not expired, auth_wrapper will return userId – the ID of the user making the request. Otherwise, it will return an HTTP exception. In this route, I have added a database call in order to retrieve the desired data about the user, according to the CurrentUser model.

We could have encoded all this data in the token and avoided the trip to the database, but I wanted to leave the JWT as thin as possible.

Now, we can test the /me route. First, let's log in with our previously registered user:

```
(venv) λ http POST 127.0.0.1:8000/users/login password="bill"
email="koko@gmail.com"
HTTP/1.1 200 OK
{
    "token": "eyJ0eXAiOiJKV1QiLCJhbGciOiJIUzI1NiJ9.eyJleHAiOj
E2NTM4Mzk1NTksImlhdCI6MTY1MzgzNzQ1OSwic3ViIjoiNjI5MzMzZDdlMzM
4NDJkOTQ5OWU2YWM3In0.
ajpoftEFBWcfn2XC1JqPDNcJMaS6OujZpaU8bCv0BNE"
}
```

Copy this token and provide it to the /me route:

```
(venv) λ http GET 127.0.0.1:8000/users/me "Authorization:
Bearer eyJ0eXAiOiJKV1QiLCJhbGciOiJIUzI1NiJ9.eyJleHAiOj
E2NTM4Mzk1NTksImlhdCI6MTY1MzgzNzQ1OSwic3ViIjoiNjI5MzMzZDdlMzM4
NDJkOTQ5OWU2YWM3In0.
ajpoftEFBWcfn2XC1JqPDNcJMaS6OujZpaU8bCv0BNE"
HTTP/1.1 200 OK
{
    "email": "koko@gmail.com",
    "id": "629333d7e33842d9499e6ac7",
    "role": "ADMIN",
    "username": "bill"
}
```

If you test the route without the bearer token, you will get a Not Authenticated error and you will be back at square one.

Finally, I will show how to insert the authentication dependency into the /cars router (or really, any other router that you might need to create). Since it will be a pretty long file, I will not explain all of it – I will rather focus on the logic used to perform authentication and authorization on a couple of routes, while the entire file is available in the book's GitHub repository. Let's see the imports for the /cars router:

```
from typing import List, Optional
from fastapi import APIRouter, Request, Body, status,
```

```
HTTPException, Depends
from fastapi.encoders import jsonable_encoder
from fastapi.responses import JSONResponse

from models import CarBase, CarDB, CarUpdate
from authentication import AuthHandler

router = APIRouter()
auth_handler = AuthHandler()
```

This part is almost identical to the `users` router – we import our Pydantic models and instantiate the router and the authentication handler class.

Our Pydantic `cars` model has changed; now it has something called `owner`, basically just the ID of the user that is supposed to sell the car. We will provide this information to the database through our authentication dependency injection. When the user attempts to insert a new instance of the entity (a car), they will have to be authenticated in order to proceed. If they are authenticated, we will just take their ID and set it as the `owner` field value:

```
@router.post("/", response_description="Add new car")
async def create_car(
    request: Request,
    car: CarBase = Body(...),
    userId=Depends(auth_handler.auth_wrapper),
):
    car = jsonable_encoder(car)
    car["owner"] = userId
    new_car = await request.app.mongodb["cars2"].insert_
        one(car)
    created_car = await request.app.mongodb["cars2"].find_one(
        {"_id": new_car.inserted_id}
    )
    return JSONResponse( status_code=status.HTTP_201_CREATED,
        content=created_car)
```

The simplest case would be the path corresponding to GET `/cars` – a route that would list all available cars, with some pagination implemented through query strings. Let's say that we want only logged users (so salespersons or admins) to access this route.

All we need to do is inject the authentication wrapper into the dependency, and FastAPI has only two choices: either the token is valid and fresh and we get a user, or HTTPException is raised; it is really as simple as that. So, let's create our route for listing cars – we're assuming that only registered users can access this route:

```python
@router.get("/", response_description="List all cars")
async def list_all_cars(
    request: Request,
    min_price: int = 0,
    max_price: int = 100000,
    brand: Optional[str] = None,
    page: int = 1,
    userId=Depends(auth_handler.auth_wrapper),
) -> List[CarDB]:
    RESULTS_PER_PAGE = 25
    skip = (page - 1) * RESULTS_PER_PAGE
    query = {"price": {"$lt": max_price, "$gt": min_price}}
    if brand:
        query["brand"] = brand
    full_query = (
        request.app.mongodb["cars2"]
        .find(query)
        .sort("_id", -1)
        .skip(skip)
        .limit(RESULTS_PER_PAGE)
    )
    results = [CarDB(**raw_car) async for raw_car in full_
        query]
    return results
```

While the whole function performs some pagination (25 hardcoded results per page) and has some nifty options for filtering by price and by brand, the gist of authentication logic is in the bold line. Also, please note that I have created a separate MongoDB collection and named it cars2, just to differentiate it from the collection used in the previous chapter, while using the same database.

Finally, let's examine the route for editing a car (just the price, in our case). We want only the owner of the car to be able to edit the price and, additionally, any admin can also step in and update the price. For this case, it would have been wise if we had encoded the role of the user as well in the JWT, as it would save us a trip to the database, but I just want to make you aware of some decisions and trade-offs that you are bound to make during the development of the API:

```python
@router.patch("/{id}", response_description="Update car")
async def update_task(
    id: str,
    request: Request,
    car: CarUpdate = Body(...),
    userId=Depends(auth_handler.auth_wrapper),
):
    user = await request.app.mongodb
        ["users"].find_one({"_id": userId})
    findCar = await request.app.mongodb
        ["cars2"].find_one({"_id": id})

    if (findCar["owner"] != userId) and user["role"] !=
        "ADMIN":
            raise HTTPException(
                status_code=401, detail="Only the owner or an
                admin can update the car"
            )
    await request.app.mongodb["cars2"].update_one(
        {"_id": id}, {"$set": car.dict(exclude_unset=True)}
    )
    if (car := await request.app.mongodb
        ["cars2"].find_one({"_id": id})) is not None:
            return CarDB(**car)
    raise HTTPException
        (status_code=404, detail=f"Car with {id} not found")
```

In this route handler, we first get the user making the request, and then we locate the car to be edited. Finally, we perform a check: if the owner of the car is *not* the user making the request and this user is not an admin, we throw an exception. Otherwise, we perform the update. FastAPI's dependency injection is a simple and powerful mechanism that really shines in the authentication and authorization domain!

In this section, we have created a simple but efficient authentication system on our FastAPI backend, we have created a JWT generator and we are able to verify the tokens, we have protected some routes, and provided the routes needed for creating (registering) new users and logging in. It is now time to see how things work on the frontend!

## Authenticating the users in React

As with the other aspects of security, authentication in React is a huge topic and is beyond the scope of this book. In this section, I will give you just a very basic mechanism that enables us to have a simple authentication flow on the client side. Everything will revolve around the JWT and the way we decide to handle it. In this chapter, we are going to store it just in memory.

The internet and the specialized literature are full of debates on what is the optimal solution for storing authentication data – in our case, the JWT token. As always, there are pros and cons to each solution and at the beginning of this section.

Cookies have been around for a very long time – they can store data in key-value pairs in the browser and they are readable both from the browser and the server. Their popularity coincided with the classic server-side rendered websites. However, they can store a very limited amount of data, and the structure of said data has to be very simple.

Localstorage and Session Storage were introduced with HTML5 as a way to address the need for storing complex data structures in single-page applications, among other things. Their capacity is around 10 MB, depending on the browser's implementation, compared to 4 KB of cookie capacity. Session storage data persists through a session, while local storage remains in the browser, even after it is closed and reopened, until manually deleted. Both can host complex JSON data structures.

Storing JWT in localstorage is nice, it's easy, and it allows for a great user experience and developer experience. It is, however, frowned upon since it opens the application to a wide array of vulnerabilities, since they can be accessed by any client-side JavaScript running in the browser.

The majority of authorities on the subject suggest storing JWT in HTTP – only cookies, cookies that cannot be accessed through JavaScript and require the frontend and the backend to run on the same domain. This can be accomplished in different ways, through routing requests, using a proxy, and so on. Another popular strategy is the use of so-called refresh tokens – we issue one token upon login and then this token is used to generate other (refresh) tokens automatically, allowing us to mitigate between security and user experience.

In this section, I will build a very simple and minimalistic React app that will just barely meet the requirements; some routes and pages should be protected unless the user logs in. I will not persist the JWT in any way – when the user refreshes the application, they are logged out. Not the most pleasant user experience, but that is not the issue right now.

Let's proceed step by step. We have our FastAPI backend running, and we are ready to create our simple frontend:

1. Navigate to your /chapter7 directory and, from the terminal, create a React app:

```
npx create-react-app frontend
```

2. Change the directory into the frontend and install Tailwind CSS:

```
npm install -D tailwindcss postcss@latest autoprefixer
```

3. Initialize Tailwind with the following command:

```
npx tailwindcss init -p
```

4. Now, it is time to edit postcss.config.js:

```
module.exports = {
  content: [
    "./src/**/*.{js,jsx,ts,tsx}",
  ],
  theme: {
    extend: {},
  },
  plugins: [],
}
```

5. Finally, delete everything in the src/index.css file and replace the content with the following:

```
@tailwind base;
@tailwind components;
@tailwind utilities;
```

These steps should be familiar by now, but now I want to take the process one step further. Tailwind has gained in popularity over the last few years, and different UI kits and utilities are based on the basic Tailwind classes. One of the most popular and usable ones is called DaisyUI (https://daisyui.com), and we will use it for prototyping our app.

6. The installation process is similar to Tailwind itself. In the terminal, type the following:

```
npm i daisyui
```

7.  When completed, we need to register `daisyui` as a Tailwind plugin in `tailwind.config.js` as follows:

```
module.exports = {
    //...
    plugins: [require("daisyui")],
}
```

8.  Finally, delete all the unneeded files (such as `App.css` and `Logo.svg`) and reduce your `App.js` file to the following in order to test that React has picked up the UI dependencies:

```
function App() {
    return (
        <div className="App bg-zinc-500 min-h-screen flex
            flex-col justify-center items-center">
            <button class="btn btn-primary">It works!</button>
        </div>
    );
}
export default App;
```

9.  Now, we can test the app and see that both Tailwind and DaisyUI are functioning correctly – you should be able to see a pretty empty page with a styled button. I had to run the following again:

**npm install postcss@latest**

Maybe by the time you are reading this, the fix will not be necessary anymore.

10. For authentication purposes, we will dive a bit deeper into the React Router 6 and we will take advantage of some of its new features and components. Stop the terminal process and bravely install the router:

**npm install react-router-dom@6**

11. We are going to set the router up in the `index.js` file as follows:

```
import React from 'react';
import ReactDOM from 'react-dom/client';
import './index.css';
import {BrowserRouter, Routes, Route} from 'react-router-
    dom'
import App from './App';
const root = ReactDOM.createRoot(document.
```

```
getElementById('root'));
root.render(
  <React.StrictMode>
    <BrowserRouter>
      <Routes>
        <Route path='/*' element={<App />} />
      </Routes>
    </BrowserRouter>
  </React.StrictMode>
);
```

We are wrapping everything in the router so that it "covers" the whole application and the path is a catch-all asterisk (*), while the element that needs to be provided to the router is the root App.js component. Now comes the tedious part of defining all the possible routes and components, but again, we are going to use React Router's new features – nested routes. Instead of wrapping each and every component into a Layout component – containing the common web page elements such as navigation or footer – we are going to use the Router's Outlet component, which just fills the component with the content of the nested component that matches the URL pattern.

12. Let's create a components folder under /src and build generic Header.jsx and Footer.jsx components, making use of our React ES6 Visual Studio Code extension (by typing _rafce):

```
const Header = () => {
  return <div>Header</div>;
};
export default Header;
```

13. Following the exact same procedure, create the following components in the /src/components folder: Footer, HomePage, Login, and Register, containing just a div returning the component's name. Layout.jsx will make use of the nested routing:

```
import { Outlet } from "react-router-dom";
import Header from "./Header";
import Footer from "./Footer";

const Layout = () => {
  return (
    <div className="App flex flex-col min-h-screen">
      <Header />
```

```
        <main className="flex-1 min-h-full flex flex-col
            align-middle justify-center items-center">
            <Outlet />
        </main>
        <Footer />
    </div>
    );
};
export default Layout;
```

The Layout component is simple but very useful: it makes use of the Outlet component that acts as a high-order component, effectively wrapping the contained routes and adding the header and the footer. I have made the page full-height using Tailwind's classes and set the display to flex. The main section is set to flex-1, to take up all the remaining space.

The App.js file is now updated as follows:

```
import {Route, Routes} from "react-router-dom"
import Layout from "./components/Layout";
import Login from "./components/Login";
import Register from "./components/Register";
import HomePage from "./components/HomePage";


function App() {
    return (
        <Routes>
            <Route path="/" element={<Layout />}>
                <Route path="/" element={<HomePage />} />
                <Route path="login" element={<Login/>} />
                <Route path="register" element={<Register/>} />
            </Route>
        </Routes>
    );
}
export default App;
```

A keen observer will immediately notice that the Route element that uses the Layout component as the rendering element is *not self-closing* – it, in fact, encloses all the remaining routes, channeling them, and in the process, adding the Header and Footer components. Excellent and elegant! You can manually try to change the URL; navigate to /login or /register or simply / (the root URL of the React site), and see whether the middle section updates. The router is set up and working. We will add more routes for the CRUD operations on cars, but they will be protected – the user will have to provide credentials in the form of a valid JWT token in order to access them (and even if they could access the React routes, without a token, the operations couldn't be performed on the backend). It is time to introduce another React hook – useContext.

Context is a way of solving the problem known as prop-drilling in React when a component that is located down in the component tree needs to accept props through a series of components – parents that do not essentially need them. Context is a method of sharing values (strings, numeric values, lists, and objects) with all the components that are enclosed in a context provider. The useContext Hook – used to interact with the context – is one of the coolest features of the new Hook-based React, and something that can handle lots of common design problems.

Using context is a bit particular, not like the useState or useEffect hook, as it involves a bit more moving parts, but we will use the simplest version, coupled with a custom Hook, for easier access.

The first step is to create a context, using createContext provided by React. This function accepts default arguments, so you could provide it with, for instance, a dictionary: {username:"Marko"}. This argument will only be used unless no value is provided otherwise. Even functions for setting or modifying the context values can be passed to the context – and that is precisely what we are going to do. We can set up an auth value that will store the logged-in user's data (if any), but also a setAuth function, called when the user logs in, that will set the user data. We could also use this function for logging the user out, by simply setting the context value of auth to a null value.

The second step is to use a context provider – a React component that allows other components to consume our context. All the consumers that are wrapped inside the provider will re-render once the context (the provider's value) changes. The provider is the vehicle for providing the content value(s) to the child component, instead of props.

Now comes the Hook, useContext, which takes a context as an argument and makes it available to the component. We will use it for accessing the context. Let's move on to the example, as it will become clearer. Follow these steps:

1.  I will create the simplest possible context with a single state variable called auth (with a useState Hook, setAuth) in the /src/context/AutProvider.js file:

```
import { createContext, useState } from "react";
const AuthContext = createContext({})
export const AuthProvider = ({children}) => {
    const [auth, setAuth] = useState({
```

```
    })
    return <AuthContext.Provider value={{auth, setAuth}}>
        {children}
    </AuthContext.Provider>
}
export default AuthContext
```

2.  Now, we can wrap our `Router` routes in the `index.js` file and make `auth` and `setAuth` available to all the routes. Edit the `index.js` file:

```
import { AuthProvider } from './context/AuthProvider';

...

<React.StrictMode>
    <BrowserRouter>
    <AuthProvider>
        <Routes>
            <Route path='/*' element={<App />} />
        </Routes>
    </AuthProvider>
    </BrowserRouter>
</React.StrictMode>
```

Finally, since we do not want to have to import both the `AuthContext` provider and `useContext` in every component, we will create a simple utility Hook that will import the context for us.

3.  In the `/src/hooks` folder, create a file called `useAuth.js`:

```
import { useContext } from "react";
import AuthContext from "../context/AuthProvider";
const useAuth = () => {
    return useContext(AuthContext)
}
export default useAuth;
```

This setup might seem complicated, but it really isn't – we just had to create one context and one hook to facilitate our job. The benefit is that now we can cover the entire area of the app and set and get the value of our `auth` variable. Let's begin using our React authentication mechanism and create the `Login` component – the one that will actually get us logged in. For the form handling, I want to introduce a third-party package: *React-Form-Hook* (https://react-hook-form.com/).

We have already seen that manual form handling in React can get pretty tedious, and there are some excellent and battle-tested solutions. In this chapter, we will get to use the React form hook. Let's begin by installing it:

```
npm install react-hook-form
```

Restart the React server with `npm run start` and fire up the `Login.jsx` component. This will arguably be the most complex component logic-wise, so let's break it down:

```
import { useForm } from "react-hook-form";
import { useState } from "react";
import { useNavigate } from "react-router-dom";
import useAuth from "../hooks/useAuth";
```

We import the `useForm` Hook, `useState` for some state variables, the `useNavigate` Hook from the router for redirecting after the login, and our `useAuth` Hook since we want to set the authentication context after a successful login. We then begin to draw our component and set up the Hook:

```
const Login = () => {
  const [apiError, setApiError] = useState();
  const { setAuth } = useAuth();
  let navigate = useNavigate();
  const {
    register,
    handleSubmit,
    formState: { errors },
  } = useForm();
```

The `ApiError` variable should be self-explanatory. I will use it to store potential errors generated from the backend in order to display them later. The `navigate` is necessary for programmatic navigation to different pages inside the router, while `react-form-hook` gives us several useful tools: `register` is used to register the form inputs with the instance of the Hook, `handleSubmit` is for, well, handling the submitting of the form, while `errors` will host the errors during the process. Let's continue with the code:

```
  const onFormSubmit = async (data) => {
    const response = await fetch("http://127.0.0.1:8000/users/
      login", {
      method: "POST",
      headers: {
        "Content-Type": "application/json",
```

```
        },
      body: JSON.stringify(data),
    });
    if (response.ok) {
      const token = await response.json();
      await getUserData(token["token"]);
    } else {
      let errorResponse = await response.json();
      setApiError(errorResponse["detail"]);
      setAuth(null);
    }
  };
  const onErrors = (errors) => console.error(errors);
```

The onSubmit is pretty similar to what we have already done manually: we send a POST request to the /login endpoint with the form data encoded as JSON. If everything is fine (an OK response, which is short for a response code in the 200–299 range), we proceed and get the token. We then feed this token to another function called getUserData. If the API sends any error, we take this error and put it in the apiError state variable. Remember, FastAPI has this nice detail key that contains the human-readable message error. The errors are simply sent to the console.

Let's take a look at the getUserData function – it is simply a call to the /me route on the backend:

```
const getUserData = async (token) => {
  const response = await fetch("http://127.0.0.1:8000/users/
      me", {
    method: "GET",
    headers: {
      "Content-Type": "application/json",
      Authorization: `Bearer ${token}`,
    },
  });
  if (response.ok) {
    let userData = await response.json();
    userData["token"] = token;
    setAuth(userData);
    setApiError(null);
    navigate("/", { replace: true });
```

```
        }
    };
```

This is the function that actually makes use of our token – we add it to the header of the request and if a user is retrieved (an OK response), we use that user's data to populate the `auth` object in `authContext`. Finally, we send the user to the home page with the help of the router. The remaining portion of the function is the markup and some utility classes:

```
return (
    <div className="mx-auto p-10 rounded-lg shadow-2xl">
        <h2 className="text-xl text-primary text-center font-bold
            my-2">
            Login page
        </h2>
        <form onSubmit={handleSubmit(onFormSubmit,
            onErrors)}>
            <div className="flex flex-col justify-center items-
                center">
                <input
                    type="text"
                    placeholder="email@email.com"
                    className="input input-bordered input-accent w-
                        full max-w-xs m-3"
                    name="email"
                    autoComplete="off"
                    {...register("email", { required: "The email is
                        required" })}
                />
                {errors?.email && errors.email.message}

                <input
                    type="password"
                    placeholder="your password"
                    className="input input-bordered input-accent w-
                        full max-w-xs m-3"
                    name="password"
                    {...register("password", { required: "The
```

```
            password is required" })}
          />
          {errors?.password && errors.password.message}
```

Finally, there is just some simple markup for displaying HTML elements:

```
          <button className="btn btn-outline btn-accent m-3
             btn-block">
            Login
          </button>
        </div>
      </form>
      {apiError && (
        <div className="alert alert-error shadow-lg">
          <div>

            <span>{apiError}</span>
          </div>
        </div>
      )}
    </div>
  );
};
export default Login;
```

It is important to note that each field in the form has a register prop that binds it to the form that is controlled by the React form hook. If we try to log in with a non-existing email or password, the API errors will be displayed, while if everything goes well, we should be redirected to the home page. In order to see the auth data, we can take a look at the React extension in Chrome after the redirect. In the **Components** tab, under **ContextProvider**, you should be able to see all the data stored in the auth object.

It will be difficult to continue developing without proper navigation, so let's visit the DaisyUI website and find a suitable navigation bar. After snooping around, I found the following solution that required some copying and some adjustments for the structure of the React Router's links:

```
import React from "react";
import { Link } from "react-router-dom";
import useAuth from "../hooks/useAuth";
```

```
const Header = () => {
  const { auth, setAuth } = useAuth();
  return (
    <div className="navbar bg-primary text-primary-content">
      <div className="flex-1">
        <Link className="btn btn-ghost normal-case text-xl"
            to="/">FARM Cars </Link>
        <span className="border-2 border-amber-500 p-1">
          {auth?.username
            ? `Logged in as ${auth?.username} - ${auth.role}`
            : "Not logged in"}
        </span>
      </div>
      <div className="flex-none">
        <ul className="menu menu-horizontal p-0">
          {!auth?.username && (
            <li className="mx-1">
              <Link to="/login">Login</Link>
            </li>
          )}
          {!auth?.username && (
            <li className="mx-1">
              <Link to="/register">Register</Link>
            </li>
          )}
          {auth?.username && (
            <li className="mx-1">
              <button className=" btn-warning">
                Logout <span className="font-semibold">{auth?.
                    username}</span>
              </button>
            </li>
          )}
        </ul>
      </div>
    </div>
```

```
    );
  };
  export default Header;
```

This is a regular navigation menu with a couple of context niceties: we import our useAuth Hook and immediately gain access to authContext. This enables us to conditionally show or hide the **Login and register** or **Logout** links. I added a small span inside the navbar to notify the user whether there's anybody logged in or not. Since the default theme is pretty bland, I am going to apply a DaisyUI theme – you can explore them on https://daisyui.com/docs/themes/. I like the autumn theme, so I am just going to find the index.html file and add data-theme="autumn" to the html opening tag.

Our **Logout** button is not doing anything useful, so let's add a logout handler in the same Header. jsx file:

```
    let navigate = useNavigate();
    const logout = () =>{
        setAuth({})
        navigate("/login", {replace:true})
    }
```

And just add the onClick handler to the **Logout** button and set it to {logout}.

We have created a very simple authentication system, but we have no routes to protect, especially routes that involve cars: updating, adding, and deleting. That is the final part of the authentication system that I want to show here. There are many ways to prevent certain components from showing or displaying conditionally in React. An elegant way is making use of the React router again – with the use of outlets.

Simply put, we will make an authentication component that will just check for the presence of the auth data – if the data is present, you will be served the outlet, the enclosed protected routes, and corresponding components, and if not, the router will send you to the login page (or whatever page you wish).

Let's create a component called RequiredAuthentication.jsx:

```
import { useLocation, Navigate, Outlet } from "react-router-
dom";
import useAuth from "../hooks/useAuth";

const RequireAuthentication = () => {
   const { auth } = useAuth();
   const location = useLocation;
```

```
    return auth?.username ? <Outlet /> : <Navigate to="/login"
/>;
};
export default RequireAuthentication;
```

The component acts as a simple switch: if the username is present in the auth object, the outlet takes over and lets the client through to any route that is enclosed. Otherwise, it forces navigation to the /login route.

This isn't much different than some other approaches that use a simple functional component and then conditionally render the reserved output or the login route.

In order to be able to see our authentication logic in practice, we need at least one protected route. Let's create a new component and call it CarList.jsx. It will simply display all the cars in the database, but in order to be accessible, the user will have to be logged in – either as an admin or a salesperson. The CarList component has some standard imports and Hooks:

```
import { useEffect, useState } from "react"
import useAuth from "../hooks/useAuth"
import Card from "./Card"
const CarList = () => {
  const { auth } = useAuth()
  const [cars, setCars] = useState([]);
```

The Card component is really not important here – it is just a card element provided by DaisyUI, similar to the one we used in *Chapter 6, Building the Frontend of the Application* in order to display the car information. The useAuth hook provides us with a fast way to check for the authenticated user information through Context. The useEffect Hook is used to make a call to the FastAPI server and populate the cars array:

```
useEffect(() => {
    fetch("http://127.0.0.1:8000/cars/", {
      method: "GET",
      headers: {
        "Content-Type": "application/json",
        Authorization: `Bearer ${auth.token}`,
      },
    })
      .then((response) => response.json())
      .then((json) => {
        setCars(json);
```

```
        });
    }, []);
```

Finally, the JSX for returning the list of cars is just a map over the array of cars:

```
return (
    <div>
        <h2 className="text-xl text-primary text-center font-
            bold my-5">
            Cars Page
        </h2>
        <div className="mx-8 grid grid-cols-1 md:grid-cols-2
            gap-5 p-4">
            {cars &&
                cars.map((el) => {
                    return <Card key={el._id} car={el} />;
                })}
        </div>
    </div>
    );
};
export default CarList;
```

In order to hook this component up with the application, we need to update the App.js file with the routes:

```
<Routes>
        <Route path="/" element={<Layout />}>
            <Route path="/" element={<HomePage />} />
            <Route path="login" element={<Login/>} />
            <Route path="register" element={<Register/>} />
            <Route element={<RequireAuthentication />}>
                <Route path="cars" element={<CarList/>} />
            </Route>
        </Route>
    </Routes>
```

Notice how we wrapped the CarList component inside the RequireAuthentication route: we could add other routes that need authentication in the same way, and we could also perform more granular control over which user can access which route. It is easy to edit the RequireAuthentication component and perform additional checks on the type of authenticated user – so we could have an area for admins only, but not for regular salespersons and so on.

Finally, let's update the Header.jsx component as well, in order to show the link to the newly created /cars route:

```
{!auth?.username && (
  <li className="mx-1">
    <Link to="/register">Register</Link>
  </li>
)}
<li className="mx-1">
  <Link to="/cars">Cars</Link>
</li>
```

I have left the link visible for all visitors – logged in or not – in order to showcase the authentication route's functionality; if you click the link without being logged in, you will be sent to the login page, otherwise, you should see a nice set of cards with the cars displayed.

There is really no need to present the remaining CRUD operations on the cars that should require authentication – we have already seen how the backend checks for the appropriate user by reading the JWT token, so it is just a matter of ensuring that the token is present and valid.

As I underlined earlier, authentication and authorization are probably the most fundamental and serious topics in any application, and they put before the developer and stakeholders a series of challenges and questions that need to be addressed early on. While external solutions (such as Auth0, AWS Cognito, Firebase, Okta, and others) provide robust and industrial strength security and features, your project might need a custom solution in which the ownership of data is under total control.

In these cases, it is important that you weigh up your options carefully, and who knows – maybe you will end up having to write your own authentication. Not all apps are made for banking, after all!

## Summary

In this chapter, we have seen a very basic but quite representative implementation of an authentication mechanism. We have seen how FastAPI enables us to use standard-compliant authentication methods and we implemented one of the simplest possible yet effective solutions.

We have learned how elegant and flexible FastAPI and MongoDB are when it comes to defining granular roles and permissions, with the aid of Pydantic as the middleman. This chapter was focused exclusively on JWT tokens as the means of communication because it is the primary and most popular tool in single-page applications nowadays, and it enables great connectivity between services or microservices.

Finally, we created a simple React application and implemented a login mechanism that stores the user data in the state in memory. I have chosen not to show any solution of persisting the JWT token on purpose – the idea is just to see how a React application behaves with authenticated users and with those who are not. Using both localstorage and cookies has its pros and vulnerabilities (localstorage more so), but they both might be viable solutions for an application that has very light security requirements.

It is important to emphasize again that the FARM stack can be a great prototyping tool, so knowing your way around when creating an authentication flow, even if it is not ideal or absolutely bulletproof, might be just good enough to get you over that MVP hump in the race for the next great data-driven product! In the next chapter, we will see how we can integrate our MongoDB and FastAPI-based backend with a robust React framework – Next.js – and we will cover some standard web development tasks such as image and file uploads, authentication with `httpOnly` cookies, simple data visualizations, sending emails, and taking advantage of the flexibility of the stack.

# Part 3 – Deployment and Final Thoughts

In this part, we will explore the Next.js framework, the Cloudinary online image service, and a couple of popular deployment options both for the frontend and the backend. We will also see some steps required for achieving functionalities such as displaying charts based on data from the backend and sending emails. We will end this part with some useful considerations and some project ideas geared towards solidifying what we have learned so far.

This part includes the following chapters:

- *Chapter 8, Server-Side Rendering and Image Processing with FastAPI and Next.js*
- *Chapter 9, Building a Data Visualization App with the FARM Stack*
- *Chapter 10, Caching with Redis and Deployment on Ubuntu (DigitalOcean) and Netlify*
- *Chapter 11, Useful Resources and Project Ideas*

# 8

# Server-Side Rendering and Image Processing with FastAPI and Next.js

We have covered a lot of ground in our FARM-stack exploration so far, but when it comes to building real, modern web applications, there are so many aspects and topics that just listing all of them would take dozens of pages.

In this chapter, I will try to focus on a couple of key topics and essential web development requirements that you are bound to run into, namely: making fast, SEO-performant, server-side, or statically generated pages, and image handling. Where possible, I will try to give concrete and deliberately simplified examples, while outlining different solutions and strategies and emphasizing the strengths specific to the MongoDB, FastAPI, and React frameworks.

In this chapter, we'll cover, or at least touch on, the following topics:

- Creating a FastAPI endpoint that can accept and process files, namely, images
- Introduction to the Next.js framework and server-side rendering
- Manipulating and uploading images to an external service
- Authentication with Next.js and API routes using FastAPI JWTs
- Deployment of FastAPI on Heroku and Next.js on Vercel

By the end of this chapter, you will have the basic knowledge required to tackle numerous web-related challenges and will know how to search for solutions autonomously, while leveraging the power and flexibility of Next.js and FastAPI.

# Technical requirements

To complete this chapter's code, the requirements are the same as for the previous chapters – you need a working Python environment (version >3.6) and a Node.js installation with npm.

You can download the complete project on GitHub here: `https://github.com/PacktPublishing/Full-Stack-FastAPI-React-and-MongoDB/tree/main/chapter8`.

# Introduction to our Sample App

In the previous chapters, we were able to dive into the basic components of our FARM stack, but web development is much more than a basic sum of its components. Full-stack web development often consists of a constant back and forth between the frontend and the backend, and their seamless communication is the key to any functional and efficient web app. In this chapter, we are going to build something a bit more realistic, while remaining on topic – a car selling application – but adhering to a slightly more complex specification. As in the previous chapters, I do not plan to propose optimized or clever solutions, but rather simple, illustrative code whose main purpose is to highlight the topic at hand. Roughly speaking, the specification is the following:

- The app should accommodate external users who do not need to be logged in to see the cars and internal users – admins and salespersons, who are able to perform CRUD operations on the car adverts

- The car listings should be rendered on the server-side (for page loading speed and SEO)

- The car entities should contain an image – in a real app, we would want an array of images, at least 5 or 10 of them, but in our case, one will do

- The images should be hosted on a cloud provider and allow for on-the-fly transformations and optimization

- We want to enable the authenticated user to remain logged in even when the browser is closed or the page is refreshed, for a predetermined period of time

- Finally, we want to explore at least a couple of possible deployment options and discuss the differences

This sounds like a lot of ground to cover, so we won't discuss the code that we have already created in the previous chapters. Rather, I will point out the new or different parts, and try to keep the features of the new technologies covered at a minimum, while providing you with useful links and books for diving deeper. We will begin with the backend.

# Managing images and files in the backend

Files, especially images, are essential to modern web applications. Apart from the usual story of an image being worth a thousand words, images have multiple functions – aesthetic (incorporated in your site branding and color schemes and conveying certain emotions), informative (in our case, the user wants to see whether the car they are considering is worth buying!), and so on. The evolution of the process of serving images has evolved with the web itself; serving optimized and fast-loading images of the right dimensions and resolution has become an essential task in web development and there are many solutions, at various levels, that help us achieve good results.

First, the images have to be stored somewhere and have to be accessible by the app. While you could be storing images on your web server and serving them pretty quickly (they are, after all, static assets), the tendency is to host them on a third-party provider and make use of their **content delivery networks** (**CDNs**). Images often make up for more than half of the total page payload, and specialized image hosting providers help us reduce that load, serving tailored images for every device, size, and network connection speed. While there are many competitors on the market, I will not delve into their differences and comparative advantages – it is a type of research that you will have to do yourself, taking into account your project. For my web development needs, *Cloudinary* – one of the market leaders – has been nothing short of excellent. It is a mature company that specializes in serving content (images, videos, and also PDFs) and optimizing it for all devices while providing image transformations on the fly, and much more. They offer a generous free tier that will allow you to get to know the platform and familiarize yourself with their APIs, available both in Python and JavaScript. Let's create an account on Cloudinary now!

## Creating a Cloudinary account

Head over to the Cloudinary website and click on the **Create Account** page. Once there, on `https://cloudinary.com/users/register/free`, you should fill in the required data: your name, email address, and a secure password. It is paramount that you choose the **Digital Asset Management** account, as that will enable you to serve your images and videos (digital assets) through Cloudinary. While Cloudinary is a feature-rich ecosystem in its own right, we will not spend time exploring it; we will just create and use the bare minimum that will allow us to store our car images and briefly touch on some transformations later.

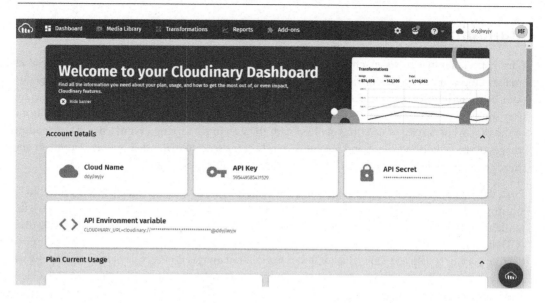

Figure 8.1 – Cloudinary account variables

After you have created your account, head over to the **Dashboard** page and take notice of the three variables that are displayed (or hidden) on the page – we will use them when creating our image-posting endpoint in FastAPI, in a similar way as the MongoDB variables. You can reveal them by clicking, and then you can copy them into a handy .txt file.

## Creating a new MongoDB database and collections

For this application, we will create a new MongoDB database and collections. Head over to the MongoDB site or fire up Compass and create a new database called nextCars with two collections inside: users and cars. Since we have covered the creation of databases and collections in *Chapter 2, Setting Up the Document Store with MongoDB*, I will not go over the process again, to save some time and space. The connection string for the database will need to be updated to match the new database name (DB_NAME=nextCars).

## Updating the FastAPI REST API

The REST API for this application is going to be mostly unaltered, and I believe that is one of the strengths of this stack – the modularity and interchangeability of the components. We will be able to reuse our entire model and our routes (and routers), while just adding the features that regard the addition of the image. Since we have decided to store our images on Cloudinary, all we have to do is provide a URL for the picture to the car model. This URL will be generated by Cloudinary upon upload, and it will enable us to generate different image sizes, according to our needs. In a more realistic scenario, you might want to create a MongoDB array field for storing a set of images (URLs), or you could pull the image out altogether into a new Pydantic and MongoDB model and then reference it –

something that would probably be the most recommended practice. Since my primary concern here is to showcase the storing and serving of images through FastAPI, and not modeling, we will stick to the single picture field inside the Cars model. In the models.py file, we will update the following:

## models.py

```
class CarBase(MongoBaseModel):
    brand: str = Field(..., min_length=3)
    make: str = Field(..., min_length=1)
    year: int = Field(..., gt=1975, lt=2023)
    price: int = Field(...)
    km: int = Field(...)
    cm3: int = Field(..., gt=600, lt=8000)
    picture: Optional[str] = None
class CarDB(CarBase):
    owner: str = Field(...)
class CarUpdate(MongoBaseModel):
    price: Optional[int] = None
```

We have just added a picture field to the Car model and set it to be an optional string that defaults to a None value. This will simplify things down the line if we want to import our cars dataset and do not provide an image right away. The CarDB model just extends our CarBase model with the user ID, while the CarUpdate model remains the same – only updating the price is possible.

The rest of the models.py file is unchanged, and I will not repeat it here. The users.py router and our main.py file are also unaltered.

On a side note, I should say that in order to get the code for this book to work, I had to modify our main.py file – the part where we implement the CORS middleware. Even though FastAPI implements the underlying Starlette's framework middleware, at the point of writing this, it seems that it is necessary to import directly Starlette's middleware. To cut things short, our main.py file looks like this now:

```
from decouple import config
from fastapi import FastAPI
from starlette.middleware import Middleware
from starlette.middleware.cors import CORSMiddleware

middleware = [
    Middleware(
        CORSMiddleware,
```

```
            allow_origins=["*"],
            allow_credentials=True,
            allow_methods=["*"],
            allow_headers=["*"],
        )
    ]


from motor.motor_asyncio import AsyncIOMotorClient
from routers.cars import router as cars_router
from routers.users import router as users_router
DB_URL = config("DB_URL", cast=str)
DB_NAME = config("DB_NAME", cast=str)
origins = ["*"]
app = FastAPI(middleware=middleware)
```

As you can see, the middleware is imported directly from Starlette and defined directly upon the app instantiation. FastAPI is still a relatively new and young framework, and it is very possible that this hack will not be necessary in the future, but I do feel the need to save you some debugging and research time.

The rest of the `main.py` file is the same as before; we include the routers and define the events for startup and shutdown:

```
app.include_router(cars_router, prefix="/cars", tags=["cars"])
app.include_router(users_router, prefix="/users",
tags=["users"])
@app.on_event("startup")
async def startup_db_client():
    app.mongodb_client = AsyncIOMotorClient(DB_URL)
    app.mongodb = app.mongodb_client[DB_NAME]
@app.on_event("shutdown")
async def shutdown_db_client():
    app.mongodb_client.close()
```

Let's open our `.env` file and set up Cloudinary. Notice that you can use Cloudinary even without providing the credentials (API and secret keys), but in order to do so, you must explicitly set that in your **Cloudinary** settings page, under the **Uploads** tab – **Enable unsigned uploading**:

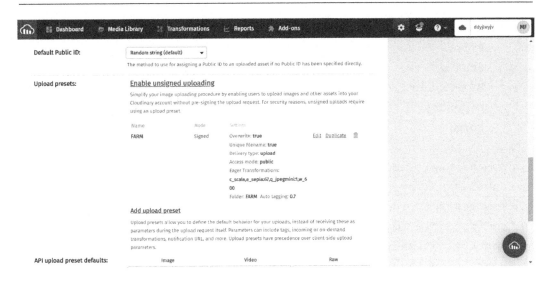

Figure 8.2 – Cloudinary settings page

In this case, I *do* want to set up a Cloudinary client and provide it with our secret keys. In the virtual environment, install the Cloudinary Python client with the following:

```
pip install cloudinary
```

Once installed, we will go to our Cloudinary management page and copy the API key and the SECRET key into our .env file, after the MongoDB credentials:

```
DB_URL=mongodb+srv://farmbook:xxxxxxxx@cluster0.fkm24.mongodb.
net/?retryWrites=true&w=majority
DB_NAME=nextCars

CLOUD_NAME=<your cloud name>
API_KEY=<your api key>
API_SECRET=<your api secret>
```

This way, we will be able to access this environment data with Python-Decouple. Since we will be using the Cloudinary API only in the /cars router, we can open the /routers/cars.py file and update it. Let's go over the entire /routers/cars.py file:

```
from typing import List, Optional
from fastapi import (
    APIRouter,
    Request,
    Body,
```

```
    UploadFile,
    File,
    status,
    HTTPException,
    Depends,
    Form,
)
from fastapi.encoders import jsonable_encoder
from fastapi.responses import JSONResponse
from fastapi.responses import StreamingResponse
from decouple import config
import cloudinary
import cloudinary.uploader
```

When dealing with file uploads, we cannot use JSON – we must accept the file through form data and we cannot mix the two (an HTTP limitation), so we imported Form, File, and UploadFile from FastAPI. The process of handling Form data is explored in *Chapter 3, Getting Started with FastAPI*, so now we have a chance to try it out; that is basically the main idea of the whole book – trying things out, even if they are not necessary, so in case you might need them, you know where to start.

The last two imports are Cloudinary's client and uploader utilities that enable our app to communicate with the online image service. Let's continue with /routers/cars.py:

```
from models import CarBase, CarDB, CarUpdate
from authentication import AuthHandler
CLOUD_NAME = config("CLOUD_NAME", cast=str)
API_KEY = config("API_KEY", cast=str)
API_SECRET = config("API_SECRET", cast=str)
cloudinary.config(
    cloud_name=CLOUD_NAME,
    api_key=API_KEY,
    api_secret=API_SECRET,
)
router = APIRouter()
auth_handler = AuthHandler()
```

We are importing our Pydantic car models and our authentication handler, which hasn't changed. After that, we need to import the Cloudinary keys and configure the library. After this is all set, we proceed to instantiate the FastAPI router responsible for cars and the authentication.

While the routes for listing all cars, getting one car by ID, deleting, and updating remain the same (so I will not list them again here), the route that is completely different is the one for creating a new car, the POST route:

```
@router.post("/", response_description="Add new car with
picture")
async def create_car_form(
    request: Request,
    brand: str = Form("brand"),
    make: str = Form("make"),
    year: int = Form("year"),
    cm3: int = Form("cm3"),
    price: int = Form("price"),
    km: int = Form("km"),
    picture: UploadFile = File(...),
    userId=Depends(auth_handler.auth_wrapper),
):
    result = cloudinary.uploader.upload(
        picture.file,
        folder="FARM",
        crop="scale",
        width=800,
    )

    url = result.get("url")
    car = CarDB(
        brand=brand,
        price=price,
        cm3=cm3,
        km=km,
        make=make,
        year=year,
        picture=url,
        owner=userId,
    )
    car = jsonable_encoder(car)
    new_car = await request.app.mongodb["cars"].insert_one(car)
```

```
    created_car = await request.app.mongodb["cars"].find_one(
        {"_id": new_car.inserted_id}
    )
    return JSONResponse(status_code=status.HTTP_201_CREATED,
content=created_car)
```

You can notice several differences from our previous route: we no longer accept JSON, but Form data, so the values (brand, make, cm3, and so on) are taken from the Form data parameters and not from parsing JSON data. We also have File and FileUpload for handling the image file, which we called picture. The file is immediately handed to Cloudinary and we get a response back upon a successful upload. Notice that here we should perform some error checking in case the upload doesn't go as planned! The uploader, if everything goes well, returns us a result and, at this point, all we care about is the URL of the image – this URL allows us not only to access the image but also to identify it and apply transformations to it!

I passed different parameters to the Cloudinary uploader along with the file: FARM is the *folder* where I want the picture uploaded (it is trivial to create custom folders inside the **Assets** page in Cloudinary); I set the picture width to 800, which means 800 px maximum, and the resizing method to scale. A complete list of parameters you can pass on upload is available on the Cloudinary website and it includes various transformations that are way beyond the scope of this book.

We then use the said URL and the user ID to construct a Car instance to be saved to our MongoDB database. This upload can take some time, so it would be a good candidate for treating with some loading spinners or other activity indicators on the frontend. Finally, we return the created car with the status 201 Created.

You can now spin the server up with the following:

```
uvicorn main:app --reload
```

Now, try to log in.

First, we need to test the /register route and create some users. You can use HTTPie to send a POST request and register a user, as we did previously:

```
venv) λ http POST "http://localhost:8000/users/register"
email="marko@gmail.com" password="marko" username="marko"
role="ADMIN"
```

I have a couple of dummy users created, so I can use HTTPIE to login and get the JWT for authentication:

```
(venv) λ http POST "http://localhost:8000/users/login"
email="marko@gmail.com" password="marko"
```

As usual, we get a JSON web token as well as the logged-in user data:

```
{
    "token": "eyJ0eXAiOiJKV1QiLCJhbGciOiJIUzI1NiJ9.eyJleHAiO-
jE2NTcwNDY3ODgsImlhdCI6MTY1NzAyNTE4OCwic3ViIjoiNjJiZjU5MWM3N-
2M3OWUxYTkwMmUwNTZhIn0.Wf7ps6IPypzDHJxrOFHJhnHw9pJkRf5QWJui-ua
e3x4",
    "user": {
        "email": "marko@gmail.com",
        "role": "ADMIN",
        "username": "marko"
    }
}
```

If we now include this JWT in our *Insomnia* client as a *bearer token* and post to the /cars endpoint some car data along with a car image it should look like as shown in the following image:

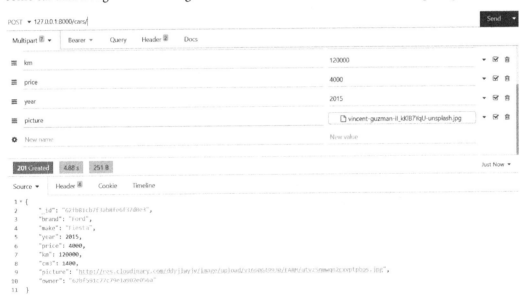

Figure 8.3 – Insomnia REST client performing a POST request

There are a couple of things to keep in mind when testing – the request type has to be set to **Multipart** and the Picture field has to be specified as a *file*. Also, do not forget to add a valid token in the **Bearer** tab; otherwise, you will get a Not Authenticated error.

The upload could take a while, depending on your connection's upload speed, but once you get a response, it will contain a picture URL. If you click it, it will display your image, reduced to a width of 800 pixels, and hosted securely on Cloudinary!

## Integrating Python Pillow for image processing

Before moving to the frontend, where we will spend most of our time in this chapter, I want to add just a little bit of code to this particular POST endpoint. While Cloudinary enables us to perform numerous image (and video!) transformations, there might be a situation in which you want or have to perform some operations yourself. One of the main advantages and selling points of the FARM stack is the availability of Python's rich and vast module ecosystem that encompasses different fields. As it happens, Python has a very powerful and mature imaging library, formerly known as PIL and now **Pillow**, which enables us to perform most filtering, resizing, cropping, watermarking, and so on, while also being able to treat images as matrices of pixels and apply complex algorithms.

In this example, I just want to show how easy it is to plug in some Pillow functionality. Let's install Pillow by stopping our FastAPI server and typing the following:

```
pip install Pillow
```

After that, we will add a couple of imports to the /routers/cars.py file:

```
from PIL import Image, ImageOps
```

Then, update the POST endpoint:

```
@router.post("/", response_description="Add new car with
picture")
async def create_car_form(
    request: Request,
    brand: str = Form("brand"),
    make: str = Form("make"),
    year: int = Form("year"),
    cm3: int = Form("cm3"),
    price: int = Form("price"),
    km: int = Form("km"),
    picture: UploadFile = File(...),
    userId=Depends(auth_handler.auth_wrapper),
):
    original_image = Image.open(picture.file)
    poster_image = ImageOps.posterize(original_image, 2)
```

```
out_image = BytesIO()
poster_image.save(out_image, "JPEG")
out_image.seek(0)
result = cloudinary.uploader.upload(
    out_image,
    folder="FARM",
    crop="scale",
    width=800,
)
```

The preceding code takes on the uploaded file using the `Image.open` method of the Pillow module, applies a simple transformation (posterizes the image), and finally, returns it as a *JPEG* to Cloudinary. If you try the exact same POST request with the Ford Fiesta image (courtesy of Vincent Guzman from Unsplash) from the previous try, you will get a transformed image. I assume you won't opt for such extreme image operations, but it is good to know how to tackle image transformation and storage with these two powerful tools. You could watermark images for an advert site, create duo-tone images that fit your branding colors, add borders or rounded corners, and pretty much anything that you can imagine.

In this section, we were able to integrate a real image-processing pipeline into our FastAPI REST API and you could use some variations of it for various image-related tasks: product galleries, systematic image processing, applying filters, and so on.

In the following section, we will begin working with Next.js – a powerful and feature-rich React-based web framework.

## Introduction to Next.js and our frontend project

In this section, we will introduce Next.js, the React web framework, and we will begin creating a project throughout the chapter. We will develop a Next.js-powered website for selling used cars, similar to what we did in the previous chapters. The backend will be powered by our FastAPI REST API, while the frontend will use various features provided by Next.js. I will gradually build up the app, adding features in a simple and, hopefully, straightforward way. The end goal of the chapter is *not* to make an optimized or production-ready app, but rather to illustrate the possibilities and features of the tools that we're going to use.

Let's speak about Next.js, one of the hottest frontend frameworks in the last couple of years. Next.js offers numerous features that cater to the modern web, and this introduction is meant only to give you an idea of what can be accomplished with it. The first problem that Next.js solves is the fact that React runs on the client-side, meaning that the pages are displayed only after being downloaded, ran in the browser, and rendered on the client. This has several drawbacks, especially with larger and more complex applications – it negatively affects Search Engine Optimization and the initial loading might take a while.

Several frameworks where not only React-based, and companies have tried to create a way of pre-rendering the resulting HTML and providing at the same time the JavaScript-based interactivity of a React (or Svelte, or Vue.js) application. Vercel's Next.js is arguably the most feature-rich and most complete out of several similar solutions (Vue.js's Nuxt.js, the relatively new SvelteKit, and so on). One young framework that looks very promising and flexible is Astro.js.

For working with Next.js, the only real requirement is that you are familiar with React since it is mostly React that we will be writing. However, Next.js provides several game-changing features that might make you switch to it for the vast majority of your projects. Let's list some of the most interesting and significant:

- File-based routing: A folder/file structure that maps directly to URLs, coupled with the Next router (with hooks!) for programmatic navigation

- Server-side rendering: The pages can be rendered on the server as well as on the client, or both, as well as statically prerendered

- Static site generation: Pages can be entirely static and Next.js can be used as part of a JAMStack site

- Image optimization: Like another React-based framework, Gatsby.js, Next.js provides us with an extremely useful `Image` component that greatly facilitates the tedious image resizing and optimizations, and the process of generating image source sets of the same image for different viewports

- Numerous other goodies: Incremental static generation (basically, the process of regenerating the site by creating only the pages that should be updated), TypeScript support, and the pluggable Node.js underlying server that can also make use of Express.js or Fastify.js (two blazingly fast Node.js frameworks)

- Configuration tools and "abstract" documents for unified layouts, plugins, and much more

I believe that this is the right place to inform you that Packt has published probably the best book ever written on Next.js – *Real World Next.js* by *Michele Riva* (`https://www.packtpub.com/product/real-world-next-js/9781801073493`) and if you wish to dive into the framework (and you should, by all means!), feel free to grab it.

## Scaffolding the application

Let's begin building our Next.js-powered car sales application. Similar to `create-react-app`, Next.js provides us with a command-line tool for scaffolding a new Next app. The only requirement for this process is having Node.js, npm, and `npx` installed on our machine.

Enter the `/Chapter8` folder, open a new terminal window (I am still using `Cmder`), and issue the following command:

```
npx create-next-app next-cars
```

This command will take some time to run, and it will create a project structure, install numerous dependencies, and give you a sample page. If everything went how it should, your terminal will instruct you to change the directory to the newly created folder (next-cars, in our case) and start the development server with the following:

```
npm run dev
```

If you visit the page at localhost:3000 (the default Next.js port), you will be greeted by the default Next.js page. Let's quickly run over the project structure – open the next-cars folder with your favorite code editor (I strongly recommend Visual Studio Code featuring the ES7 React snippets plugin!).

The /pages folder is where the magic happens. To put it as simply as possible, if you create a page, which is really a React component, name it index.js, and put it in the /pages/cars/mazda folder, it will render this page/component at the /cars/mazda URL. If you create another component in the same /mazda folder and name it 3.js, it will render a component for the /cars/mazda/3 URL, and so on. Another feature that is important to emphasize immediately is the fact that you can name a page [slug].js, with the use of square brackets. Square brackets are used to capture url parameters, so a file located at the location of /cars/[slug].js will render the component for every request matching the URL /cars/anything, while passing the parameter slug (equal to "anything" in this case) as a prop to the component..

### *Styling with Tailwind CSS*

Let's install Tailwind CSS since I want to keep the styling work to an absolute minimum and, as we did before with React, the process is practically identical. Stop the Next.js development server and type the following command:

```
npm install -D tailwindcss postcss autoprefixer
npx tailwindcss init -p
```

The second command will initialize a tailwind.config.js file, so open it and replace the content with this:

```
module.exports = {
  content: [
    "./pages/**/*.{js,ts,jsx,tsx}",
    "./components/**/*.{js,ts,jsx,tsx}",
  ],
  theme: {
  },
  plugins: [
  ],
}
```

Finally, delete Home.module.style in the /styles folder and replace the global styles with the following Tailwind directives:

```
@tailwind base;
@tailwind components;
@tailwind utilities;
```

I usually like to immediately test the home page. Open the /pages/index.js file, the one that will map to the root URL (/), and create a generic React component by using the _rafce shortcut:

```
const index = () => {
  return (
    <div className="bg-orange-500 text-white p-5">
      FARM Cars
    </div>
  )
}
export default index
```

Restart the server and you should see a simple page with one div element, an orange background with white text; that means Tailwind is installed. Just in case, keep in mind that Tailwind maintains excellent documentation, so head over to the guides at https://tailwindcss.com/docs/guides/nextjs in case anything changes in the future versions.

### Customizing the _app.js component

When building our React app, we used a custom layout component to wrap the pages and achieve a consistent look across the application. Next.js, among other useful things, provides us with a special component called App that lives in the /pages/_app.js file. This component is used for initializing pages and provides different capabilities, such as the said layout consistency (header, footer, and page content), but can also be used for keeping track of the state while navigating the app, injecting additional data, and so on. For now, we will use it just to create a page skeleton. Let's create a folder called /components in the root folder (the same level as /pages) and create two generic components (Header.jsx and Footer.jsx) with just the text header and footer, respectively.

Then, let's alter the _app.js component:

```
import '../styles/globals.css'
import Header from '../components/Header'
import Footer from '../components/Footer'
function MyApp({ Component, pageProps }) {
  return (
```

```
    <div className="flex flex-col justify-between items-stretch
        min-h-screen">
      <Header />
      <div className="flex-1">
        <Component {...pageProps} />
      </div>
      <Footer />
    </div>
  )
}
export default MyApp
```

All the content of our pages will be rendered into the highlighted component, while we added a wrapping div, set it to a flex column display using Tailwind, and made the header and footer stick to the top and bottom.

Next.js provides us with a very nifty Link component that optimizes the navigation within the application with features such as page preloading, dynamic routes variable handling, and more.

This basic setup provided us with some useful features – we have a layout component, and we didn't have to make one from scratch or manually wrap components.

### Setting up the environment variables

Next.js allows us to make use of environment variables and it does so in a very simple and elegant way, following a few conventions. Why do we need environment variables? Well, in our case, we do not want to hardcode the URL of our API everywhere in the code – we are working with a local API (on localhost:8000) during development, then we will eventually deploy our Python API on Heroku or some other server, and we will have another address. Finally, when we deploy our Next.js application, we will want to provide the URL of our production server as an environment variable to Vercel or Netlify, depending on our deployment solution.

Next.js will read the .env.local file, located in the root of our project, and load its variables into the current environment. These variables will not be available to the client unless they start with NEXT_PUBLIC_. In our case, we just want to save our API_URL that will be served by FastAPI. So, let's put that in the file, bearing in mind that it *should* be available to the clientside:

```
NEXT_PUBLIC_API_URL=http://127.0.0.1:8000
```

If we wanted to add other environment variables, they would have to be stacked below this one. It is important not to add the trailing slash at the end of the URL when dealing with Heroku or the requests will crash.

### Scaffolding the required pages

Our strategy now will be the following:

- We will create all the pages needed for our application: the car list and the individual car pages (server-side rendered), the register and login pages, and the create new car page. For brevity's sake, we will skip the pages for updating and deleting cars, but you are more than welcome to implement them yourself as a useful exercise.

- After all the pages and the navigation have been scaffolded, we will create a more robust authentication mechanism, using Next.js API routes, `httpOnly` cookies, and the React Context API. The users will be able to log in and log out, and only admins and salespersons will be able to create new cars (a similar logic would be implemented for updating and deleting cars). We will not implement a registration page and that would also be a great exercise for you – it shouldn't be harder than coding the login route, depending on whether you opt to automatically log the newly created users in or not.

We have just wrapped the whole application inside a div and added the footer component at the end. If you take a look at the app now, on `http://localhost:3000` with the Next.js server running, you should be able to see the text *footer* after the FARM Cars title from `index.js`, our only page for now. I will apply the exact same process for building the header component, which will contain just a menu bar. Let's now update a `Header.jsx` component in the `/components` folder:

```
const Header = () => {
  return <div
      className="text-orange-600 p-2 font-bold">
      Header</div>;
};
export default Header;
```

I have just added a minimal amount of Tailwind style just so we can see where the header is. Now, we will include it in the `_app.js` file, as we did with the footer:

```
import '../styles/globals.css'
import Header from '../components/Header'
import Footer from '../components/Footer'
function MyApp({ Component, pageProps }) {
  return (
    <div>
      <Header />
      <Component {...pageProps} />
      <Footer />
```

```
      </div>
    )
  }
export default MyApp
```

Finally, we can make the header and footer stick to the top and bottom of the page, respectively, by applying Tailwind classes; we will make the whole app a flex container, and we will set the minimum height to screen height while allowing the App component to take up as much space as needed:

```
import '../styles/globals.css'
import Header from '../components/Header'
import Footer from '../components/Footer'
function MyApp({ Component, pageProps }) {
  return (
    <div className="min-h-screen flex flex-col">
      <Header />
      <div className="flex-1"><Component {...pageProps} />
      </div>
      <Footer />
    </div>
    )
  }
export default MyApp
```

Having the layout in place, now we can create a simple navigation menu in the header with the help of the Next.js Link component. Let's reiterate: we need the following links – home (/), cars (/cars), login (/account/login), and register (/account/register) – for now. Later on, we will display some links conditionally depending on the user – whether a user is logged in or not, whether they're an admin or salesperson, and so on.

### Creating the header navigation

Let's create this navigation, using the Link component and the Tailwind classes:

```
import Link from "next/link"
const Header = () => {
  return (
    <div className=" text-orange-600 p-2 font-bold flex flex-
        row justify-between items-center">
      <div>
        <Link href="/">
```

```
            <a>FARM Cars</a>
          </Link>
        </div>
        <ul className="flex flex-row space-x-4 ">
          <li>
            <Link href="/cars">
              <a>Cars</a>
            </Link>
          </li>
          <li>
            <Link href="/about">
              <a>About</a>
            </Link>
          </li>
          <li>
            <Link href="/account/register">
              <a>Register</a>
            </Link>
          </li>
          <li>
            <Link href="/account/login">
              <a>Login</a>
            </Link>
          </li>
        </ul>
      </div>
    );
};
export default Header;
```

These links are downright ugly, and they all point to non-existing locations, but while we won't delve into aesthetic enhancements, we will create all the pages now and just scaffold them with the help of the ES7+ React/Redux/React-Native snippets Visual Studio Code extension we installed earlier. I will not list all the code here, but just go over the following files: in the /pages directory, create a /cars folder, and inside index.js, add the following:

```
const cars = () => {
  return (
```

```
    <div>Cars page</div>
  )
}
export default cars
```

I will repeat this exact process and create an /accounts folder in the /pages folder and inside it, I will create the **Login** and **Register** pages.

## Authentication with API routes and httpOnly cookies in Next.js

We should be able to navigate using our navigation in the header. It is now time to introduce an important feature of Next.js – the API routes. Put simply, Next.js allows us to write API endpoints by using a special folder called /api located inside the /pages directory. Inside this /api folder, we can make use of the folder and file-based Next.js router, so an API route that lives in a /api/user.js file will be available at the http://localhost:3000/api/user endpoint, and so on. *Note that these files are not React components, but simple Node.js request/response functions.*

While the API routes are powerful Node-based mechanisms that allow you to write your backend entirely without ever leaving Next.js, they can have different uses in different cases and scenarios. For instance, we can use these API routes as a proxy for our FastAPI backend, thus hiding it completely from the frontend in case we want to perform some client-side data fetching. Coupled with the concept of middleware – essentially, functions that intercept the request and response cycle – we can use them for securing the entire application or just parts of it and do so in a granular way. While you can (and by all means should) inspect the API routes documentation on the Next.js website, let's see how it can help us with our task of authenticating and authorizing users.

In the previous chapter, we have seen how JWT-based authentication works, and, since we were using React, we opted for a rather extreme solution – we didn't save the JWT anywhere, so any page refresh or browser closing resulted in a logout, since the JWT was stored only in the Context API. We could have used the browser's local storage but there are many reasons to believe that these solutions are too insecure and risky. Since Next.js API routes run on the same server as our frontend, we can use a more elegant and secure method and persist the state of the logged user throughout the application. We will use httpOnly cookies, which are available only through HTTP and are inaccessible to JavaScript. Since both the frontend and the "backend" (in this case, Next.js' API routes, not our real backend) will run on the same server (in development: localhost:3000 by default), we can set cookies easily. After we get the cookie, we will use it to store the JWT token and provide it to any subsequent request. Our FastAPI /me route will be used to read the JWT and tell us whether the user exists or not, whether it's a regular user or an admin, and so on, and then we will model the page's behavior accordingly.

Having laid out our main strategy, let's move on and tackle the first task: we want to create a Next.js API route, call it login, and enable it to just POST the credentials data (in FastAPI, we opted for a combination of email and password) to our real backend (Python) and, if the request should be successful, send a cookie with the JWT.

Before we begin refreshing our Node.js knowledge (it is really the bare minimum – just request and response), we need to stop the Next.js server and install the cookie package in order to be able to set cookies (note that this package isn't particularly tied to Next.js itself):

```
npm i cookie
```

In the /pages/api folder, create a file called login.js (the naming is important!) and start writing some Node.js code:

```
import cookie from 'cookie'
export default async (req, res)=>{
    if (req.method==='POST'){
        const {email, password} = req.body
        const result = await fetch
          ('http://127.0.0.1:8000/users/login', {
            method:'POST',
            headers:{'Content-Type':'application/json'},
            body:JSON.stringify({email, password})
        })
        const data = await result.json()
        if (result.ok){
            const jwt = data.token
            res.status(200).setHeader('Set-Cookie',
              cookie.serialize(
                'jwt',jwt,
                {
                    path:'/',
                    httpOnly: true,
                    sameSite:'strict',
                    maxAge:30

                }
            )).json({
                'username':data['user']['username'],
                'email':data['user']['email'],
                'role':data['user']['role'],
                'jwt':jwt
            })
```

```
        } else {
            data['error'] = data['detail']
            res.status(401)
            res.json(data)
            return
        }
    } else {
        res.setHeader('Allow', ['POST'])
        res.status(405).json({message: `Method ${req.method}
          not allowed`})
        return
    }
}
```

The code is pretty straightforward; there are just a couple of checks that make it a bit longer, but they are important. Let's see how it works: first, it is a typical Node.js async request/response function – we first check whether the method is right as we do not want to proceed with anything that is not a POST request. After having read the body of the request (the email and password pair), we pass them to a fetch request to our FastAPI server, making sure to set the content type to JSON and the method to POST. After we get the response from FastAPI, we check whether it's OK and proceed to set a cookie through the header. The options passed to the cookie serializer are the following: path set to /, which means that the cookie will be sent throughout the entire application, all the URLs, httpOnly is true since this was the whole point, so to speak, sameSite is set to strict, and maxAge is the duration of the validity of the cookie in seconds – here, I opted for a very short amount of time, just 30 seconds, so we can test things out, but ideally it should match the duration of the JWT itself and be around 60*60*24*7 minutes or about a week for this type of website.

Test the following endpoint with HTTP:

```
(venv) λ http POST http://localhost:3000/api/login
email="marko@gmail.com" password="marko"
```

You should get a response similar to this one:

```
HTTP/1.1 200 OK
Set-Cookie: jwt=eyJ0eXAiOiJKV1QiLCJhbGciOiJIUzI1NiJ9.eyJleHAiO-
jE2NTcxNDUxOTYsImlhdCI6MTY1NzEyMzU5Niwic3ViIjoiNjJiZjU5MWM3N-
2M3OWUxYTkwMmUwNTZhIn0.JKn-QcQ3DVaUZA_tAzQaDZnylFPY40qQDtWd-
FSOYdVA; Max-Age=30; Path=/; HttpOnly; SameSite=Strict
Vary: Accept-Encoding
{
```

```
    "email": "marko@gmail.com",
    "role": "ADMIN",
    "username": "marko"
}
```

All the data seems to be there – the set cookie and the data that we passed along with the cookie. We can now head over to the `/pages/login.jsx` page – a "proper" page – and create our `login` component. It is going to be very simple – just a form connected to the previously created `/api/login` API route. Once the correct credentials are provided, the cookie will be set. Later, we will discuss how we are going to use this cookie, but for now, let's just set it from our frontend. Let's now update our `Login.jsx` page in the `/pages` folder and enable the user to actually log in, using our `login` API route. Open the `Login.jsx` page and edit it:

```jsx
import { useState } from "react";
const login = () => {
  const [email, setEmail] = useState("");
  const [password, setPassword] = useState("");
  const handleSubmit = async (e) => {
    e.preventDefault();
    const res = await fetch('api/login', {
      method: "POST",
      headers: { "Content-Type": "application/json" },
      body: JSON.stringify({ email, password }),
    });
    const data = await res.json();
  };
```

We aren't doing anything special here. I am using just a couple of state variables in order to have two controlled inputs in our form, preventing the form from submitting by default and sending the email/password combination to our API route through a POST request to the Next.js API route. The rest of the functional component is mainly used for rendering the form:

```jsx
return (
    <div className="flex flex-col justify-center items-center
        h-full">
      <h2 className=" text-orange-500 font-bold text--
          lg">Login</h2>
{error && (
        <div className="border-2 text-red-700 font-bold p-5">
```

```
            {error.detail}
          </div>
       )}
       <div>
         <form className=" max-w-md flex flex-col justify-center
             items-center"
           onSubmit={handleSubmit}>
           <label className="block">
             <span className="text-gray-700">Email</span>
             <input
               type="email"
               className="mt-1 block w-full"
               placeholder="your email"
               required
               onChange={(e) => setEmail(e.target.value)}
               value={email}
             />
           </label>
           <label className="block">
             <span className="text-gray-700">Password</span>
             <input type="password" required
               className="mt-1 block w-full"
               onChange={(e) => setPassword(e.target.value)}
               value={password}
             />
           </label>
           <button className=" bg-orange-500 text-white p-2 m-3
               w-full rounded-lg">Log in</button>
         </form>
       </div>
     </div>
   );
 };
export default login;
```

If we test this page and submit our credentials, we will get an HTTP-only cookie and ideally, we should redirect the user to the home page. We are also displaying the error from FastAPI in case the email and password do not match, but this is all less important now. We have the cookie, and it will persist through page refreshes and the app being closed! While we're at it, let's implement a rather rudimentary but effective way of destroying the cookie – we will create an API route called `logout.js` in the API folder:

```
import cookie from 'cookie'
export default async (req, res)=>{
    res.status(200).setHeader('Set-Cookie', cookie.serialize(
        'jwt','',
        {
            path:'/',
            httpOnly: true,
            sameSite:'strict',
            maxAge:-1
        }
    )
    ).end()
}
```

This rather silly route doesn't take any parameters and doesn't return anything useful. Rather, it sets the token to a blank value and makes it expire instantly (`maxAge:-1`).

We are now able to obtain and destroy cookies that are HTTP only, therefore, not accessible through JavaScript, and we made sure that our FastAPI routes in the backend are secured.

Now, we face two different but highly related problems: we want to be able to keep track of this logged-in status and the type of user throughout the entire application, and we want to be able to filter out some pages completely, depending on the role of the authenticated user. I want to point out again that all this code is by no means meant for any kind of production site and that we cannot hope to be able to replicate the robustness, security, and ease of use of branded solutions such as Auth0, Amazon Cognito, Firebase, and the like. It is just a, hopefully, useful introduction to what is possible with Next.js and really any REST API that is secured via JWT, since we are not doing anything Python-specific at this point.

### React Context API and custom hook

In order to make our app at least a bit more pleasant to work with, we will create (again) a Context for authentication, and it will not differ very much from what we did with plain React. Create a folder called /context in the root of our project and create an AuthContext.js file inside:

```
import { createContext, useState } from "react";
const AuthContext = createContext({})
export const AuthProvider = ({children}) => {
    const [user, setUser] = useState(null)
    const [authError, setAuthError] = useState(null)
    const [loading, setLoading] = useState(false)
    return <AuthContext.Provider value={{user, setUser,
        authError, setAuthError, loading, setLoading}}>
        {children}
    </AuthContext.Provider>
}
export default AuthContext
```

This mechanism was already dissected in *Chapter 7, Authentication and Authorization*, so I will not repeat the explanations. As with the React project, we will create a custom hook in order to make the context easier to work with. Create a folder called /hooks in the root of the project, and create the useAuth.js file:

```
import { useContext } from "react";
import AuthContext from "../context/AuthContext";
const useAuth = () => {
    return useContext(AuthContext)
}
export default useAuth;
```

The hook enables us to plug into the context quickly anywhere we might need it. In Next.js, the most logical place to put the context is the _app.js component, since it encompasses the entire app. Open _app.js and edit it:

```
import '../styles/globals.css'
import Header from '../components/Header'
import Footer from '../components/Footer'
import {AuthProvider} from '../context/AuthContext'
function MyApp({ Component, pageProps }) {
```

```
  return (
    <AuthProvider>
      <div className="min-h-screen flex flex-col container
        p-5">
        <Header />
        <div className="flex-1 "><Component {...pageProps}
          /></div>
        <Footer />
      </div>
    </AuthProvider>
  )
}
export default MyApp
```

### Updating the Login.jsx component

Now our whole application is "aware" of the context and we provided just a couple of state variables and their setters: `user`, `setUser` for the user, the same for the error, and a pair of `setLoading` and *loading* for the loading stage since we're going to try to get the user from the /me route from the cookie's JWT. Now we can modify the `Login.jsx` page to accommodate the context. The rendered part is not altered, only the function:

```
import { useState } from "react";
import { useRouter } from "next/router";
import useAuth from "../../hooks/useAuth";
const login = () => {
  const [email, setEmail] = useState("marko@gmail.com");
  const [password, setPassword] = useState("marko");
  const [error, setError] = useState(null);

  const { setUser } = useAuth();
  const router = useRouter();
  const handleSubmit = async (e) => {
    e.preventDefault();
    const res = await fetch("/api/login", {
      method: "POST",
      headers: { "Content-Type": "application/json" },
      body: JSON.stringify({ email, password }),
```

```
    });
    if (res.ok) {
      const user = await res.json();
      setUser(user);
      router.push("/");
    } else {
      const errData = await res.json();
      console.log(errData);
      setError(errData);
    }
  };
```

In this new version, the Login function does a bit more – after obtaining (hopefully!) the user data, it sets the context to the logged-in user and redirects us to the home page, making use of the Next Router, a simple hook that enables programmatic navigation.

While we're at it, let's create a Logout.jsx component for logging the user out. The procedure is the same – destroy the cookie by making it expire immediately, set the context to a null user, and redirect to the home page:

```
import { useRouter } from "next/router";
import { useEffect } from "react";
import useAuth from "../../hooks/useAuth";
const logout = () => {
  const { user, setUser } = useAuth();
  const removeCookie = async () => {
    const res = await fetch("http://127.0.0.1:3000/api/logout",
{
      method: "POST",
      headers: { "Content-Type": "application/json" },
    });
  };
  const router = useRouter();
  useEffect(() => {
    removeCookie();
    setUser(null);
    router.push("/");
  }, []);
```

```
    return <></>;
};
export default logout;
```

Now it is time to update our `Header.jsx` file and make our navigation user-aware; if the user is logged in, we want to display their username and maybe enable some menu items that would otherwise be unavailable. But more importantly, we want to check whether the cookie containing a (valid) JWT is present and if so, load the user automatically by using the `useEffect` hook. Open up `Header.jsx` and begin editing it:

## components/Header.jsx

```
import Link from "next/link";
import useAuth from "../hooks/useAuth";
import { useEffect } from "react";
const Header = () => {
  const { user, setUser, authError, setAuthError, setLoading,
loading } = useAuth();
  useEffect(() => {
    setLoading(true);
    (async () => {
      const userData = await fetch("/api/user");
      try {
        const user = await userData.json();
        setUser(user);
      } catch (error) {
        setUser(null);
      }
    })();
    setLoading(false);
  }, []);
```

After importing our `useAuth` custom hook, we get access to all of our context data and we can conditionally show or hide menu items. If there is no user logged in, we want to show the register and login menu items, otherwise, the logout button and maybe some information on the current user. We also take this opportunity to insert a `useEffect` hook, a function that will fire off and try to verify our cookie. If a cookie is found and a valid user is retrieved, we set the `setUser` function to that user and it will be available throughout the app; if not, we set the user to be null. In between, I threw some `isLoading` states in case we want to inform the user that we are trying to retrieve the data from the API. The rest of the component is similar to what was previously written, except for some user-checking logic:

```
return (
    <div className=" text-orange-600 py-2 font-bold flex flex-
        row justify-between items-center">
        <div>
            {loading ? <span>Loading...</span> : ""}
            <Link href="/">
                <a>
                    FARM Cars
                    {user ? (
                        <span>
                            {user.username} ({user.role})
                        </span>
                    ) : (
                        ""
                    )}
                </a>
            </Link>
        </div>
        <ul className="flex flex-row space-x-4 ">
            <li>
                <Link href="/cars">
                    <a>Cars</a>
                </Link>
            </li>
            {user && user.role === "ADMIN" ? (
                <li>
                    <Link href="/cars/add">
                        <a>Add Car</a>
                    </Link>
                </li>
            ) : (
                ""
            )}
```

```
      {!user ? (
        <>
          <li>
            <Link href="/account/register">
              <a>Register</a>
            </Link>
          </li>
          <li>
            <Link href="/account/login">
              <a>Login</a>
            </Link>
          </li>
        </>
      ) : (
        <>
          <li>
            <Link href="/account/logout">
              <a>Log out {user.username}</a>
            </Link>
          </li>
        </>
      )}
    </ul>
  </div>
);
},
export default Header;
```

## Next.js middleware

The menu now works as expected and the **New Car** item will not be visible in the menu. However, the page still exists, and it can be reached even if we are not logged in; you can try to navigate to the page, and it will load. You shouldn't be able to insert new car ads because, without the cookie, you will not have a valid JWT to provide to the FastAPI server, but we do not want to give access to the page anyway. Yes, I know that the page doesn't contain any form or means to input data; the point is that the page shouldn't be available to anonymous users. While we could use our context API and verify the absence or presence of users and act accordingly, we could also use higher-order components, as we did with React Router. Instead, I want to showcase another very cool and useful feature of Next. js – the middleware.

Next.js middleware is essentially a set of user-defined functions that allows us to tap into the request-response cycle of Next.js and perform various operations, such as performing checks, setting and reading cookies, redirecting and modifying responses, and so on. While the features are documented on the Next.js website (`https://nextjs.org/docs/advanced-features/middleware`), you might be familiar with a similar concept if you have ever used Django or Express. Bear in mind that even FastAPI has a very similar feature of the same name! Let's follow the instructions from the documentation. As with other "special" files such as `_document.js` and `_app.js`, middleware lives in a file called `middleware.js` at the same level as our `/pages` folder. I will just make a half-functional example here. I want to check for the mere existence of a cookie named `jwt`. If this cookie is present, users can proceed to the `/cars/add` page; otherwise, they will be redirected to the login page when trying to reach the said page:

```
import { NextResponse } from "next/server";
export function middleware(req){
    const url = req.url
    const cookie = req.cookies.get('jwt')
    if(url.includes('/cars/add') && (cookie===undefined)){
        return NextResponse.redirect('http://localhost:3000/
            account/login')
    }
    return NextResponse.next()
}
```

We imported just the `NextResponse` class from the `"next/server"` but feel free to explore other middleware goodies. After the import, we export a single function called middleware (again, the name is important) that takes in the request object and the response, which we won't use, so it is omitted. We then take the URL of the request (which will match every request on the site because middleware runs on every request) and try to find a cookie named `jwt`. Finally, there goes our condition – if the URL includes `/cars/add` and there is no cookie called `jwt` (matches undefined), we redirect to `/account/login`. Otherwise, we call the `next()` page.

Now, if you are not logged in and try to go to the `/cars/add` page, you should immediately get redirected to the `/account/login` page. Middleware in Next.js is still a pretty new feature, but it is very powerful and can be used for many advanced use cases. Notice that here we are redirecting to our development localhost address, so this code should be refactored and the Next.js server address should be included in the `.env.local` site!

Implementing authentication flows by ourselves is a good learning experience and we should probably leave it at that. I want to point out again that there are numerous excellent authentication solutions both for the React/Next.js world and for FastAPI. Still, if you are new to the React Context API and to the world of hooks, implementing even a rudimentary authentication solution similar to the one presented in this chapter can help you grasp the majority of the moving parts involved in a full-stack project (in our case, a FARM stack project) and help you even in other similar technologies (Vue.js, Svelte, Node.js, Django REST framework, and so on).

## Creating the page for inserting new cars

To complete our Next.js app, we are going to add just a couple of pages – the ones that actually have something to do with our initial purpose: building a car sales app. First, we need to create a page for adding cars, and this page is already "protected" by our Next.js middleware – only logged-in users can access the page and we know that only logged-in users can POST to our FastAPI backend. For this page, we are going to install two new Node.js packages: Axios (for structuring our API calls) and cookies-next, for reading our cookie from Next.js, extracting the JWT, and supplying it to the API call for creating a new car via a POST request. Stop the Next.js server and install the packages:

```
npm i axios cookies-next
```

Now we have everything in place, and we can begin creating our add.jsx page in the /cars folder:

```
import { useState } from "react";
import axios from "axios";
import { useRouter } from "next/router";
import { getCookie } from "cookies-next";
export const getServerSideProps = ({ req, res }) => {
  const jwt = getCookie("jwt", { req, res });
  return { props: { jwt } };
};
```

We are using useState for making our form inputs controlled, axios for the API call, the Next Router for navigating away from the page when we are done, and the getCookie function from the cookies-next package because we want to read the server-side cookies. In order to be able to use data from the server-side directly, Next.js provides us with a custom function called getServerSideProps that will be the centerpiece of our server-side page generation process.

getServerSideProps is one of the most important custom functions in the Next.js universe, as it enables us to get data from the server, pass it to the page as props, and then pre-render the page at request time. Normally, we use it to get data about the entity or group of entities that we want to display on a page, but in this case, we use it a little differently; we read the value of our JWT from the cookie that we obtained when logging in and we pass it to the page through *props*.

Next, we set up a bunch of stateful values for our form, but this should really be handled by a form library, as we did previously in the chapter on React:

```
const add = ({ jwt }) => {
  const [brand, setBrand] = useState("");
```

```
const [make, setMake] = useState("");
const [year, setYear] = useState("");
const [cm3, setCm3] = useState("");
const [price, setPrice] = useState("");
const [km, setKm] = useState("");
const [picture, setPicture] = useState(null);
const [loading, setLoading] = useState(false);
const router = useRouter();
```

Besides the form fields, we set up a loading state and instantiate the Next router – the React hook we already used for programmatic navigation when the request is completed. Now, we get to the important part of the component:

```
const handleSubmit = async (e) => {
    e.preventDefault();
    const formData = new FormData();
    formData.append("brand", brand);
    formData.append("make", make);
    formData.append("year", year);
    formData.append("km", km);
    formData.append("cm3", cm3);
    formData.append("price", price);
    formData.append("picture", picture);
    setLoading(true);
```

The handleSubmit function will fire up when the user tries to submit the form, so first, we prevent the default form submit action and then we create a new FormData instance, appending all the values obtained from the states. Next, we try to make our API call, in this case using Axios instead of Fetch (which we have used until now):

```
    try {
        const response = await axios({
            method: "POST",
            url: "http://localhost:8000/cars/",
            data: formData,
            headers: {
                "Content-Type": "multipart/form-data",
```

```
        Authorization: `bearer ${jwt}`,
      },
    });
  } catch (error) {
    console.log(error);
  }
  setLoading(false);
  router.push("/cars");
};
```

The important part is that now (since we have an image, thus, a file, to send), we must use `multipart/form-data` – that is why we made our Python FastAPI REST server accept form data instead of JSON. We also set the authorization using the JWT coming from the cookie. The function ends up redirecting us to the `/cars` page. In a realistic app, a friendly message for the user would be nice. Finally, we get to construct the form:

```
{!loading ? (
  <form
      className=" max-w-md flex flex-col justify-center
          items-center"
      onSubmit={handleSubmit}
  >
      <label className="block">
        <span className="text-gray-700">Brand</span>
        <input
          name="brand"
          id="brand"
          type="text"
          className="mt-1 block w-full"
          placeholder="car brand"
          required
          onChange={(e) => setBrand(e.target.value)}
          value={brand}
        />
      </label>
```

I will omit the remaining fields (for the make, year, cm3, price, and km) for brevity, since they are identical – except the numeric ones are, well, set to number inputs. The `picture` field, however, is the following:

```
<label className="block">
    <span className="text-gray-700">Picture</span>
        <input name="picture" id="picture" type="file"
           className="mt-1 block w-full"
           onChange={(e) =>setPicture(e.target.files[0])}
           required />
</label>
<button className="bg-orange-500 text-white p-2 m-3 w-full
    rounded-lg ">Submit</button>
</form>
        ) : (
         <></>
        )}
        {loading && (
<div className=" bg-orange-600 w-full min-h-full text-white
    flex flex-col justify-center items-center">
<p className=" text-xl">Inserting new car</p>
</div>
        )}
    </div>
  );
};
export default add;
```

The `file` field provides an array of files by default, so we take the one with the index equal to zero (the first one) and we send it to the `useState` function. All the fields are required in the HTML, although additional validation would be necessary. Finally, we use the loading variable to display an ugly loading div while the file is being uploaded (for large pictures, it can take some time, depending on your connection!).

If you test the `/cars/add` page, you should be able to insert some car pictures (or really any pictures) and some data, and the images should be resized (by Cloudinary) and posterized by Python Pillow! Let's create the most important pages now – the list of all cars and the individual car pages. I will not spend any time making them pretty, so be warned.

## Creating the car list page

I have already mentioned that Next.js allows us to use three distinct page rendering methods: pure client-side rendering with React, server-side rendering, where pages are prerendered on the server and then sent to the browser (similar to Django and other old-school frameworks), or completely **statically generated** (SSG). For the car list page, we will use server-side generation, while the individual pages will be statically generated.

We will make use of the `getServerSideProps` function to get the cars from our API and then use them to construct our page – the function we've already used in order to get the cookie. We could have opted for a different strategy, but this is the most common approach in our type of scenario – we have a semi-dynamic website, so to speak: data should change and be updated, but not very often, so users will not miss important last-minute notifications. Let's open the `/cars/index.jsx` page:

```
import Card from "../../components/Card"
export const getServerSideProps = async () => {
  const res = await         fetch(`${process.env.NEXT_PUBLIC_API_
URL}/cars/`);
  const cars = await res.json();
  return {
    props: {
      cars,
      revalidate: 10,
    },
  };
};
```

After importing a still non-existing `Card` component that will be used for displaying the cars, we implemented a very simple async `getServerSideProps` function; it just makes a call to the API (we do not need any cookies or a JWT since this endpoint is not protected!), returns the resulting array of cars as JSON, and sets the `revalidate` to 10 seconds. This is the amount of time after which a page will be regenerated. The `cars` variable in props will be passed to our component:

```
const Cars = ({ cars }) => {
  return (
    <div>
      <h1>Cars</h1>
<div className="grid lg:grid-cols-4 grid-cols-3 gap-3">
        {cars.map((car) => {
          const {_id, brand, make, picture, year, km, cm3,
            price} = car
```

```
            return (
              <Card
                  key={_id}
                  brand={brand}
                  id={_id}
                  make={make}
                  url={picture}
                  year={year}
                  km={km}
                  cm3={cm3}
                  price={price}
                  />
              );
          })}
        </div>       </div>
    );
};
export default Cars;
```

The rest of the component is trivial; we pass all the individual car props to the Card component and we lay them in a grid. For the Card component, I wanted to plug in another way of using Cloudinary: the npm package called cloudinary-build-url. The package works together with Next.js and helps us create transformations, apply filters, or resize images on a component or page level. Stop the server and install the package:

**npm i cloudinary-build-url**

Card.jsx lives in the /components folder and is rather simple, with a little twist:

```
import Image from 'next/image'
import Link from 'next/link'
import { buildUrl } from 'cloudinary-build-url'
const transformedUrl = (id)=> buildUrl(id, {
    cloud: {
      cloudName: '<my cloud name>',
    },
    transformations: {
      effect: {
        name: 'grayscale'
```

```
        },
        effect: {
          name: 'tint',
          value: '60:blue:white',


        }
     }});
```

Our images are getting completely mauled by the various filters and transformations, but I wanted to showcase the different stages at which you can apply image transformations – at the upload stage, before the upload stage with Python and Pillow, and even when we are already in Next.js. buildUrl is straightforward: you need to create a function that will take in the ID or URL of your image, provide the cloud name, and list the transformations that you wish to apply. In a real-world scenario, one of these image stages should be more than enough:

```
const Card = ({brand, make, year, url, km, price, cm3, id}) =>
{
  return (
    <Link href={"cars/" + id}>
        <div className="max-w-sm rounded overflow-hidden
          shadow-lg cursor-pointer hover:scale-105
            transition-transform duration-200">
        <div className="w-full"><Image src=
          {transformedUrl(url)} alt={brand} height={300}
            width={600} /></div>
        <div className="px-6 py-4">
            <div className="font-bold text-xl mb-2">{brand}
              {make}</div>
            <p className="text-orange-600 font-bold">Price:
              {price} EUR</p>
            <p className="text-gray-700 text-base">
            A detailed car description from the Cars FARM
              crew.
            </p>
        </div>
    <div className="px-6 pt-4 pb-2">
      <span className="inline-block bg-gray-200 rounded-full
        px-2 py-1 text-sm font-semibold text-gray-700 mr-2
```

```
            mb-2">made in {year}</span>
        <span className="inline-block bg-gray-200 rounded-full
          px-2 py-1 text-sm font-semibold text-gray-700 mr-2
          mb-2">Cm3:{cm3}</span>
        <span className="inline-block bg-gray-200 rounded-full
          px-2 py-1 text-sm font-semibold text-gray-700 mr-2
          mb-2">Km:{km}</span>
      </div>
    </div>
    </Link>
    )
}
export default Card
```

The rest of the component is really just a bunch of Tailwind classes. If we try this, however, we will get a pretty descriptive error, stating that we haven't whitelisted the Cloudinary domain in the Next.js settings and thus our images cannot be displayed. Head over to the next.config.js file in the root of our project and edit it quickly:

```
module.exports = {
  images: {
    domains: ['res.cloudinary.com'],
  },
}
```

This way, we are able to show images from the Cloudinary domain and if we should add other media sources, we would have to list them in this file.

## Creating statically generated pages for individual cars

Our final part of this application will be to create individual pages for the cars. Since we will fetch our cars by their unique IDs generated by MongoDB and then converted to a plain string, we will make use of Next.js's dynamic routes. Similar to React Router, Next.js offers a simple and effective way of creating pages based on a URL query. All we need is a special name for the page, enclosed in brackets, with the name of the parameter that we want to use for querying. In plain words, if we name a page/component [slug].jsx in a /articles folder, we will be able to reference the slug value in a URL in the form /articles/first in our code as a variable slug equal to "first." Please do not take my contorted explanation for granted and head over to the Next.js routing tutorial, https://nextjs.org/docs/routing/introduction; it is thorough and simple.

Let's create a new page in our /pages/cars folder, name it [id].jsx, and start editing it:

```jsx
import Image from "next/image";
export const getStaticPaths = async () => {
  const res = await fetch(`${process.env.NEXT_PUBLIC_API_URL}/
      cars`);
  const cars = await res.json();
  const paths = cars.map((car) => ({
    params: { id: car._id },
  }));
  return { paths, fallback: "blocking" };
};


export const getStaticProps = async ({ params: { id } }) => {
  const res = await fetch(`${process.env.NEXT_PUBLIC_API_URL}/
      cars/${id}`);
  const car = await res.json();
  return {
    props: { car },
    revalidate: 10,
  };
};
```

After importing the Next Image component for rendering the picture, we have a Next.js function, getStaticPaths, which makes an API request and has to return all our unique identifiers that will be used for constructing the single car pages. Since we opted for the ID as the unique identifier, we are making a fetch request to get all the cars and then mapping through the array of cars in order to get just the IDs. In other cases, you might use unique article slugs based on the title and some combination of date or author. It is important, however, to keep this array filled with unique values that will enable us to get to the respective pages to be generated on the server side. This function returns a variable called paths enclosed in an object and additional options. The Next.js documentation recommends using getStaticPaths when statically pre-rendering pages that use dynamic routes – data coming from CMSs, databases, filesystems, and so on – so it perfectly fits our needs. We want the individual car pages to be statically rendered, indexed by crawling engines, and fast.

getStaticProps is the function that must be used with getStaticPaths and is responsible for generating the individual pages, based on the paths provided by the previous function. In our case, it takes the IDs as parameters, performs fetch requests in order to get the necessary data, and passes it to the page under props. From there on, we are creating a normal React, albeit static, page with the incoming car props:

```
const CarById = ({ car }) => {
  return (
    <div className="flex flex-col justify-center items-center
        min-h-full">
      <h1 className="text-xl font-bold text-gray-700">
        {car.brand} - {car.make}
      </h1>
      <div className=" bg-white p--5 shadow-md rounded-lg">
        <img src={car.picture} width={700} height={400} />
      </div>
      <div className=" text-gray-500 m-5">{`This fine car was
          manufactured in ${car.year}, it made just ${car.km}
              km and it sports a ${car.cm3} cm3 engine.`}</div>
      <div className="text-gray-500 font-bold">Price: {car.
          price} eur</div>
    </div>
  );
};

export default CarById;
```

Again, just an ugly page for the car, but prerendered on the server for all the cars in the database (or in the query).

There are numerous other features and even bare minimum requirements that our app is lacking, but we have no space to implement them all. We would probably want a **Registration** page in case users should register, and we lack basic interactions – messaging, comments, inquiries, or similar. That is not the point here, however; the sole purpose of the section was to give you a taste of the powerful FastAPI/MongoDB/Next.js combination. With server-side rendering, our applications can be blazingly fast, but only if we use the tools at our disposal correctly!

It is worth mentioning that the page completely lacks any meta information, but the documentation on using the Head component (https://nextjs.org/docs/api-reference/next/head) is extensive and straightforward.

# Deployment to Heroku and Vercel

To conclude this chapter and have a well-rounded, albeit incomplete, project, we will now deploy our backend (FastAPI) to Heroku and our frontend to **Vercel**, a Platform-as-a-Service and hosting company that is, incidentally, the creator of Next.js.

You should already have a Heroku account if you followed the workflow described in *Chapter 3, Getting Started with FastAPI* so we will now proceed and create an account on Vercel. You can and should log in with your GitHub account since your deploys will be automatic from your repository once you set up the project. The process of deploying FastAPI to Heroku has already been discussed in *Chapter 5, Building the Backend for Our Application* – we just need to pass additional environment variables from our /backend/.env file, the new MongoDB database name, and Cloudinary data.

> **A personal note**
>
> Heroku seems to dislike when the requirements.txt file contains the packages' version numbers – I guess it needs to figure the dependency tree by itself, so if you want to save yourself some time, try to remove the version numbers.

We will now turn our attention to Vercel. After creating an account by logging in with GitHub, you should already have added a repository within your /next-cars folder. If not, do it now, stop the Next.js server, and add the code:

```
git add .
```

Then, create a commit:

```
git commit -m "deployment to Vercel"
```

After you create the repository on GitHub and add the origin, you can push the changes to your main branch:

```
git push origin main
```

Now, heading over to Vercel, click the blue **Deploy** button and head over to https://vercel.com/new. Here, we can choose our next-cars repository and import it. The next step is to insert our environment variables; in my case, the API address on Heroku was https://calm-cove-22493.herokuapp.com (without the trailing slash!), so I used it for NEXT_PUBLIC_API_URL.

After hitting the **Deploy** button, the process will begin and you will be able to monitor it throughout the stages – preparation, generations of pages, and so on. Vercel is very verbose, so in case of some problems, you should be able to debug it and fix the issues.

After a, hopefully, successful deployment, Vercel will throw some confetti around and guide you to test the website on a custom URL. The application for this chapter is deployed on https://next-cars-two.vercel.app/.

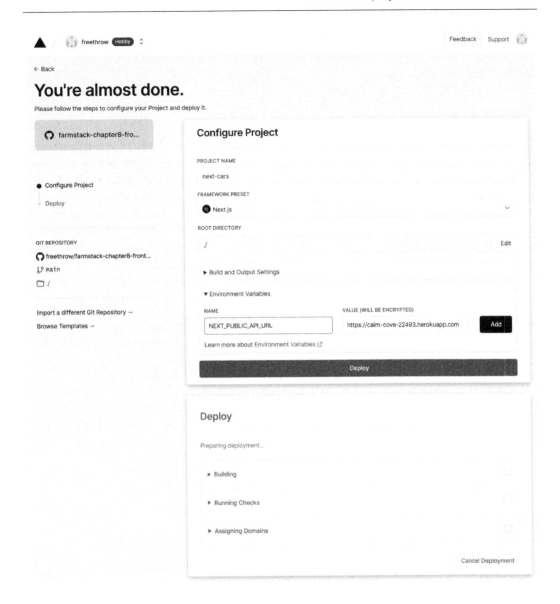

Figure 8.4 – The Vercel project configuration page and the Deploy button

The Vercel deployment page (*Figure 8.4*) is very informative and dynamic. It allows us to set environment variables and customize the deployment settings (we won't do it here, though) and it informs us of the deployment status as it goes through various stages. Errors, should they arise, are displayed in the tabs below the **Deploy** title and allow for a quick and informative log-checking.

The deployment of Next.js on Netlify is very similar, with the environment variables setting process and the automatic deploys from GitHub, but we will examine this process with React.js in the forthcoming chapter.

## Summary

In this chapter, you were introduced to Next.js – an incredibly feature-rich and powerful React-based framework, suitable for building all kinds of websites and apps. We covered **server-side generation (SSG)** and **server-side rendering (SSR)**, as well as a more robust authentication system, using httpOnly cookies and API routes. You have learned the very basics of Next.js development and are now familiarized with the most interesting features and differences from plain React development. You have learned different ways of integrating images (or media files in general) into a complex pipeline, based on Cloudinary and Python Pillow and the powerful Next Image component. Finally, you were able to deploy your Next.js app on Vercel, a premier deployment solution, and put the GitHub repository into a continuous delivery and deployment pipeline. We've covered a lot of ground!

In the next chapter, we are going to go back to plain React and explore some topics that really set our FastAPI background apart from other REST API solutions, such as a (super-simple) regression system, some dashboard/data visualization, report generation, and serving them through an API.

# 9

# Building a Data Visualization App with the FARM Stack

We have covered a lot of ground – we have seen how FastAPI and React can blend and allow our MongoDB data store to shine, passing data back and forth.

In this chapter, we will build yet another little application that should enable us to showcase other, different types of functionalities that might be easier to achieve with this particular stack than with other technologies. We will create an admin application in React using Create React App (as we learned about in *Chapter 4, Setting Up a React Workflow*) and we will try to quickly achieve some goals by creating a simple reporting application with fast pagination and some data visualizations. During the process, we will try to leverage Python's vast package ecosystem, as well as the simplicity of the MongoDB aggregation framework.

We will try to examine the process of data fetching and data visualization from different aspects and discuss the possibilities, while we *implement* a rather simple, yet effective solution. In this chapter, we will also discuss FastAPI's Background Tasks feature and how it can help us when dealing with long-running processes that shouldn't be awaited by the user while using the website. Stay tuned, because this should be fun!

In this chapter, we will cover the following main topics:

- **Stale-while-revalidate (SWR)** – a better way of data fetching with the SWR library, including result pagination, cache invalidation, data refreshing, and more
- Revisiting the MongoDB aggregation framework and creating a couple of endpoints (URLs) for our analytics application
- Data visualization options and a few simple implementations with Chart.js
- Setting up an email service with SendGrid and integrating it with our REST API
- Integrating a simple Machine Learning algorithm

# Technical requirements

The technical requirements for this chapter are no different than for the previous chapters – you will need to have a working Python installation (version 3.6 or later, but for package compatibility reasons, it would probably be better to have a newer one, such as 3.9+), and to have Node.js and npm installed (Node.js version 14 or later). The code in this chapter will be deployed on a Ubuntu server, so having access to a Linux – Debian machine would be beneficial, although if you want to perform the actual deployment on a DigitalOcean Droplet in the next chapter, you can use **Secure Shell (SSH)** from Windows. If you want to follow the part where we integrate a machine learning pipeline, install scikit-learn.

# The specification

I have always felt that it is better if I know upfront upon reading something what I shall be building and what its goal is. Even a vague specification is better than no specification at all, so in this spirit, let's turn to our imaginary scenario again:

*The management would like to have a way to quickly browse all the cars in the database and have an overview of them – how many Volkswagens or Fiat Puntos are available, what the average production year is, and so on (this one is pretty vague, but we get the idea). The management would also love to receive and be able to send automated reports about cars that have been added in the last 7 or 30 days.*

Armed with our FARM stack knowledge, we know that we can tackle this, but what's more important is that we know that we will also be able to address future requests, modifications, and features, while using the same technologies and finding a very cheap (or free!) deployment solution to kickstart our project. Let's begin.

# Creating the backend

While we will be working with the same data, this chapter will employ a significantly simplified backend for our purposes, as we do not need to repeat things that have already been covered. We will create a new, simpler backend with just some READ routes (GET requests) as we will not need to update, create, or delete any cars. We will also insert a pretty hefty number of cars into our database – we need data to work with and we need a realistic number of entities in order to showcase the dashboard functionalities.

Our plan will be the following:

* Create a new collection inside our Mongo database
* Import the provided sample data from a **Comma-Separated Values (CSV)** document
* Create a new Python environment and install the required packages
* Scaffold our FastAPI application

- Create some MongoDB aggregations and map them into a FastAPI endpoint
- Finally, we will add some backend functionality that isn't going to be directly included in our request/response cycle for sending emails using SendGrid

Let's start and repeat all the steps that we have already covered in the previous chapters, since I would like to have a rather self-contained and complete project with a description of all the necessary steps (especially when it comes to deployment). So, create a folder (mine is called `Chapter09`), another folder inside of it called `/backend`, and follow these steps:

1.  From this `/backend` folder, let's create a new Python environment:

    ```
    python -m venv venv
    ```

    The preceding command will create our virtual environment called `venv`.

2.  We can now proceed to activate it by entering into the `/venv/Scripts` directory and typing the following:

    ```
    activate
    ```

3.  Let's return to our `/backend` directory and install the first dependencies, `fastapi`, `uvicorn`, `motor`, and `python-decouple` for environment variables and `dnspython` for connecting to Mongo:

    ```
    pip install fastapi uvicorn motor python-decouple
    dnspython
    ```

4.  Now, we can fire up our Visual Studio Code and open the `/backend` folder. Let's start with the `.gitignore` and `.env` files. The `.gitignore` file is the one that we copied or created in the previous FastAPI chapters, while the `.env` file will contain the data about our MongoDB collection and, later, our `SendGrid` API key for sending emails.

5.  For now, let's just add the new database name – I called mine `dashboard`, but you can get more creative. Now, we will leave Visual Studio Code and open Mongo Compass. Log in to your MongoDB account, create a new database called `dashboard`, and a collection named `cars` inside.

6.  Select the `cars` collection inside the `dashboard` database in the menu on the left and find the big, green **Import data** button in the middle. It is of paramount importance that you set the column data types to numbers before proceeding to import for all the columns except for `brand` and `make` – so `cm3`, `price`, `km`, and `year` should all be numbers.

> **Important Note**
>
> Beware! If you decide to import your data through the MongoCompass interface, the IDs of the documents (cars) will be `ObjectId`, so our API will not be able to find them by the string ID. I have included a simple Python script for importing the data cast into our model so we can get nice simple string `_id` fields. In this project, we will not be making use of any individual car endpoints, but I feel that it is important to emphasize this fact.

After hitting the **IMPORT** button, you should have a little below 4,000 records to play with. That would be a pretty successful company, indeed!

7. Now, we are done with *Compass* and we can turn to Visual Studio Code – let's update our `.env` file, with our own database credentials:

```
DB_URL=mongodb+srv://<username>:<password> @cluster0.
fkm24.mongodb.net/?retryWrites=true&w=majority
DB_NAME=dashboard
```

8. Now that we have a database (we will only be reading from it, no writing!), we can begin building our API. Let's create a `main.py` file in the root of the `/backend` folder:

```
from decouple import config
from fastapi import FastAPI
from starlette.middleware import Middleware
from starlette.middleware.cors import CORSMiddleware
```

As we did previously, we are just importing the bare necessities: FastAPI, *decouple*'s `config` class in order to be able to read our `.env` variables, and *Starlette*'s middleware in order to be able to add CORS middleware:

```
middleware = [
    Middleware(
        CORSMiddleware,
        allow_origins=["*"],
        allow_methods=["*"],
        allow_headers=["*"],
    )
]
from motor.motor_asyncio import AsyncIOMotorClient
from routers.cars import router as cars_router
DB_URL = config("DB_URL", cast=str)
DB_NAME = config("DB_NAME", cast=str)
origins = ["*"]
```

Again, by now, this will have become second nature to you – we are defining the middleware and allowing all possible origins (again: not to be done in real production systems!).

9.  After these lines, we are importing our faithful `motor` asynchronous client, a `cars` router that we haven't written yet, and read the `.env` variables that should allow us to connect to MongoDB. Let's finish the `main.py` file:

```
app = FastAPI(middleware=middleware)
app.include_router(cars_router, prefix="/cars",
tags=["cars"])
@app.on_event("startup")
async def startup_db_client():
    app.mongodb_client = AsyncIOMotorClient(DB_URL)
    app.mongodb = app.mongodb_client[DB_NAME]


@app.on_event("shutdown")
async def shutdown_db_client():
    app.mongodb_client.close()
```

Again, nothing really new: we are instantiating our app with the middleware the *Starlette way*, adding the router that we are yet to create, and connecting and disconnecting the Mongo client on startup and shutdown, respectively. I don't know about you, but I am always eager to start the API server and right now, we cannot do that – we have to create the `cars` router.

10. But before that, we need to have our models. Let's create our `models.py` file in the `root` folder:

```
from bson import ObjectId
from pydantic import Field, BaseModel, validator


class PyObjectId(ObjectId):
    @classmethod
    def __get_validators__(cls):
        yield cls.validate
    @classmethod
    def validate(cls, v):
        if not ObjectId.is_valid(v):
            raise ValueError("Invalid objectid")
        return ObjectId(v)
    @classmethod
    def __modify_schema__(cls, field_schema):
        field_schema.update(type="string")
```

```python
class MongoBaseModel(BaseModel):
    id: PyObjectId = Field(default_factory=PyObjectId,
                           alias="_id")
    class Config:
        json_encoders = {ObjectId: str}
```

This is the standard procedure (I hesitate to call it a hack since I don't believe it fits that moniker) for converting our MongoDB `ObjectIDs` and I wouldn't comment it again. Let's see the actual `CarBase` model:

```python
class CarBase(MongoBaseModel):
    brand: str = Field(..., min_length=2)
    make: str = Field(..., min_length=1)
    year: int = Field(..., gt=1975, lt=2023)
    price: int = Field(...)
    km: int = Field(...)
    cm3: int = Field(..., gt=400, lt=8000)
```

The `CarBase` model is deliberately simplified: we don't have the `userId` and we don't have the Cloudinary picture file, since we won't be needing them for the functionality that we want to show.

11. Now, we can maintain our application structure from before and create a folder, `routers`, in the `/backend` folder. Inside, create an empty `__init__.py` indicating that it is a Python module. Then, in the `/routers` directory, create a `cars.py` file:

```python
from typing import Optional
from fastapi import APIRouter, Request
from models import CarBase
router = APIRouter()
```

12. These are our imports – the `CarBase` model and the instantiation of `APIRouter`. Let's add just one endpoint that lists all the cars (or a subset defined by the query parameters) and allows for some querying – the same as in the previous chapters:

```python
@router.get("/all", response_description="List all cars")
async def list_all_cars(
    request: Request,
    min_price: int = 0,
    max_price: int = 100000,
    brand: Optional[str] = None,
    page: int = 1,
```

```
) -> List[CarBase]:
    RESULTS_PER_PAGE = 25
    skip = (page - 1) * RESULTS_PER_PAGE
    query = {"price": {"$lt": max_price,
                       "$gt": min_price}}
    if brand:
        query["brand"] = brand
```

In this query, we also want to have the number of pages, based on our RESULTS_PER_PAGE variable for a pagination functionality. For instance, if our query yields 52 results, we will have three pages: two full pages of 25 results each and one third page with just the last 2 results. So, we need to get the total number of pages and return it along with the data:

```
    pages = ceil(
        await request.app.mongodb["cars"].count_
documents(query) / RESULTS_PER_PAGE
    )
    full_query = (
        request.app.mongodb["cars"]
        .find(query)
        .sort("km", -1)
        .skip(skip)
        .limit(RESULTS_PER_PAGE)
    )

    results = [CarBase(**raw_car) async for raw_car
               in full_query]

    return {"results": results, "pages": pages}
```

13. ceil is the Python function that rounds a decimal number up, so 52/25 becomes 3. Finally, we have one endpoint that we can test! Start the Uvicorn web server with the following:

```
uvicorn main:app --reload
```

Make sure to issue the command in the root /backend folder with the activated virtual environment. Now, you should be able to test the http://localhost:8000/cars endpoint and make sure that it behaves in the way you expect. You will see that the response returns the number of pages, along with the data itself.

## The MongoDB Aggregation Framework

We have addressed the aggregation framework, but we haven't really made much use of it until now. While it might seem complicated at first sight, it is really intuitive and easy once you get the hang of it. Instead of delving into the theory and syntax, here you should read about it on the excellent MongoDB website anyway: `https://www.mongodb.com/docs/manual/aggregation/`. I will just describe the endpoints that I want to have for this dashboard and then, we are going to assemble them within an aggregation pipeline.

The first analytical endpoint that we are going to need is the one that returns us the average prices of the various car models (the makes) for a fixed brand. This is easily accomplished within the aggregation pipeline and can be broken into discrete steps:

- Select all cars with a brand matching the desired brand – `$match`.

- From this selected group of cars, only keep the car features that we actually need – in our case, the price and the make (or model) – `$project`.

- Now, we want to group and apply an actual aggregation function! What do we want to group by? Well, the car model – that's obvious. What is our aggregation function going to be? Um… average? Right! And what are we averaging? The price, of course – using `$group` – but maybe we would want to do so by kilometers. Or the year of production. It would be nice if we could make this generic – a function that accepts all of our numerical car features.

- Nobody likes when the query set returns without ordering – at least, I don't. So, to finish things off, let's order our aggregation results by (average) price, starting from the cheapest – `$sort`.

Broken into steps, the aggregation doesn't seem so intimidating, and writing it just requires plain Python dictionaries and dollar signs for the *MongoDB*-reserved words:

```
query = [
    {"$match": {"brand": brand}},
    {"$project": {"_id": 0, "price": 1, "make": 1}},
    {
        "$group": {"_id": {"model": "$make"},
                   "avgPrice": {"$avg": "$price"}},
    },
    {"$sort": {"avgPrice": 1}},
]
```

The only thing that I had some trouble remembering was the mandatory `group` and `id` parts, but we have it covered in the introduction to MongoDB. The rest is pretty straightforward – including the use of ones and zeros for selecting or deselecting fields to display.

Once we have the pipeline in a form of a list of dictionaries, it is no different than a regular query. In the following code, we have parametrized the price into a generic numeric value called `val` that we wish to aggregate upon – it can take values of `price`, km, cm3, or `year`, our numerical attributes:

```
@router.get("/brand/{val}/{brand}", response_description="Get
brand models by val")
async def brand_price(brand: str, val: str, request: Request):
    query = [
        {"$match": {"brand": brand}},
        {"$project": {"_id": 0}},
        {
            "$group": {"_id": {"model": "$make"},
                       f"avg_{val}": {"$avg": f"${val}"}},
        },
        {"$sort": {f"avg_{val}": 1}},
    ]
    full_query = request.app.mongodb["cars"].aggregate(query)
    return [el async for el in full_query]
```

This query, when the `http://127.0.0.1:8000/cars/brand/price/Honda` endpoint is hit, returns a JSON response in the following format:

```
[
    {
        "_id": {
            "model": "HR_V"
        },
        "avgPrice": 2350.0
    },
    {
        "_id": {
            "model": "Jazz"
        },
        "avgPrice": 4565.555555555556
    }, ...
```

In which `_id` contains the model or make of the car (the brand is fixed and in this case, it is Honda), and `avg_price` contains the result of the averaging aggregation. This format is easy to parse and can be fit into various visualization solutions, as we will see later.

> **Important Note**
>
> We could have gotten rid of this index dictionary right here in Python, but we chose to let it go up into the frontend. Later, we are going to see that there are many decisions, similar to this one, that can make or break an application – choosing where to perform certain transformations and data processing. Remember, we have the MongoDB querying and aggregation layers, then we have the powerful Python layer – with all imaginable data processing goodies – and finally, we have ES6, itself a pretty powerful language for data wrangling…

Now, we have a reusable endpoint that aggregates all of our numerical variables! Let's create a few more endpoints – we want, for example, to display a pie chart (yes, I know they are evil!) in order to show how many cars fall into which brand. This is probably the first information that someone in the company would want to know right away. Essentially, we want to count the number of cars of each brand:

```python
@router.get("/brand/count", response_description="Count by brand")
async def brand_count(request: Request):
    query = [{"$group": {"_id": "$brand",
                "count": {"$sum": 1}}}]
    full_query =
        request.app.mongodb["cars"].aggregate(query)
    return [el async for el in full_query]
```

Finally, let's add another endpoint that we will call /sample – it will come in handy later when we implement a caching solution. This function returns a sample of the queried collection, with the only restriction on the car production year. There are some restrictions and guidelines on how to use sampling (https://www.mongodb.com/docs/manual/reference/operator/aggregation/sample/) but for our purposes, we just need to know that the endpoint should return a reasonable amount of cars (less than 100, for instance). Armed with a knowledge of how to integrate aggregation pipelines into FastAPI routes, this one is simple:

```python
@router.get("/sample/{n}", response_description="Sample of N cars")
async def get_sample(n: int, request: Request):
    query = [
        {"$match": {"year": {"$gt": 2010}}},
        {
            "$project": {
                "_id": 0,
            }
        },
```

```
            {"$sample": {"size": n}},
            {"$sort": {"brand": 1, "make": 1, "year": 1}},
    ]
    full_query =
        request.app.mongodb["cars"].aggregate(query)
    return [el async for el in full_query]
```

Later on, we will add another endpoint that will perform some tasks in the background, but for now, we have more than enough endpoints to start building our dashboard and our pagination functionality.

# Building the frontend with SWR and Charts.js

Now, we will proceed to build our frontend with two goals in mind: we want to have a way of paginating through our cars with the usual previous or next buttons and we want to find a way of displaying the data from our MongoDB aggregations – whether by the average price of models by brand or something else. In order to be able to start tinkering with the user interface, we will create a new React App using our faithful friend: the `create-react-app` script and I will (again) install Tailwind CSS. Since we have already seen this procedure a couple of times, I will not repeat it here. After installing Tailwind, we are going to need *React Router 6* as well, so go ahead and install it. Now, it is time to set up the router and the three pages that will be displayed in our analytics application. Follow these steps:

1.  Edit the `index.js` file in the `/src` directory:

    ```
    import React from 'react';
    import ReactDOM from 'react-dom/client';
    import {BrowserRouter,Routes,Route,
    } from "react-router-dom";

    import './index.css';
    import Layout from './components/Layout';
    import Home from './components/Home';
    import Dashboard from './components/Dashboard';
    import Report from './components/Report';
    ```

    After importing the `Router` components, we are also reporting four components that we have yet to create – the `Layout` component will be used for the same purpose as in *Chapter 4, Setting a React Workflow*, while `Home`, `Dashboard`, and `Report` will be virtual pages in our single page app, and they will all live in the `/components` folder.

2.  Let's finish the router setup in the same file:

```
const root = ReactDOM.createRoot(document.
getElementById('root'));
root.render(
  <React.StrictMode>
    <BrowserRouter>
    <Layout>
      <Routes>
        <Route path="/" element={<Home />} />
        <Route path="/dashboard"
          element={<Dashboard />} />
        <Route path="/report" element={<Report />}
        />
      </Routes>
    </Layout>
    </BrowserRouter>
  </React.StrictMode>
);
```

3.  Now, it's time for the `Layout.jsx` component: we will make a standard `flex` layout with the header and footer at the top and the bottom of the page, respectively:

```
import Header from "./Header";
import Footer from "./Footer";
const Layout = ({ children }) => {
  return (
    <div className="flex flex-col h-screen">
      <Header />
      <div className="flex-1 flex flex-row
        justify-center items-start mx-auto container
          my-10">
        {children}
      </div>
      <Footer />
    </div>
  );
```

```
};
export default Layout;
```

4.  Feel free to get creative with the footer, while the header will contain just a navigation menu:

```
import { NavLink } from "react-router-dom";
const Header = () => {
  return (
    <div className="fixed bg-white w-full">
      <div className="flex flex-row
        justify-center space-x-4 h-10 items-center
          text-red-800 font--bold text-lg">
        <NavLink to="/">Cars</NavLink>
        <NavLink to="/dashboard">Dashboard</NavLink>
        <NavLink to="/report">Report</NavLink>
      </div>
    </div>
  );
};
export default Header;
```

The virtual pages, Dashboard, Report, and Home, can just be scaffolded with generic React functional components for now. Make sure the navigation works as advertised and that the content of the Layout component changes after clicking the links. I have added a couple of classes just to see whether the pages work.

One other important step that we need to take at this point is to set up an .env.local environment file, in which we will specify the URL of our API. Since now we are in development mode, this file will simply point to our development FastAPI local server (at http://127.0.0.1:8000), but once we deploy our React application, the API will be served from a server on the internet (in this case, we will deploy to *DigitalOcean*'s Ubuntu Droplet, but it could be *Heroku* as well). In order to be accessible from the process.env variable, the environment variable has to start with REACT_APP, so in our case, the .env.local file will look as follows:

**REACT_APP_API_URL=http://127.0.0.1:8000**

Now, instead of hardcoding our API URL, we will just reference the REACT_APP_API_URL variable and when the time for deployment comes, we will simply provide our production API to the deployment service of choice (Netlify or Vercel, for example) and the React bundler will set things up accordingly.

## React pagination and SWR

The first page that we'll tackle is the Home page, and this should allow us to quickly navigate or paginate through all the records on the page. In this application, we will not implement context, nor local storage solutions, so we will not be able to preserve any kind of state on page refreshing, but that is not the point here. We have seen that making requests to the API server and then implementing the useEffect or useState dance on every page can quickly become a bit cumbersome. In this application, we will use the concept (and the library) called SWR. The library bears the same name as the concept, so do not get confused. We will use *Vercel's* relatively lightweight library, which enables us to handle data fetching from the server in a more pleasant, stable, and quicker way, while providing data caching, prefetching (fetching data that has yet to be displayed in the app after a user interaction that hasn't yet occurred), and validation. Different implementations are available for React – one very popular and feature-rich implementation is *React Query*, but we will use *SWR* (https://swr. vercel.app/).

Before diving into the *Home* page that is supposed to display all our cars, let's create two simple React components that will be reusable across the app – first, a really bland Card.jsx component for displaying the individual car:

```
const Card = ({ car }) => {
  const { make, brand, km, cm3, price, year } = car;
  return (
    <div className=" shadow-md rounded-md flex flex-col
      justify-center p-2 bg-green-100 items-center">
      <div className="font-bold">
        {brand} - {make} ({cm3}cm3)
      </div>
      <div>{km} Km / Year: {year}</div>
      <div>Price: {price} eur</div>
    </div>
  );
};
export default Card;
```

Then, we need a reusable CarsDropdown component, a simple select element with the car brands as possible values, and a custom onChange handler:

```
const CarsDropdown = ({ selectHandler, allCars }) => {
  const carBrands = ["Fiat","Opel","Renault","Peugeot",
    "VW","Ford","Honda","Toyota"];
  return (
```

```
  <select
    onChange={selectHandler}
  value={elValue}
    className=
        "px-2 py-1 my-2 mx-2 rounded-lg form-select
        md:w-1/6"
  >
    {allCars && <option value="">All brands</option>}
    {carBrands.map((brand) => {
      return (
        <option value={brand} key={brand}>
          {brand}
        </option>
      );
    })}
  </select>
  );
};
CarsDropdown.defaultProps = {
  allCars: false,
  elValue: "",
};
export default CarsDropdown;
```

This is just a simple `select` component that we parametrized for our purposes: it is populated with the selected car brands (ideally, this brands array would come from a `distinct` query from the database) and it is passed a `handler` function through props. We have also used a `defaultProp` – the `allCars` flag. This is just a way to indicate whether we want the `allCars` option included or not – on the first pagination page we want to include all the brands, while in the charts that display data for a particular brand, it wouldn't make much sense.

We now have all the ingredients to build our simple pagination Home.jsx page. Let's set up SWR and see how it does its magic with the querying:

```
import { useState } from "react";
import useSWR from "swr";
import Card from "./Card";
import CarsDropdown from "./CarsDropdown";
const fetcher = (...args) => fetch(...args).then((res) => res.
```

```
json());

const Home = () => {
  const [pageIndex, setPageIndex] = useState(1);
  const [brand, setBrand] = useState("");
  const { data, error } = useSWR(
    `${process.env.REACT_APP_API_URL}/cars/
all?page=${pageIndex}&brand=${brand}`,
    fetcher
  ); if (error) return <div>failed to load</div>;
  if (!data) return <div>loading...</div>;
```

Setting up SWR is rather simple – we just need a pretty generic `fetcher` function that will use the arguments provided to make the API call. This function can use *Axios* as well, but here, we use just `fetch` and make a couple of `then` clauses in order to get the result in JSON. We then make use of the `useSWR` hook, which is very simple to use – it provides a `data` object or an `error` object, depending on the result of the query. You can play around with it and try stopping the FastAPI server or making an intentional typo in the URL – the page will be cut short to a loading or an error message.

In our case, we follow the documentation and immediately short-circuit the functional component: if there is an error, we return a `div` with the notification, and if there is no error, but no data either, we display a loading message. The third option is that we got the data – and this data can be treated pretty much the same way as with the `useEffect` and `useState` combination before. Every time the URL changes to accommodate a selected car brand or a query page number, SWR will fetch the new data. It gets even better – SWR will prefetch data if we play our cards right and it will provide caching, noticeable even in our lightweight application. The SWR documentation suggests a neat trick (`https://swr.vercel.app/docs/pagination`): we should basically request the next paginated content just to make SWR make the API call, without displaying the content on the current page. By doing this, we drastically improve our user experience. Let's update the previous code and make this call (to the `pageIndex+1` page, the next page) – we'll just dump the retrieved data into an invisible `div`:

```
const { nextData, nextError } = useSWR(
  `${process.env.REACT_APP_API_URL}/cars/all?page=${
    pageIndex + 1
  }&brand=${brand}`,
  fetcher
);
const { data, error } = useSWR(
```

```
    `${process.env.REACT_APP_API_URL}/cars/
        all?page=${pageIndex}&brand=${brand}`,
    fetcher
  );
  if (error) return <div>`failed to load {process.env.REACT_
    APP_API_URL}`</div>;
  if (!data) return <div>loading...</div>;
```

Let's now build the controls for our Home page – the brand selector and the **Previous** and **Next** page buttons:

```
return (
    <div className="w-full p-8 my-10">
      <h1 className="font-bold text-lg text-center
        p-8 border border-gray-500">Explore Cars</h1>
<div className="hidden">
This will not be displayed!
    {JSON.stringify(nextData)} {JSON.stringify(nextError)}
</div>
      <div className="flex flex-row justify-between my-3">
        <CarsDropdown
          selectHandler={(event) => {
            setBrand(event.target.value);
            setPageIndex(1);
          }}
          allCars={true}
          elValue={brand}
        />
        <div className="">
          {pageIndex > 1 ? (
            <button
              className=" bg-red-800 text-white font-bold
                          p-3 m-1 rounded-md w-40"
              onClick={() => setPageIndex(pageIndex - 1)}
            >Previous</button>
          ) : (
            <></>
```

```
        )}
      </div>
```

In the preceding snippet, we are putting our custom select, `CarsDropdown`, to good use, passing it a simple handler that sets the selected brand and restarts the pagination – setting the page to `1` every time the brand is changed. After the selector, we use simple logic to conditionally display the **Previous** button – if the page index is not greater than `1`, then there is no previous data. We use the same logic for displaying the **Next** button, relying on the total number of pages provided by our API.

The last part is just displaying a bunch of cards and iterating over the data:

```
    <div className="flex flex-row justify-center items-center">
        Brand:
        <span className=" font-bold text-lg mx-2
          text-gray-500">
          {brand ? brand : "All brands"}
        </span>
        Page:
        <span className=" font-bold text-lg mx-2
          text-gray-500">
          {pageIndex} of {data.pages}
        </span>
      </div>
    </div>
    <div className="grid grid-cols-4 lg:grid-cols-5
      gap-2">
      {data.results.map((car) => (
        <Card car={car} key={car._id} />
      ))}
      </div>
    </div>
  );
};
export default Home;
```

As useful feedback for the user, we are also displaying the selected brand and the number of pages, as well as the current page they are viewing.

You will notice that SWR does a lot of things under the hood – it takes care of the data and the error automatically, performs caching, and validates the data on page focus.

# Building the dashboard with Chart.js

We have finished creating our FastAPI analytical endpoints that perform aggregations, and we managed to return nice and simple arrays of data ready to be displayed in our dashboard. Now, we will use one of the most popular charting solutions – Chart.js – in order to create our dashboard, a page filled with charts that display our data and shed some light on it.

## Data visualization with React

Over the course of the last decade, we have witnessed incredible development when it comes to data visualization – Python itself provides numerous interesting solutions that often blend with some JavaScript in order to produce interactivity (such as Bokeh and Altair), along with older staples such as Matplotlib and Seaborn. JavaScript and React specifically are very well-suited for web-based visualizations that look great and have a good speed, even on mobile devices, and are often integrated into mobile applications.

Data visualization solutions can be generally categorized by how much they can accomplish, but also by their level of customization. Some D3.js visualizations are simply impossible to reproduce with any other tool and require a pretty high level of proficiency. Others, such as Chart.js – the charting solution that we will be using for our application – are relatively easy to use and provide a sufficient level of customization for the majority of cases. I must also mention the growing popularity of particular data visualization frameworks, especially *Plotly Dash* and the up-and-coming *Streamlit*: these are two Python-based frameworks that allow even novices to create production-level quality data applications, and showcase datasets, exploratory analyses, and data processing algorithms, which truly democratizes and opens up the field. The *FARM stack*, in my humble opinion, provides similar possibilities, although not in a framework-based environment. The recent technique of combining D3.js and React, where D3 is used to display data and React takes control of the DOM, has given us some amazing solutions, and there is no reason why the backend shouldn't be based on MongoDB and Python.

Let's get back to our simple dashboard. The dashboard page is meant to host a couple of charts – but once you get the hang of it, you are free to experiment and add others as well. The page itself will be a mere container, as the charts will be independent from one another and will each sport a different state:

```
import BrandCount from "./BrandCount";
import ModelCount from "./ModelCount";
import BrandValue from "./BrandValue";
const Dashboard = () => {
  return (
    <div className=" w-full p-8 my-10">
      <h1 className="font-bold text-lg text-center
        p-8 border border-gray-500">
        DashBoard
```

```
      </h1>
      <div className="grid 2xl:grid-cols-2 gap-2">
        <BrandValue val={"price"} />
        <BrandValue val={"km"} />
        <BrandValue val={"cm3"} />
        <BrandValue val={"year"} />
      </div>
    </div>
  );
};
export default Dashboard;
```

Again, the Tailwind styles applied are not here to make the app look pretty, but rather, to enable us to differentiate between various components and not get in the way too much. Now, we will try and build a `BrandValue` component, which will be used to display a chart based on the aggregation data that it receives from our endpoint.

Just to be clear, we are building a `Charts.js` chart, a simple bar chart, with only one dataset (we could potentially put more than one brand on display), and we have two values that determine the data – the brand of the car (which will be provided by our custom dropdown brand selector) and the numerical value that we will pass as props. We could have made just another dropdown menu for the numeric values that we want to aggregate upon (km, cm3, `price`, and `year`) and just create one big chart, but I want to showcase more visualizations side by side, and maybe users will want to see and compare different charts at the same time.

Let's stop the server and install `React Charts 2` and `Charts.js`:

```
npm i react-chartjs-2 chart.js
```

At this point, you really should go over to the Chart.js documentation site and get acquainted with the way that they deal with charts. As mentioned previously, Charts.js is definitely more of a pre-canned visualization solution, in the sense that it allows you to pass numerous properties and options to the chart object, but you are confined by the charts that are offered. For our case, and really for cases when you do not need super customized solutions with brand-matching colors or a particularly weird chart type, Chart.js is a great solution.

Open up a new React component in the `components` folder and call it `BrandValue.jsx`. We will begin with the imports:

```
import { useState } from "react";
import useSWR from "swr";
```

```
import {
  Chart as ChartJS,
  CategoryScale,
  LinearScale,
  BarElement,
  Title,
  Tooltip,
  Legend,
} from "chart.js";
import { Bar } from "react-chartjs-2";
import CarsDropdown from "./CarsDropdown";
```

We are importing `useState` and this will be used to keep track of the selected brand, since the aggregation target is already passed via props. `useSWR` will be used to fetch data, as we did with our pagination page, while the remaining imports are all from Chart.js – basically, every bit of functionality that will be needed has to be imported. In the end, we import our `CarsDropdown` as well, as it will be used for selecting the car brand. Let's now register the various parts of a Chart.js chart:

```
ChartJS.register(CategoryScale, LinearScale, BarElement,
  Title, Tooltip, Legend);
```

The next and arguably the most important step is passing the `options` object to our chart. As you can see from the documentation, it is a simple object with some nested values, and it takes care of the title and the axes. Now, `Chart.js` is very good at setting our axis values – but we have an edge case: the production year. This is a good example of a variable that has a very limited range compared to its total value – and in fact, if we leave it to Chart.js, it will draw us a list of rectangles with *so little* variation of height that it will be virtually impossible to tell them apart (let's say, comparing rectangles of 2,010 mm and 2,005 mm).

For this reason, you may want to create a simple function that returns the `options` object before passing it to the chart itself. In this case, I just went to the documentation site and saw that we can actually pass a minimum value for the *y*-axes – everything is possible and relatively easily achievable with `Chart.js`. Let's see this `options` function:

```
export const options = (val) => {
  let optObj = {
    responsive: true,
    plugins: {
      legend: {position: "top",},
      title: {
```

```
          display: true,
          text: `Average ${val} of car models by brand`,
        },
      },
    };
    if (val === "year") {
      optObj["scales"] = {
        y: {
          min: 1980,
        },
      };
    }
    return optObj;
};
```

We used the `val` prop provided to the component in two places actually – for setting the `title` of the chart and for checking whether the aggregation variable is equal to the `year` string. If it is, we simply add a `scales` key with a value of `1980` for the *y*-axis – which just means that for the `year` aggregation only, the *y*-axis will begin at `1980`. Feel free to experiment and see what works best for you. After defining our usual `fetcher` function for the SWR library, we are ready to begin crafting the component itself:

```
const fetcher = (...args) => fetch(...args).then((res) => res.json());
const BrandValue = ({ val }) => {
  const queryStr = `avg_${val}`;
  const [brand, setBrand] = useState("Fiat");
  const { data, error } = useSWR(
      `${process.env.REACT_APP_API_URL}/cars/brand/${val}/${brand}`,,
    fetcher
  );
  if (error) return <div>failed to load</div>;
  if (!data) return <div>loading...</div>;
```

The preceding code just declares our functional component function and at the start, we create a `queryStr` variable. Since the component prop that is passed will be, say, km, we need a way to access the values in the API and they would be under the `avg_km` key in this case. These values will be used when creating our data object to be passed to the `Chart.js` instance. We then proceed to initialize the state variable brand and set up our SWR data-fetching mechanism, as we did with the pagination page. Finally, we get to create the `chartData` object – the data that `Chart.js` will use to actually build the chart:

```
const chartData = {
    labels: data.map((item) => {
      return item["_id"]["model"];
    }),
    datasets: [
       {
         label: brand,
         data: data.map((item)=>Math.round(item[queryStr])),
         hoverBackgroundColor: ["#aaff99"],
       },
    ],
  };
```

Again, I strongly suggest that you visit the Chart.js documentation (it is excellent, by the way) in order to understand how the library expects data to be passed. Our case is a pretty simple one – we need the labels and these are just the car model names to be spread across the categorical *x*-axis, so we can just map over the data (that SWR was kind enough to provide!) and extract the ID model. Again, we could have lost the ID part while we were in Python. Chart.js by default expects more datasets than just one, so the variable name is `datasets` (plural), and this is useful when comparing datasets with the same labels. We, however, need just one dataset and that is the rounded value of our aggregation – km, cm3, year, or `price`. This is where our `queryStr` variable generated from the component props comes into play – it allows us to access the data from the API. As a nice touch, I added a hover background color for the bars – it is just a *HEX* value. With all this in place, writing the component becomes simple:

```
return (
  <div className="w-full shadow-md my-5">
    <h1 className=" text-red-700 font-bold text-center">
      {val.toUpperCase()} by model for a given
        brand - {brand}
    </h1>
```

```
        <div className=" w-full text-center">
          <CarsDropdown
            selectHandler={(event) =>
              setBrand(event.target.value)}
            elValue={brand}
          />
        </div>
        <div className="p-5 min-w-full">
          <Bar options={options(val)} data={chartData} />
        </div>
      </div>
    );
  };
export default BrandValue;
```

We display the value that we are aggregating, the `CarsDropdown` component with the handler, and the value (so the component doesn't re-render to the default state!), and we insert the options and the data objects into the `BarChart` component. Chart.js does the bulk of the work in the preparation stage. The page should display four identical bar charts for each numerical data value. The charts are independent and can be set to different brands.

Before leaving the dashboard, let's create a pie chart and display the number of cars for each brand. The management loves pie charts! The procedure will be very similar, except we will not accept any props. Pie charts, however, often present another challenge – the color contrast of adjacent segments should be significant enough to clearly distinguish the data. For this reason, we will borrow some colors from `D3.js` – their excellent chromatic scale package essentially maps an array of numbers or a segment of values between 0 and 1 into appropriate colors. We typically pass the index of the data or a normalized or scaled variable value to the scale and use the resulting color code to paint. Install the scale with the following:

```
npm i d3-scale-chromatic
```

Now, we can create a `BrandCount.jsx` component in the `/components` folder:

```
import useSWR from "swr";
import { Chart as ChartJS, ArcElement, Tooltip, Legend } from
"chart.js";
import { Pie } from "react-chartjs-2";
import { schemePastel1 } from "d3-scale-chromatic";
const colors = schemePastel1;
```

```
ChartJS.register(ArcElement, Tooltip, Legend);
const fetcher = (...args) => fetch(...args).then((res) => res.
json());
```

After importing useSWR, we take what we need from Chart.js – the chart itself, ArcElement, which is a core element of a pie chart, and the usual Tooltip and Legend. The pie comes from the react-chartjs-2 library. We then instantiate a color scale – I opted for some pastel colors but feel free to explore the whole set. After registering the components of the chart, we define our fetcher for SWR. Let's make the pie:

```
const BrandCount = () => {
  const { data, error } = useSWR(
    `${process.env.REACT_APP_API_URL}/cars/brand/count`,
      fetcher
  );
  if (error) return <div>failed to load</div>;
  if (!data) return <div>loading...</div>;
  const chartData = {
    labels: data.map((item) => {
      return item["_id"];
    }),
    datasets: [
      {
        data: data.map((item) => item.count),
        backgroundColor: data.map((item, index) =>
          colors[index]),
        borderWidth: 3,
      },
    ],
  };
```

The code is pretty intuitive after having dealt with the bar charts – the only thing that is different is the fact that we are using our D3 color scale to map through the indices of the data and pick a color for each data point. Here, I just bumped the border between the slices, but you are free to experiment and bake a different flavor pie. In the GitHub repo with the code from this book, you will find an additional, very similar pie chart that lists the models within a given brand and uses our CarsDropdown selector.

## Background Tasks

FastAPI provides a very nifty feature called *Background Tasks* – it is a simple mechanism that allows us to pass one or more operations (functions, really) that should run after a request, but shouldn't be awaited by the client making the requests: they can happen in the background. It is another feature provided by *Starlette*, and the recommendation is to use them for lighter tasks, such as sending email notifications. It is not a drop-in replacement for serious task or message brokers such as RabbitMQ and Celery.

In order to finish our analytics application, we are going to use FastAPI Background Tasks to achieve the following functionality. The user makes a POST request sending an email address and a number of cars to be included in the report. This situation is really *just a simulation* of a real analytics pipeline – the email could be a list of all the salespeople or managers, or perhaps a list of registered customers that want to receive information about new cars that are available or some flash sales. The cars selected for the report will be drawn as a random sample, while in a real-world scenario, they could be selected according to some more or less complex criteria – vehicles marked for a discount, inserted only in the past couple of days, and so on. After the user submits the data (in our case – just an email address and a number of companies!), we will take advantage of Python's ecosystem to perform some operations. We could, for instance, create some charts and send the results to the selected email address. This will enable us to see how Background Tasks handle these potentially long-running and processor-intensive operations while sending a quick response to the user.

We will break this operation down into simple steps. First, let's open our React project (the frontend) and create the `Report.jsx` page:

```
import { useState, useEffect } from "react";
const Report = () => {
  const [email, setEmail] = useState("");
  const [carsNum, setCarsNum] = useState(10);
  const [message, setMessage] = useState("");
  const [loading, setLoading] = useState(false);

  const handleForm = async (e) => {
    e.preventDefault();
    setLoading(true);
    const res =
      await fetch("http://127.0.0.1:8000/cars/email", {
      method: "POST",
      headers: { "Content-Type": "application/json" },
      body: JSON.stringify({ email, cars_num: carsNum }),
    });
    if (res.ok) {
```

```
            setLoading(false);
            setMessage(`Report with ${carsNum} cars sent to
                    ${email}!`);
        }
    };
```

This page is going to be very rudimentary, without any validation in order to save some space. I just added four state variables – `email` and `carsNum` are the parameters that we are sending to the API, while the `loading` and `message` variables are used for managing the user interface. Upon submission, we set the `loading` flag to `true` and after receiving an `ok` response (and, beware, we will *always* receive it, because this response has no way of knowing how Background Tasks will end), it displays a gentle message informing the user that the report is about to be created and sent to the desired email address. We aren't even validating the email address – I repeat, this is just a proof of the concept. Be sure to only send emails to yourself and not to spam random people, as your SendGrid account will quickly (and rightfully) be terminated if so! Let's finish the component and page:

```
return (
    <div className="w-full p-8 my--10">
      <h1 className="font-bold text-lg text-center p-8
        border border-gray-500 w-full ">Generate Report</h1>
      <div className="flex flex-col justify-center
        items-center h-full py-5">{loading && (
      <div className="border border-green-600 w-2/3 p-10
        text-center font-thin my-4 text-lg animate-pulse">
        Generating and sending report in the background...
      </div>
        )}
{message && (
    <div className="border border-green-600
      w-2/3 p-10 text-center font-thin my-4 text-lg
      animate-pulse">
          {message}
        </div>
        )}
```

Finally, we can add the form for sending the email:

```
{!loading && !message && (
        <form className="flex flex-col justify-center"
          onSubmit={handleForm}>
          <label htmlFor="email">Email</label>
          <input
            type="text"
            id="email"
            name="email"
            value={email}
            onChange={(e) => setEmail(e.target.value)}
            className="px-2 py-1 my-2 rounded-full"
          />
          <label htmlFor="carsNum">Number of cars</label>
          <input
            type="number"
            id="carsNum"
            name="carsNum"
            max={50}
            min={5}
            value={carsNum}
            onChange={(e) => setCarsNum(e.target.value)}
            className="p-2 py-1 my-2 rounded-full"
          />
          <button
            type="submit"
            className="block rounded-md bg-green-600
                       text-white px-3 py-1 m-4
                       text-lg hover:bg-green-500
                       transition-colors duration-300"
          >Send report</button>
        </form>
      )}
    </div>
  </div>
);
```

```
};
export default Report;
```

The component is really simple – a form with two fields and a handleSubmit function that, when called, hits an API endpoint.

Let's move on to Python now. First, we need to create the endpoint that will accept the email and the number of cars fields – our substitute for a potentially complex and smart query – and trigger the background task. For simplicity's sake, I will add the route to the existing /cars router, but it should probably be wiser to create a brand-new router and group various similar analytic routes under it. Let's edit the /routers/cars.py router:

```
@router.post("/email", response_description="Send report")
async def send_mail(
    background_tasks: BackgroundTasks,
    cars_num: int = Body(...),
    email: str = Body(...),
):
    background_tasks.add_task(report_pipeline,
                             email, cars_num)
    return {"Received": {"email": email, "cars_num":
        cars_num}}
```

Do not forget to import Background Tasks from FastAPI at the top of the file:

```
from fastapi import APIRouter, Request, Body, HTTPException,
BackgroundTasks
```

The Background Tasks syntax is straightforward – we just have to declare the background_tasks variable as a BackgroundTasks type (you can name it whatever you like, however) and then use the add_task method to add a function to be executed, followed by the arguments. This way, we can add multiple, logically ordered tasks. In our case, we are calling a report_pipeline function– yet to be defined – with the email and cars_num variables that we are promptly extracting from the body of our POST request. We finish the endpoint with a generic message that simply acknowledges that the server received the POST variables, with a (default) *200 OK* status.

Go ahead and create a new folder called /utils in the root of the project (the /backend folder) and inside of it, create an empty __init__.py file, transforming the directory into a Python module. We will approach this top-down, although it would be wiser to start with the low-level functions and start testing, testing, and then do some more testing! Inside /utils, let's create our first Python file, report.py, in the /utils directory:

```python
from time import sleep
def report_pipeline(email, cars_number):
    sleep(5)
    print(email, cars_number)
```

Go ahead and try this route out – either with *Insomnia* or *HTTPie* or through our React App, if you left it running. You should see an immediate response, while, if you look closely at the Python terminal running FastAPI, you will notice a delay of 5 seconds, after which the email and the number of cars will be printed: this is the whole point of Background Tasks – the HTTP response is sent immediately, while the server (although not the part involved in the request/response cycle) is left doing the hard, or simply time-consuming, work.

We will carry out an example – a simple one, but also something that you could easily extend and adapt to some pretty complex analysis.

First, let's install pandas – the basis of any Python analysis and data wrangling:

```
pip install pandas
```

Let's finally make a new file in the /utils directory and name it report_query.py. This file will contain the functionality needed to connect to the database (synchronously, because there is no need to make it asynchronous), perform some simple data wrangling (you can think of this as part of a simple ETL pipeline), and return some data for the report:

```python
from pymongo import MongoClient
from decouple import config

import pandas as pd
DB_URL = config("DB_URL", cast=str)
DB_NAME = config("DB_NAME", cast=str)
client = MongoClient(DB_URL)
db = client[DB_NAME]
cars = db["cars"]
```

After importing the synchronous *MongoDB* driver, *PyMongo*, and setting it up using the environment variables, we can define our simple data-processing function:

```
def make_query(cars_number: int):
    query = [
        {"$match": {"year": {"$gt": 2010}}},
        {
            "$project": {
                "_id": 0,
            }
        },
        {"$sample": {"size": cars_number}},
        {"$sort": {"brand": 1, "make": 1, "year": 1}},
    ]
    full_query = cars.aggregate(query)
    results = [el for el in full_query]
    return pd.DataFrame(results).to_html(index=False)
```

The function simply makes a sample query – it picks `cars_num` at random, with the only condition that the year has to be greater than 2010, but you could make it as complex as needed of course. After making the aggregation, we are left with a list of dictionaries, something pandas has no problem turning into a DataFrame. We then use the simplest possible functionality and transform the DataFrame with the aggregation data into an HTML table, while removing the zero-based index.

> **Important Note**
>
> It is worth remembering that at this stage, we could potentially do anything with this data – transform it, interpolate it, or create static PNG or SVG charts and save them into files to be attached or embedded into PDF or DOCX documents.

Feel free to test the previous function by adding a `print` statement at the bottom of the file and actually invoking it from `/utilities`:

```
print(make_query(5))
```

It should display a valid HTML table with five random cars inside it.

Let's move on – so, we want to incorporate the email-sending functionality and for that, we need an emailing solution. While there are numerous options on the market, the choice really boils down to a couple of big companies that provide similar solutions. Here, I opted for SendGrid, one of the leaders in email management and a part of the *Twilio* company. They provide a free tier (the number of emails that we can send and test the service before committing is currently fixed at 100 emails per day) and a very friendly API for sending emails. Head over to the sign-up page `https://signup.sendgrid.com/` and fill in the required data.

*SendGrid* is a serious service and emails are tricky – you need to make sure that you are not spamming people, and that your emails are not marked as spam, deleted, or never opened. You will eventually need to validate your domain (the domain that will be used for sending real emails, in production). There is really a lot of work to be done to set up a production-grade email system, especially when you are targeting outside users that subscribe or create an account. This topic is a bit beyond the scope of this book and this chapter, so I will just stick to the very basics – in order to be able to send an email with SendGrid, you will need to verify your (free) account and provide a phone number for SMS validation. After that, you should make your first API key – once logged in, head over to the page, `https://app.sendgrid.com/settings/api_keys`, and create a Full Access API key. By now, you know the drill – copy the key in a secret `txt` file, and after that, update the `.env` file in the `/backend` directory:

```
SENDGRID_ID=SG.<very long string, like really looooong>
```

We also need to install the `sendgrid` Python library using the following:

```
pip install sendgrid
```

The relevant documentation is available on GitHub: `https://github.com/sendgrid/sendgrid-python`.

Now, let's create a file that will assemble and send the email – let's call it `send_email.py` – in the `/utils` folder:

```
from decouple import config
import sendgrid
from sendgrid.helpers.mail import *
SENDGRID_ID = config("SENDGRID_ID", cast=str)
```

We are importing the `decouple` library in order to access `SENDGRID_ID`, our API key, and after that, all the various `sendgrid` helpers. Let's proceed and build our email:

```
def send_report(email, subject, HTMLcontent):
    sg = sendgrid.SendGridAPIClient(api_key=SENDGRID_ID)
    from_email = Email("your@email.rs")
    to_email = To(email)
    subject = "FARM Cars daily report"
    content = Content(
        "text/plain", "this is dynamic text, potentially
            coming from our database"
```

```
    )
    mail = Mail(from_email, to_email, subject, content,
                html_content=HTMLcontent)
```

Most of the helpers are self-explanatory: first, we instantiate the client (`sg`) and then, we gradually add settings – `from_email`, `to_email`, `subject` (which we're going to customize later), the text content (which is mandatory, as is `html_content`) – that are going to generate our table converted from the pandas DataFrame.

> **Important Note**
>
> At this point, it is important to emphasize the fact that we are free here to craft any type of HTML within the reasonable email-imposed limits – we could (and should!) use an email design tool (there are many and they are usually WYSIWYG) and for the HTML, we can use the powerful Jinja2 templating language, which will be able to convert even the most complex data structures into HTML with ease. This is all just the tip of the iceberg – with the power of pandas and the Python data-wrangling ecosystem, we can create charts with Plotly, Matplotlib, Bokeh, or Altair, save them as PNGs or SVGs, and embed them in documents, whether PDFs or DOCXs (with the excellent `doxc-tpl` module), or in plain HTML! Charts could also potentially be saved on Cloudinary – the possibilities are endless.

Let's finish our email-sending file:

```
try:
    response =
        sg.client.mail.send.post(request_body=mail.get())
except Exception as e:
    print(e)
    print("Could not send email")
```

We now have both ingredients for our simple pipeline – we have a function that generates reports (or tables, rather) from the database and we have an email-sending function. All that's left to do is to connect the two. Edit the `utils/report.py` file:

```
from .report_query import make_query
from .send_report import send_report
def report_pipeline(email, cars_number):
    try:
        query_data = make_query(cars_number)
    except Exception as e:
        print(e)
```

```
        print("Couldn't make the query")
try:
        send_report(email=email, subject="FARM Cars
                Report", HTMLcontent=query_data)
except Exception as e:
        print(e)
```

I have wrapped the code into some `try` and `except` blocks, as errors are bound to happen. In a production system, we would want to log these errors in a verbose way since the FastAPI server will not take care of it and nobody likes diving through log files on Unix servers.

You should be able to test the React page now – so fire up the React server. If you enter your email and select a number, you should receive an ugly-looking email with a single HTML table inside. The functionality, however, can be easily extended at various points – we could embed machine-learning algorithms, cool static or dynamic visualizations, or create PDFs, Word reports, and Excel files with a predefined structure. Finally, with a little help from a package called FastAPI-utils, we can simulate a cron job and perform certain actions periodically. We are not trying to replace a full-fledged solution such as Streamlit or Plotly Dash – both excellent Python-based data analytics web solutions – but you can already see that the FARM stack allows you to achieve most of this functionality and flexibility. Coupled with a combination of D3.js and React, the types and the granularity of the dashboards, visualizations, and analyses that you can generate are practically unlimited.

Finally, as a bonus, and just to show how easily we can make our application not only buzzword-compliant but also more useful, we will implement a very simple machine-learning algorithm. Let's suppose that the management would love to have a basic prediction, a baseline, for the price of a car that has just been listed. We could train a model – a simple one or an incredibly complex stacked combination of different models – and embed it in our FastAPI server through a simple `/predict` endpoint. This part of the chapter is really optional and if you aren't into machine learning models, feel free to skip this section.

The endpoint is really simple – it just accepts the brand, make, year, cm3, and km values for a car and, based on this data, tries to predict the price of said car. The admin or the salesperson can then based on this predicted price, act accordingly – choose it as a minimum sale price or as a basis to compare to the price that the owner gave, for example. First, we need to install two Python libraries in our FastAPI virtual environment:

```
pip install pandas joblib
```

Let's build the endpoint now – in the `cars` router, add the following endpoint:

```
@router.post("/predict", response_description="Predict price")
async def predict(
    brand: str = Body(...),
```

```
    make: str = Body(...),
    year: int = Body(...),
    cm3: int = Body(...),
    km: int = Body(...),
):
    loaded_model =
       joblib.load("./random_forest_pipe.joblib")
    input_data = {
        "brand": brand,
        "make": make,
        "year": year,
        "cm3": cm3,
        "km": km,
    }

    from_db_df = pd.DataFrame(input_data, index=[0])
    prediction = float(loaded_model.predict(from_db_df)[0])
    return {"prediction": prediction}
```

The preceding code takes in the car data from the request body and converts it into a pandas DataFrame with just one row. After that, it is passed to a loaded `joblib` model, which is previously trained and saved in scikit-learn using the `Joblib` library for saving (or dumping) models.

The simple Python code used for generating this model, based on the data from our database, is contained in a Jupyter Notebook on the internet and should you be so inclined, you are free to explore it and modify it accordingly. The dataset that I used in this book is clean and overly simplified – features are eliminated, the number of brands is very restricted, and outliers have been removed, so it will not be difficult to achieve pretty high metric scores. Real-life data is messy, dirty, and full of interdependencies, so models should have increased complexities. This is just an example of how easy it would be to connect a machine-learning pipeline with our pluggable FastAPI server.

Now, it is time to push our code to GitHub, since this is where we are going to feed it to DigitalOcean and Netlify.

## Summary

This was a pretty long chapter, but I hope that it wasn't boring. After having covered more conventional web apps in the previous chapters, we were able to dig in a little deeper here and see what this particular stack had to offer. We created some API endpoints based on MongoDB aggregations and we were able to turn them into visualizations with Chart.js, but you should feel comfortable enough to plug in your visualization solution of choice. We have seen how to leverage SWR- and React-specific fetching strategies in order to make our sites snappy and performant. We have also explored the Background Tasks feature that FastAPI provides and how it can help us perform some time-consuming tasks – we used it to implement a simple email-sending system, while introducing SendGrid, a powerful enterprise-level emailing solution.

In the next chapter, we are going to deploy our analytics application – we will serve FastAPI from a robust Ubuntu server featuring Nginx and Gunicorn, while the frontend will be hosted on Netlify, the most popular static-hosting continuous integration solution. While we're at it, we will implement a simple cache with Redis, making our FastAPI application potentially even faster!

# 10

# Caching with Redis and Deployment on Ubuntu (DigitalOcean) and Netlify

In this chapter, we are going to explore yet another deployment setup – a robust Uvicorn/Gunicorn/Nginx solution that has been tried and tested with Django and other WSGIs but also ASGI web applications. This should give you more than enough choices when starting your next FARM stack project. We will also add a simple caching solution with Redis, relieving MongoDB from some requests that could (and should!) be cached and served directly. Finally, we will deploy our React-based frontend on Netlify, another very popular deployment option, whose simplicity matches its flexibility.

In this chapter, we will cover the following topics:

- Creating an account on DigitalOcean (optional)

- Preparing our Ubuntu server with Nginx

- Deployment of a FastAPI instance through Uvicorn, Gunicorn, and Nginx

- Caching with Redis

- Creating a free account on Netlify

- Deployment of the React Frontend on Netlify

By the end of this chapter, you should feel confident when it comes to deploying FARM stack-based applications on a variety of serving platforms, including a bare-bones Ubuntu (or any Linux) server. You will be able to recognize where and how to add caching and implement it effortlessly with Redis. Finally, with the knowledge of possible deployment solutions, you will be able to make solid decisions when the time comes to deploy your application.

# Deploying FastAPI on DigitalOcean (or really any Linux server!)

In this section, we are going to take our simple analytics application and deploy it on a Ubuntu server on *DigitalOcean* (www.digitalocean.com) as an **Asynchronous Server Gateway Interface (ASGI)** application. We are going to end up with a pretty robust and customizable setup that includes our development web server – Uvicorn – but also Gunicorn (https://gunicorn.org), an excellent and robust web server that plays very nicely with *Nginx*, and a virtual machine running Ubuntu – a *DigitalOcean* droplet. Though in this example we are going to use DigitalOcean, the procedure should apply to any Debian or Ubuntu-based setup; you can try it out on your own machine running Ubuntu. The following instructions rely heavily on the excellent tutorials on setting up an Ubuntu server on *DigitalOcean* by Brian Boucheron (https://www.digitalocean.com/community/tutorials/initial-server-setup-with-ubuntu-20-04) and on deploying an Async Django application by Mason Egger and Erin Glass (https://www.digitalocean.com/community/tutorials/how-to-set-up-an-asgi-django-app-with-postgres-nginx-and-uvicorn-on-ubuntu-20-04). You should read them as they are very useful and well written!

> **Important Note**
>
> In this section, we will make heavy use of SSH – the Secure Shell Protocol. SSH is a cryptographic protocol developed for accessing secure network services over insecure networks. If that doesn't make much sense, do not worry – there are plenty of great resources on basic SSH operations on the internet. If you are willing to dive a bit deeper into DevOps, you can read the following book: https://www.amazon.com/Mastering-Ubuntu-Server-configuring-troubleshooting/dp/1800564643. *Mastering Ubuntu Server* is an excellent guide on the subject. In the following pages, we will just log into a DigitalOcean droplet, which is nothing more than a remote Ubuntu computer that we will be able to control. While I will show the procedure for deploying a fully functional FastAPI instance on a DigitalOcean droplet, the best way to try out this procedure would be to practice on your Ubuntu-based server. If you have a spare box (even an older one), install Ubuntu and try connecting to it from your main computer.

The deployment procedure will be broken into easy steps.

*DigitalOcean* is one of the leaders in providing cloud computing and **Infrastructure as a Service (IaaS)**. Users can benefit from different types of virtual machines that can be modeled according to our needs. In our case, we just want a solution for hosting our FastAPI server, similar to how we did with Heroku in the previous chapters.

While *DigitalOcean* doesn't provide a completely free tier, it is reasonably cheap to get started (around 4 USD per month). It has a flexible and scalable system where you can easily scale up or down according to your needs and it offers complete control of the virtual machines – droplets, a fact that brings us a whole new level of flexibility, a word that we often used in this book. Another advantage of *DigitalOcean* is its excellent community and an endless list of well-written articles on any service or setup you may want to achieve, so it represents a good place to start if you are entering the world of deployment, database setup, and so on. Just to be clear, *DigitalOcean*, as well as its competitors (Linode, for instance) is perfectly able to host our complete full-stack setup – we could install MongoDB on the server as well, add Node.js and Next or a React frontend, and orchestrate everything through Nginx, a powerful and fast server. In this example, however, we only want to serve our FastAPI instance and showcase a different type of deployment. Follow these steps:

1. Create an account on DigitalOcean! Head over to the DigitalOcean signup page at `https://cloud.digitalocean.com/registrations/new` and fill in your data. You can sign in with GitHub or Google if you wish, and you can use a referral code if you have one so that you can try out the service for a determined time. Once you submit your data (and once you have some credit to spend – be it from a referral program or after you connect your credit card), you will be able to create your first droplet.

2. Create a droplet. I have used a Ubuntu 22.04 x64 Ubuntu distribution, the plan is Basic (the cheapest), and the CPU options are $4/month with 512 MB/1 CPU (you will have to hit the left arrow to find this plan!). Since I am in Europe, I selected the Frankfurt data center region. Finally, to simplify things, I opted for password authentication, so I entered a root password (that I am not going to disclose here!). I gave the hostname a name – `farmstack`. Although we will be using the IP address to access this brand-new machine through SSH, it is useful to have a user-friendly machine name.

   Give DigitalOcean some time to prepare your droplet. After about 30 seconds, you will be able to click on the lefthand menu under **Droplets** and you will be taken to a page that displays information about your droplet. You now have a Ubuntu-based server under your control!

3. To verify that you are indeed able to log in as root on your brand-new machine, click on the IP address of the droplet to copy it, open **Cmder** (or whatever shell you have been using this whole time) on Windows or a bash/shell if you are on Linux or macOS, and try to access the droplet:

   ```
   ssh root@<your_IP_address_that_you_just_copied>
   ```

4. *Cmder* will kindly inform you that the authenticity of the host cannot be established, which is normal at this stage, and ask you if you want to continue connecting. Type `yes`; you will be greeted with a shell that should read as follows:

   ```
   root@farmstack:~#
   ```

5. It is good practice to create a new user account that will have all the necessary privileges so that we don't use the root account for our web hosting. Let's create an account called `farmuser`:

   ```
   adduser farmuser
   ```

6.  You will be asked to provide a password (twice), a name, and some other information, such as a room number (!). It is important to remember the password! This newly created user will need to be able to perform various administrative tasks, so we should grant them adequate privileges. In the same SSH session, type the following:

```
usermod -aG sudo farmuser
```

After this, when we log in as `farmuser`, we will be able to just type `sudo` before performing actions that require superuser powers.

We will make use of the *UFW* firewall to make sure that only certain types of connections to our server are permitted. There are different options when it comes to DigitalOcean's firewalls, but this should be more than enough and easy to set up on different machines. Things may get tricky, though – we need to make sure that when we leave our SSH root shell, we *will* be able to get back in with our `farmuser` account!

7.  To be sure that OpenSSH is allowed to access the machine, type the following:

```
ufw allow OpenSSH
```

8.  You should see a message saying **rules updated**. Now, let's enable `ufw` and check its status:

```
ufw enable
ufw status
```

The preceding commands should warn you that they may disrupt existing *SSH* connections; confirm the first one anyway. The second should just inform you that the service is active.

9.  Great. Now, **Keep the SSH session alive** and open a new terminal so that we can test our connection with our regular yet highly privileged `farmuser`:

```
ssh farmuser@<your_IP_address_that_you_just_copied>
```

You should be greeted with a prompt; that is, `farmuser@farmstack:~$`. That's great – now, we can proceed with this (regular) user and use `sudo` when we need to do tricky stuff!

It is time to update our Ubuntu packages and add some more. Logged in as `farmuser` (or whatever your regular, non-root username was), issue the following command:

```
sudo apt update
sudo apt install python3-venv nginx curl
```

`sudo` will prompt you for a password – your regular `farmuser` password – so kindly provide it. Apart from Python 3, we are installing `Nginx`, our powerful web server and reverse proxy solution, and `curl` (to test our API service locally).

Now, we are entering the second, project-related phase of our deployment. It is time to create a virtual environment, just like we did numerous times during the development phase. This is a bare-bones server, so we have to do everything manually. There is no helpful guiding hand like there was with *Heroku* or *Vercel*. Follow these steps:

1.  Let's create a directory called `apiserver` in our home folder and `cd` into it (you can always see where you are currently located with PWD!):

    ```
    mkdir ~/apiserver
    cd ~/apiserver
    ```

2.  Now, let's create a Python 3 environment:

    ```
    python3 -m venv venv
    ```

3.  After the setup has finished, go ahead and activate this environment with the following command:

    ```
    source venv/bin/activate
    ```

    You should see `venv` prepending the command prompt.

4.  It is time to grab the address of the GitHub repository that you created for the backend and change the directory to our `/apiserver`. Now, clone the GitHub repo inside to get all the code:

    ```
    git clone <your repo address>
    ```

    This will create a folder with the same name as the repository – in my case, it is a bit cumbersome: `FARM-chapter9-backend`. Cloning the code from the repo will not copy the `.env` file with the necessary keys for MongoDB and Sendgrid (and Cloudinary in the previous app).

5.  Although we could set the environment variables manually through the shell, we are just going to blatantly copy them using the secure copy `scp` command. Make sure you're in your local computer's `/backend` folder and take note of the remote folder. Then, issue the following command:

    ```
    scp .env farmuser@207.154.254.114:~/apiserver/FARM-
    chapter9-backend
    ```

6.  Now try out the `ls` command to make sure that the folder with the code is indeed there, but keep in mind that the `.env` file will not be shown! You will have to use something such as nano `.env` to verify that the file is indeed there and that it contains the necessary information. If you don't want to mess with `scp`, you can just create and type in the `.env` file using nano – the powerful command-line text editor provided by Linux systems.

7.  Once the code is in the Ubuntu droplet, `cd` into the directory and install all the dependencies with the following command:

    ```
    pip install -r requirements.txt
    ```

> **Important Note**
>
> After committing the code for the backend, you should update the `requirements.txt` file by typing `pip freeze > requirements.txt`, while being within the activated virtual environment on your local machine. This file should then be committed to GitHub – it will be our magic ingredient for recreating the same virtual environment on other machines, including our droplet!

8. Once the dependencies have been installed, we can test our application with the standard Uvicorn command:

```
uvicorn main:app -reload
```

The prompt should inform you that Uvicorn is running on `http://127.0.0.1:8000` but that we cannot access it yet from the outside.

9. Stop the server with *Ctrl + C*. To be able to test that the API is working, we have to disable our UFW firewall. To do that, you have to `sudo` your way through it:

```
sudo ufw disable
```

> **Notice**
>
> This is a dangerous practice – a bit like leaving your front door open.

Now, if you try to rerun the *Uvicorn* server, you should be able to access your API with a REST client or a browser at the IP address of your droplet, on port `8000`! So far, we are only trying out what we have been doing throughout this book on DigitalOcean. Now, it is time to introduce Gunicorn.

> **Important Note**
>
> **Gunicorn** is a mature and battle-tested WSGI Python server for UNIX. It is often used in conjunction with Uvicorn since it is highly configurable and able to handle Uvicorn workers efficiently. The Uvicorn documentation itself recommends a setup that includes Gunicorn and Nginx and that is exactly what we are going to do! Gunicorn is an interesting and powerful project in its own right and its documentation is is a useful read (`https://gunicorn.org/`).

Let's build our deployment now. Follow these steps:

1. Install `gunicorn` with a simple call to `pip`:

```
pip install gunicorn
```

2.  After installing `gunicorn`, we can start our API server with the following command (while staying in the source code directory!):

    **`gunicorn --bind 0.0.0.0:8000 main:app -w 4 -k uvicorn.`**
    **`workers.UvicornWorker`**

    The preceding command starts a *gunicorn* server with four *uvicorn* workers. Gunicorn provides also load balancing functionality for our Uvicorn servers – an async request that might be taking a bit too long won't hog up the system. Now, we can test our app on port 8000.

    Now, we are going to use Linux's powerful `systemd` service and socket files to make the server start and stop programmatically.

    > **Important Note**
    >
    > **systemd** is a process and system manager for Linux systems. If you wish to get to know its capabilities and functionalities, I can recommend (another) very useful article from the DigitalOcean knowledge database: `https://www.digitalocean.com/community/tutorials/systemd-essentials-working-with-services-units-and-the-journal`. Again, in these pages, we will only explain the commands that we will be using – starting, stopping, and enabling and disabling services, servers, and so on.

3.  We are going to have to use a bit of `nano`, the command-line text editor of choice for the majority of Linux distributions. Stop the `gunicorn` server with *Crtl + C* and deactivate the virtual environment with a simple `deactivate`. The prepended `venv` should be gone.

4.  Now, let's create a `gunicorn` socket. Sockets are simply communication points on the same or different computers that enable systems to exchange data. When we create a Gunicorn socket, it is just a way of telling the system that the created socket can be used to access data that the server will provide:

    **`sudo nano /etc/systemd/system/gunicorn.socket`**

    The file's content should be as follows (fully adapted from the aforementioned ASGI Django guide):

    ```
    [Unit]
    Description=gunicorn socket

    [Socket]
    ListenStream=/run/gunicorn.sock

    [Install]
    WantedBy=sockets.target
    ```

5.  To leave nano, just type *Ctrl + X* and type `yes` when asked to confirm. The filename should remain the same as what we gave it initially.

6.  Now, we are going to create the `gunicorn.service` file. Again, fire up *nano* with the following command:

    ```
    sudo nano /etc/systemd/system/gunicorn.service
    ```

7.  Begin typing the following:

    ```
    [Unit]
    Description=gunicorn daemon
    Requires=gunicorn.socket
    After=network.target


    [Service]
    User=farmuser
    Group=www-data
    WorkingDirectory=/home/farmuser/apiserver/FARM-chapter9-
    backend
    ExecStart=/home/farmuser/apiserver/venv/bin/gunicorn \
            --access-logfile - \
            -k uvicorn.workers.UvicornWorker \
            --workers 3 \
            --bind unix:/run/gunicorn.sock \
        main:app


    [Install]
    WantedBy=multi-user.target
    ```

    I have highlighted the essential parts and paths that you should triple-check before saving. It is important to emphasize that the working directory is the directory *hosting our code*, while `execstart` is referring to the `virtualenv` directory. In our case, they are side by side inside the `apiserver` folder! This should be enough for `systemd`.

8.  Save the file and let's try it out. Start and enable the newly created `gunicorn` socket with the following commands:

    ```
    sudo systemctl start gunicorn.socket
    sudo systemctl enable gunicorn.socket
    ```

9. If everything went right, there shouldn't be any errors. You should, however, check the status of the socket:

```
sudo systemctl status gunicorn.socket
```

10. You should also check for the existence of the `gunicorn.sock` file:

```
file /run/gunicorn.sock
```

11. Now, activate the socket:

```
sudo systemctl status gunicorn
```

12. With that, we should be able to (finally!) test our API with `curl`:

```
curl --unix-socket /run/gunicorn.sock localhost/cars/all
```

You should get a bunch of cars flooding the terminal since we've hit our `cars` endpoint!

We're nearly there, hang on! Now, we will use Nginx to route the incoming traffic. Follow these steps:

> **Important Note**
> Nginx is an extremely powerful, reliable, and fast web server, load balancer, and proxy server. At its most basic, Nginx reads its configuration and, based on this information, decides what to do with each request that it encounters – it can simultaneously handle multiple websites, multiple processes, and the most diverse configurations that you throw at it. You may have a bunch of static files, images, and documents in one location on the server, a Node.js API managed by PM2, a Django or Flask website, and maybe a FastAPI instance all at once. With the proper configuration, Nginx will be able to effortlessly take care of this mess and always serve the right resource to the right client. At least some basic knowledge of how Nginx operates can be a very useful tool to have under your belt, and the `nginx.org` website is a great place to start.

13. Nginx operates in server blocks, so let's create one for our `apiserver`:

```
server {
    listen 80;
    server_name <your droplet's IP address>
    location = /favicon.ico { access_log off; log_not_
found off; }

    location / {
        include proxy_params;
        proxy_pass http://unix:/run/gunicorn.sock;
```

```
        }
    }
```

Once you get used to Nginx's server block syntax, you will be serving websites (or processes, to be precise) in no time. In the preceding code, we instructed Nginx to listen on the default port (80) for our machine (IP address) and to redirect all traffic to our Unix Gunicorn socket!

14. Now, enable the file by copying it to the `sites-enabled` folder of Nginx, as follows:

```
sudo ln -s /etc/nginx/sites-available/myproject /etc/
nginx/sites-enabled
```

There is a very handy command that allows us to check if the Nginx configuration is valid:

```
sudo nginx -t
```

15. If Nginx is not complaining, we can restart it by typing the following command; then, we should be good to go:

```
sudo systemctl restart nginx
```

16. The last thing we must do is set up the `ufw` firewall again, allow Nginx to pass through, and close port `8000` by removing the rule that allowed it:

```
sudo ufw delete allow 8000
sudo ufw allow 'Nginx Full'
```

Congratulations! You are now serving your API through a robust setup that consists of Uvicorn, Gunicorn, and Nginx. With this setup, we have a plethora of options. You could serve static files (images, stylesheets, or documents) blazingly fast through Nginx. You could also set up a Next.js project and manage it through PM2 (https://pm2.keymetrics.io/), a powerful Node.js process manager. We will stop here, although there are many – not so complicated – steps to go through before we have a production-ready system.

## Adding caching with Redis

Redis is among the top technologies when it comes to NoSQL data storage options, and it is very different from MongoDB. Redis is an in-memory data structure store, and it can be used as a database, cache, message broker, and also for streaming. Redis provides simple data structures – hashes, lists, strings, sets, and more –and enables scripting with the Lua language. While it can be used as a primary data store, it is often used for caching or running analytics and similar tasks. Since it is built to be incredibly fast (much faster than MongoDB, to be clear), it is ideal for caching database or data store queries, results of complex computations, API calls, and managing the session state. MongoDB, on the other hand, while being fast and flexible, if it scales sufficiently, could slow down a bit. Bearing in mind that we often (as is the case in this chapter) host MongoDB on one server (Atlas Cloud) and our FastAPI code on another one (DigitalOcean or Heroku), latency also might affect the response times. Imagine if we wanted to perform a complex aggregation instead of the simple ones that we have created in this chapter. By throwing in some data science, such as algorithms with interpolations or machine learning algorithms, we could be in trouble should our website become popular (and it will!).

Caching to the rescue! What is caching? It is a really simple concept that has been around for decades – the basic idea is to store some frequently requested data (from a Mongo database, in our case) in some type of temporary storage for some time until it expires. The first user requesting said resource (a list of cars) will have to wait for the whole query to complete and will get the results. These results will then automatically be added to this temporary storage (in our case, Redis, the Usain Bolt of databases) and served to all subsequent requests for the same data. By the same data, we usually imply the same endpoint. This process persists until the data stored in Redis (or any other caching solution that you may use) expires – if valid data is not found in the cache, the real database call is made again and the process repeats.

The expiry time is of crucial importance here – in our case, if we are working with a car-selling company, we can be generous with caching and extend the expiry period to 10 minutes or even more. In more dynamic applications, such as forums or similar conversational environments, a much lower expiry time would be mandatory to preserve functionality.

Installing Redis on Linux is quite simple, while on Windows it is not officially supported. You could follow the official guide for installing Redis for development purposes on Windows (`https://redis.io/docs/getting-started/installation/install-redis-on-windows/`) but that is beyond the scope of our application. We will, however, install Redis on our DigitalOcean Linux box and add caching to our FastAPI application!

Connect to your DigitalOcean box (or to your Linux system of choice – if you are developing on Linux or Mac, you should install it there as well) by following the steps from this chapter, while using SSH from a terminal:

1.  Now, install Redis by typing the following command:

```
sudo apt install redis-server
```

> **Important Note**
> In a production environment, you should secure your Redis server with a disgustingly long password. Since Redis is fast, an attacker could potentially run hundreds of thousands of passwords in mere seconds against it during a brute-force attack. You should also disable or rename some potentially dangerous Redis commands. In these pages, we are only showing how to add a bare-bones, not-secured Redis instance to our setup.

2.  Now, we should restart the Redis service. Although it should happen automatically, let's make sure by typing the following command:

```
sudo systemctl restart redis.service
```

3.  Test it by typing the following command to see if it is working:

```
sudo systemctl status redis
```

The Terminal will send an ample response, but what you are looking for is the green word **Active** (running). It should also be started automatically with every reboot – so we get that going for us, which is nice.

4.  The traditional way to test that Redis is responding is to start the client:

```
redis-cli
```

Then, in the Redis shell, type `ping`.

Redis should respond with `pong` and the prompt should say **127.0.0.1:6379**. This means that Redis is running on localhost (the Linux server) on port `6379`. Remember this address, or better, write it down somewhere (I know, I know). We are going to need it for our FastAPI server.

There are many ways to make Redis talk to Python, but here, we will opt for a simple module aptly named *Fastapi-cache* (`https://github.com/long2ice/fastapi-cache`). Now, we will have to edit our backend code in the `/backend` folder. When we're done, we will push the changes to GitHub and repeat the deployment procedure. Or, if you just want to quickly try out the caching, you could edit the files on *DigitalOcean* directly by navigating to the directory and using *nano*.

Anyway, activate the virtual environment of your choice and install the package and *aioredis* (the async Python Redis driver):

```
pip install fastapi-cache2 aioredis
```

Now, our FastAPI project structure dictates which files need to be updated. We need to update our `main.py` file and add the following imports:

```
import aioredis
from fastapi_cache import FastAPICache
from fastapi_cache.backends.redis import RedisBackend
```

Then, we need to update our startup event handler:

```
@app.on_event("startup")
async def startup_db_client():
    app.mongodb_client = AsyncIOMotorClient(DB_URL)
```

```
app.mongodb = app.mongodb_client[DB_NAME]
redis = aioredis.from_url(
    "redis://localhost:6379", encoding="utf8", decode_
        responses=True
)
FastAPICache.init(RedisBackend(redis), prefix="fastapi-
    cache")
```

The code makes sense – we're getting a Redis client, just like we did with Mongo, and we are passing the URL and a couple of (suggested) settings. Finally, we initialized the *FastAPICache*. Now, we need to add the caching decorator to our endpoints, which are located in the /routers/cars.py file. We will add one import:

```
from fastapi_cache.decorator import cache
```

Now, we can decorate the routes that we wish to cache (only GET requests, but that's all we have in this project really). Edit the /sample route:

```
@router.get("/sample/{n}", response_description="Sample of N
cars")
@cache(expire=60)
async def get_sample(n: int, request: Request):
    query = [
        {"$match": {"year": {"$gt": 2010}}},
        {
            "$project": {"_id": 0,}
        },
        {"$sample": {"size": n}},
        {"$sort": {"brand": 1, "make": 1, "year": 1}},
    ]
    full_query = request.app.mongodb["cars"].aggregate(query)
    results = [el async for el in full_query]
    return results
```

This route is now cached, which means that when it's hit, it will provide a sample of size *N* and then, for all subsequent requests in the next 60 seconds, it will send the same cached response. Go ahead and try it out, either on your DigitalOcean API or local environment, depending on where you implemented caching. Try *hitting* the API for 1 minute – you should always get the same result until the cache expires. Congratulations – you have just added a top-of-the-class caching solution to your API!

# Deploying the Frontend on Netlify

Similar to Vercel, Netlify is one of the top companies providing services for static web hosting and serverless computing, but also a rather simple CMS and goodies such as form handling. It is widely regarded as one of the best solutions for hosting *JAMStack* websites and its **content delivery network (CDN)** can speed up the hosted websites significantly. It is also one of the easiest ways to host a React application. This is what we are going to use it for in this section.

After logging in with your Google or GitHub account, you will be presented with a screen that offers you the possibility to deploy a new project:

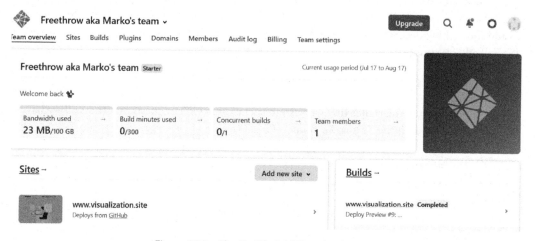

Figure 10.1 – The Netlify Add New Site button

Next, you will be asked whether you are importing an existing project (yes!); you should choose your React frontend project from GitHub. If you logged in with GitHub, you won't have to authorize Netlify again – if not, please authorize it:

Figure 10.2 – The Import and existing project page on Netlify

After browsing through your GitHub projects, point Netlify to the React frontend and leave all the defaults that Netlify was able to cleverly infer from the project. You will be presented with a page on which you could potentially modify any deployment setting, but we will limit ourselves to just adding a single environment variable. You've guessed it – it's the handy `REACT_APP_API_URL`!

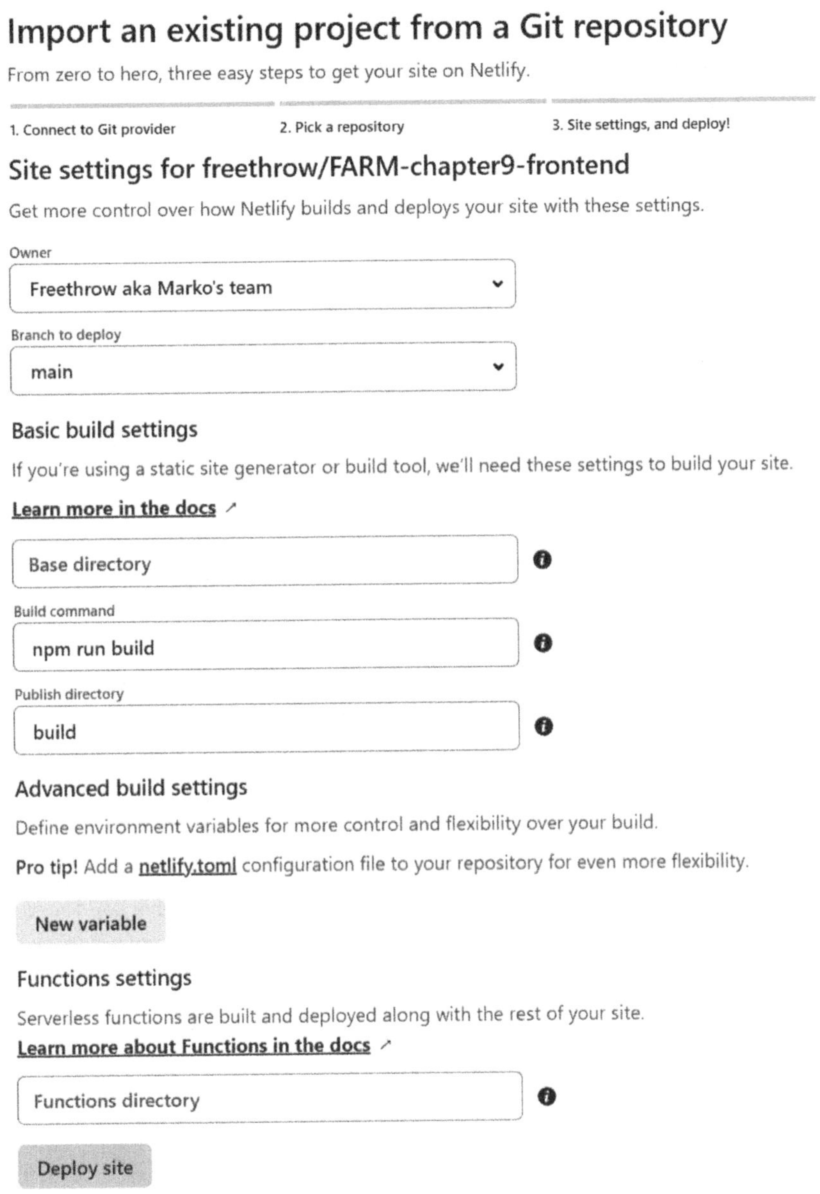

## Import an existing project from a Git repository

From zero to hero, three easy steps to get your site on Netlify.

| 1. Connect to Git provider | 2. Pick a repository | 3. Site settings, and deploy! |
|---|---|---|

### Site settings for freethrow/FARM-chapter9-frontend

Get more control over how Netlify builds and deploys your site with these settings.

Owner
> Freethrow aka Marko's team            ⌄

Branch to deploy
> main            ⌄

### Basic build settings

If you're using a static site generator or build tool, we'll need these settings to build your site.

**Learn more in the docs** ↗

> Base directory            ⓘ

Build command
> npm run build            ⓘ

Publish directory
> build            ⓘ

### Advanced build settings

Define environment variables for more control and flexibility over your build.

**Pro tip!** Add a **netlify.toml** configuration file to your repository for even more flexibility.

[ New variable ]

### Functions settings

Serverless functions are built and deployed along with the rest of your site.

**Learn more about Functions in the docs** ↗

> Functions directory            ⓘ

[ Deploy site ]

Figure 10.3 – Netlify's pre-deployment setting page

You will have to add just one variable in the advanced settings: you've guessed it – REACT_APP_API_URL. Create a **New variable** by hitting the respective button and name it REACT_APP_API_URL. The value should be https://yourdomain.com:

## Basic build settings

If you're using a static site generator or build tool, we'll need these settings to build your site.

**Learn more in the docs** ↗

| Base directory | ⓘ |
|---|---|

Build command

| npm run build | ⓘ |
|---|---|

Publish directory

| build | ⓘ |
|---|---|

## Advanced build settings

Define environment variables for more control and flexibility over your build.

**Pro tip!** Add a **netlify.toml** configuration file to your repository for even more flexibility.

| Key | Value |
|---|---|
| REACT_APP_API_URL | http://207.154.254.1  👁  ⊗ |

Figure 10.4 – Adding the new environment variable in Netlify

After some time, maybe a minute or so, you will have your deployment ready for the world to see! In case of any problems (and there will be problems), you should inspect Netlify's deployment console and watch for hiccups.

Your React frontend with all its fancy charts and fast pagination will now be served from Netlify's fast **content delivery network (CDN)** while operating on a FastAPI (cached) backend served by Nginx on DigitalOcean. Throw in our previously explored Heroku and Vercel deployments and you have a lot of options to start tinkering!

This doesn't mean that these are your only deployment options! A popular and rock-solid choice is to use a Docker container and containerize your application (together or separately) and provide this Docker image to some of the giants – **Amazon Web Services (AWS)**, Microsoft Azure, or Google App Engine. This type of deployment isn't much different from the Heroku deployment, although it requires creating the proper type of account and setting the environment the right way. These solutions also tend to have higher upfront costs.

# Summary

In this chapter, we added a very simple yet powerful caching solution based on Redis – an incredibly powerful product in its own right. We went through the tedious but often necessary procedure of hosting the API on a Ubuntu server behind Gunicorn and the mighty Nginx – a server that offers so much flexibility and configurability that it simply has to be put in the conversation of the FARM stack. As a bonus, we explored yet another cheap (well, free) frontend hosting option – Netlify – which offers premiere continuous deployment and plays very nicely with all our frontend solutions, be it plain React or Next.js or maybe, in the future, React-Remix. Now, you should feel confident enough to dive head-first into your next project and peruse the numerous options that FastAPI, React, and MongoDB have to offer by playing nicely with each other.

In the next chapter, we will try to address some of the best practices that pertain to the components of the stack in every project, as well as some topics that we haven't touched on but are equally important, such as testing, using static templates with Jinja2, site monitoring, and more.

# 11

# Useful Resources and Project Ideas

In the final chapter of this guide to building applications with FastAPI, React, and MongoDB, we will use the FARM stack components to briefly touch on or cover topics that are important, often crucial, but haven't been discussed in the previous chapters, as well as reccomend some further further actions that you could partake if you want to deepen your understanding of the technologies that build up this interesting and flexible stack.

We will provide you with some guidelines when it comes to building data-driven or data-intensive applications, as well as some practical advice when working with the FARM stack and maybe some ideas for projects where the FARM stack (or very similar stacks) could fare pretty well. As a side note, I will add a couple of thoughts on learning and finding your way in the ever-growing and always-changing web development and analytics fields. This will be helpful for those who come from the most diverse backgrounds, but their jobs or maybe their newfound passion drives them to find a path through the data-driven world of the 21st century.

In this chapter, we will cover the following topics:

- MongoDB Considerations
- FastAPI and Python Considerations
- React Practices
- Other Topics
- Some project ideas to get started

# MongoDB considerations

In *Chapter 2, Setting Up the Document Store with MongoDB*, we provided a concise introduction to MongoDB that should be enough to get you started with simpler projects. However, MongoDB is a complex ecosystem employed by enterprise-level companies, so diving deeper into its features and patterns will only benefit your developer's abilities and understanding of the NoSQL paradigm.

One of the first steps in this direction is data modeling or schema design – and it is often said that your data model should reflect how your application will see the data and its flow, starting from the queries you will be making. There are advanced design patterns that apply to MongoDB schemas that are beyond the scope of this book.

Some of the more popular MongoDB document modeling suggestions were mentioned in *Chapter 2, Setting Up the Document Store with MongoDB*, but let's add some more, formulated differently – they tend to sound a bit like Haiku poetry:

- Objects should be combined, in the same document, if they are meant to be used together

- When separating objects into different documents, try not to make JOINs necessary, although simple LEFT JOINS are possible through the Aggregation Framework

- The frequency of the data use cases should dictate the schemas – the most frequent data flows should be the easiest to access

Coming from the relational database world, modeling relationships often boils down to the choice between *embedding and referencing*. In our simple application of used cars, we opted to reference the user ID when we made the CRUD application with the users since it was the simplest thing to do, but that could probably apply to a real-world setting as well. There are numerous empirical rules, so to speak – if the *many* sides of a *one-to-many* relationship could contain hundreds of items, embedding is probably not the best way to go, and so on.

As one of the numerous and useful MongoDB guides provided by the Mongo Team itself states, in a semi-joking tone, embedding should be preferred in relationships that are *one-to-one*, *one-to-few*, and *one-to-many*, while referencing should be used in *one-to-very-numerous-many* and *many-to-many* cases (`https://www.mongodb.com/developer/products/mongodb/mongodb-schema-design-best-practices/`).

As a side note, Python drivers such as *PyMongo* and its async sibling, *Motor*, play extremely nicely with MongoDB. Given Python's rich data structure system and data processing capabilities, it is relatively easy to change and mix things up, change schemas on the fly, and try out different types of documents until you find the optimal (or suboptimal, but good enough) solution for your particular use case.

I want to finish this section by mentioning two interesting projects that could be included in some of your applications: **Beanie** (`https://roman-right.github.io/beanie/`) is an **Asynchronous Python object-document mapper** (**ODM**) for *MongoDB based on Motor and Pydantic* that can speed up the creation of CRUD applications. Another interesting project is **Mongita** (`https://github.com/scottrogowski/mongita`), which dubs itself as a SQLite for MongoDB. It could be particularly interesting as an embedded database for lighter cases in which you want the keep the data local, or for prototyping even before having to set up MongoDB or Atlas.

# FastAPI and Python considerations

This book intentionally omits a brief Python tutorial and there are several reasons why this was a decision from the start. Apart from becoming ubiquitous and omnipresent, it Python encompasses data and text processing, web development, data science, machine learning, numerical computations, visualizations, and virtually every possible aspect of computing (it has even had a brief excursion into the browser's world, the Kingdom of JavaScript). Python is a truly beautiful and peculiar language, built with a purpose and developed over the years into the modern versions (3.6+ at the time of writing) that we use now. Although its syntax and keywords are simple and the language has been written with clarity in mind, it takes some time to learn and then some practice to learn the *Pythonic* way of doing things. Being so popular as Python is, it has various benefits, so there are excellent Python books and courses that emphasize the proper use of Python's rich data structures and the way it treats objects and functions, as well as the modern async paradigms that are often used in FastAPI and when interacting with MongoDB. So, dedicating it a mere chapter or two couldn't do it justice, in my humble opinion.

What is considered good practice in Python is valid in FastAPI. However, because FastAPI itself translates simple Python functions (or even classes, inspired by Django's class-based views) into REST API endpoints so seamlessly, you don't have to do anything out of the ordinary. FastAPI is built in a way that favors you, the developer, giving you the necessary flexibility and smoothness that you may even forget that you're writing an API.

Some fairly generic considerations that should be part of your FastAPI development process are as follows:

- Use *Git* and *GitHub*, learn a simple workflow, and stick to it. It is easier to learn one workflow and use it until you get used to it and then switch, rather than trying to learn all the commands at once, especially if you're a one-man-band trying to automate or *REST-ify* a business process!

- Keep your environment variables in `.env` files, but also back them up somewhere (API keys, external services credentials, and so on).

- If you haven't already, even if you're a seasoned Python developer or you have maybe written just a text processing script or two, learn Python's *type hinting* system. It is closely related to *Pydantic* and it adds a layer of robustness to your overall code. It is also an integral part of coding a FastAPI application.

- *Structure* your application properly. Although it is very easy and tempting to create even a feature-rich application in a single file, especially if you do not have a clear specification, resist this urge. The FastAPI documentation site has an excellent page on structuring larger applications and the internet already has some variations of it.

The main idea is to break the application into routers and Pydantic models so that they have separate directories (we had a `/routers` directory in the book, so we should have had a `/models` directory as well). These directories should each have an empty `__init__.py`, making them Python modules. I put external service utilities either in a separate file or in a `/utils` directory, but you could go granular, depending on the complexity of your app. Keep in mind that you will always end up with an ASGI application that is the only endpoint referenced by your server of choice, be it Uvicorn or something else.

## Testing FastAPI applications

I have left out the most important topic that was not covered in this book for last – testing. Put simply, testing is necessary to ensure that our application behaves the way it was supposed to. Without delving into the theory of **test-driven development** (TDD) in which tests are written before the actual code, here, I will just point out some specific issues that you may run into when working with the async MongoDB driver (Motor) and FastAPI. Unit testing your API is essential and, to be honest, isn't even difficult to set up –every endpoint should be tested, and they should perform the tasks that they are supposed to perform. While unit testing in Python already has several mature frameworks, such as *unittest* and *pytest*, some FastAPI-specific points are worth mentioning.

The FastAPI documentation recommends (at the time of writing) that you use the *TestClient* provided by Starlette. *Francois Voron*, in his excellent book published by *Packt* on FastAPI (*Building Data Science Applications with FastAPI*), recommends a slightly more advanced setup using *HTTPX* (an async HTTP library similar to Requests, developed by the Starlette team) and *pytest-asyncio*, making the whole process completely asynchronous.

The inclusion of Pydantic makes testing FastAPI applications a pleasant experience and it enforces certain practices that tend to produce more stable software. FastAPI's automatic documentation, on the other hand, is an incredibly helpful tool (that we haven't used much in this book, since I opted for REST clients) that saves you time and frequent trips between the code editor and the client.

## React practices

In *Chapter 1, Web Development and the FARM Stack*, we chose React for our frontend because of its apparent simplicity and flexibility. Don't be fooled by this apparent simplicity - writing serious React applications is a complex endeavor! React is constantly at the top of the most used, loved, and popular frontend technologies, so there is a plethora of React resources, books, courses, and tutorials covering every facet of the library (if you are a visual learner, try the video course by *Academind GMBH* and its main author, the eloquent and humorous *Maximilian Schwarzmüller – React – The Complete Guide*).

We haven't even scratched the surface of what is possible and what it means to begin developing performant and maintainable React apps. Solid knowledge of JavaScript and ES6 is the best foundation for becoming a better React developer, but it is also important to dive a bit deeper into some fundamental React concepts and explore the Hooks mechanism, the components life cycle, and the components hierarchy. Familiarize yourself with other hooks – in this book, we just glimpsed over two or three of the most popular, but there are many more, and knowing how they work and especially why they work the way they do will make you a better React developer.

As of 2022, React functional components (the only ones that we have seen in this book) are generally preferred to older class-based ones as they are more concise, maintainable, and generally flexible. This would also be my personal preference.

# Other topics

In this section, we will further emphasize some other important points that might work in our favor when using the FARM stack. While technically there is no barrier, you should be able to use the FARM stack for virtually any type of web application that you can think of – as any tool, the stack might be more suitable for some types of apps and less for others.

## Authentication and authorization

An entire chapter in this book is dedicated to implementing a possible JWT-based authentication solution with FastAPI and its consequent application in React. Yet, as mentioned in that chapter, that might not be the best or even a viable solution – you may need to revert to a third-party provider such as Firebase, Auth0, or Cognito. Before committing to a third-party solution, be sure to fully understand the pros and cons and the consequences of a potential lock-in, especially if you are planning to scale the application!

## Data visualization and the FARM stack

We have built a couple of rather simple visualizations, but you can already imagine that with properly formatted and granular JSON responses and React as the frontend, almost anything is achievable. This possibility to practically mold the data in the way that you might need it for a particular visualization opens, in my opinion, a great playground where you can test, tinker, and try out different solutions, maybe through iterations, until you reach the type of data visualization that you are satisfied with.

There is a broad spectrum of visualization requirements and there is probably no need to try and craft a Shirley Wu D3.js piece of art where a simple two-color stacked run-of-the-mill bar chart could have done the job. However, with the availability of a fast backend and MongoDB accommodating virtually any type of data structure that you might throw at it, you are ready for any task. D3's *Observable* wrapper has a very interesting interface and abstracts much of D3.js mechanisms, so it might be a good place to start. Displaying high-res static charts may also be a very good option.

## Relational databases

If your business problem needs the complexity of relational databases and their strict structure, querying with SQL and other features that only a relational database can provide doesn't mean that you have to ditch the FARM stack altogether! Given the modularity of FastAPI and using some of the deployment options that we explored throughout this book, nothing is stopping you from plugging in a relational database (Postgres, MySQL, and so on), exploring the documentation of SQLAlchemy or some async database Python drivers, and simply adding said functionality while managing the users, for instance, through MongoDB.

# Some project ideas to get started

To end this book on a creative note, we will suggest some project ideas if you are willing to dive deeper into the possibilities of the FARM stack and hone your skills, but above all, unleash your creativity.

## Old School Portfolio website

This is a weird little project just to show off that FastAPI, React, and MongoDB are perfectly capable of handling simple portfolio sites – an about page, service, gallery, contact form – the usual stuff. Create a nice design (or steal one that you like and try to recreate it in Tailwind CSS!), plug in React-Router or Next.js if you want to make it fast, and make use of server-side generation and image optimization. For the content, define a couple of Pydantic models: a blog post, portfolio item, article – whatever fits your needs – and then create simple routes for serving them via GET requests. Since this is a hardcore developers blog, you don't even need to create an authentication system and POST or PUT routes: text-related content will be entered directly into MongoDB (Atlas or Compass) and images will go to separate folders on *Cloudinary*, queried directly through the API. Of course, this is a bit of a joke, but it would be great practice, nevertheless. Try incorporating *markdown* – a powerful text pre-processor that converts simple text (markdown) into valid HTML. Both Python and ES6/React have excellent libraries for handling markdown, so try to find a good combination.

## React Admin Inventory

The idea is to try and create an inventory system built on top of *React-Admin* (`https://marmelab.com/react-admin/`), with authentication from Auth0 or Firebase, and a public-facing interface. React-Admin provides an admin interface similar to the one used by Django and it is based on CRUD verbs: each resource (or item) that exposes interfaces for POST, PUT, GET, and DELETE operations can be edited, deleted, and read and new instances can be created. Explore the package and try to think of some type of collection that you may want to manage. Bear in mind that there are excellent tools such as *Airtable* (an online spreadsheet-like application) that expose REST APIs that can be called from your FastAPI routes!

# Plotly-Dash or Streamlit – like exploratory data analysis application

Pick a dataset that you are familiar with – when I was starting to play with data, I always felt most confident with basketball-related data from the NBA: it is easy to spot correlations and outliers with the bare eye when you know where the data comes from and how it was generated. For instance, it's rare to find a player that shoots like Steph Curry but dunks like Russell Westbrook. Try creating an input pipeline that programmatically accepts data (and test it out thoroughly!) – be it from a little web or, better, API scraper or from an input file that uploads a JSON or CSV file. Clean the data, preprocess it, and insert it into the MongoDB datastore. From there, and based on the structure of the data at hand, try to figure out some useful filters and controls, not unlike enterprise tools such as Tableau or Google Data Studio – if you're already familiar with data like that, you will know what to expect. The only difference here is that you are free as a bird and you can build your way up while exploring, coding, and having fun. To return to my NBA players example, you could prepare MongoDB queries that separate players by position, team, age, and years of experience as a first stage. After that, you can fire up a Jupyter notebook, install a couple of visualization libraries (I like Plotly!), and see what types of correlations or groupings can come up. After you have found some interesting pandas-driven data wranglings, you can just extract them into separate functionalities, test them out a bit, and then incorporate them into FastAPI endpoints, ready to be visualized with D3.js or Chart.js. Finally, you could deploy your application and share it with your friend that manages your fantasy team to show him the data backing your draft decisions. We have seen how easy it is to embed a machine learning model built with Scikit-Learn, so give it a go: try embedding a neural network model, if that's your thing, with Keras or try out some simple linear regression!

Previous knowledge of data visualization and exploration frameworks such as Streamlit or Dash will help you.

# A document automation pipeline

I don't know about you, but I have always been surrounded by repetitive documents that have the same structure – be they Word documents with a branded header and footer and three colors and five font sizes, or Excel reports with the same column headers and colors and maybe even some (Excel) charts inside of them. Try to think of a document server based on the docx-tpl package, which allows you to define a Word template, formatted as it should be, and then pass a context containing all the data that needs to be in the document – text, images, tables, paragraphs, and titles – all while maintaining the initially defined styles. Similar and even more powerful automation can be achieved with Excel – using pandas for complex calculations, pivoting, and merging different documents into one. After creating the templates, try to think of some FastAPI endpoints that would perform POST requests and save the posted data to a MongoDB database, along with the data (for instance, the title of the document, the author, the data, and so on), and then trigger a DOCX or XLSX document render. Save the file with a recognizable name (maybe by adding the current time or the UUID library, for uniqueness) in a directory and ensure this directory is servable, either by FastAPI directly (via the static files functionality) or, in case you plan to have a significant number of heavy documents, maybe even an entire Nginx server block – after all, this is what Nginx excels at (pun intended). These files could then be accessible to all the team members or even sent directly via mail with a CRON job or something similar. Seemingly silly projects like this often result in incredible work time reductions in the long run.

# Summary

In this brief chapter, we added some pointers for further development and fortifying your FARM stack knowledge and experience, as well as some project ideas that you should customize and use as a starting point for your very own projects.

It has been quite a ride! We have made the case for a new and modern stack – the FARM stack – and we have introduced the protagonists.

You have learned how to perform simple and not-so-simple operations with MongoDB and create, read, query, and aggregate data that will later be converted into endpoints for your applications. You should also be comfortable setting up a MongoDB document store in the cloud or locally and wrangling data through the shell, the Compass GUI, or code.

We introduced FastAPI – probably our first billed actor in this web development action movie – a simple, clean, and fast Python framework that allows us to bridge the gap between our ideas and our code in an elegant, fast, and developer-friendly way, using the experience of the most successful Python web solutions from the past and the present.

You are now able to create user interfaces that match the workflow of your application and, more importantly, your data flow. Even though we barely explored the very basics of React, you should be able to take it from here and dive deeper and deeper into concepts such as state management – local and global, custom hooks, component life cycles, and much more.

We have created numerous simple or mildly complex applications to showcase the capabilities and the flexibility of the stack, but also as a way of helping you get started quickly – we explored server-side rendering and image optimization with Next.js, sent emails, manipulated images, and performed data visualizations as a part of what can easily be achieved with the FARM stack.

Finally, we deployed our web applications through a myriad of free or very cheap services, since I strongly believe that without that last step, the development process, especially while learning new concepts, isn't as gratifying as it could and should be.

I believe that the FARM stack has a bright future as a stack of choice for professional development teams and data wranglers or freelancers who just need to tell a story through a web application. I hope you have enjoyed this journey as much as I have, and I look forward to you building some FARM stack apps!

# Index

# V

# W

Packt.com

Subscribe to our online digital library for full access to over 7,000 books and videos, as well as industry leading tools to help you plan your personal development and advance your career. For more information, please visit our website.

## Why subscribe?

- Spend less time learning and more time coding with practical eBooks and Videos from over 4,000 industry professionals

- Improve your learning with Skill Plans built especially for you

- Get a free eBook or video every month

- Fully searchable for easy access to vital information

- Copy and paste, print, and bookmark content

Did you know that Packt offers eBook versions of every book published, with PDF and ePub files available? You can upgrade to the eBook version at packt.com and as a print book customer, you are entitled to a discount on the eBook copy. Get in touch with us at customercare@packtpub.com for more details.

At www.packt.com, you can also read a collection of free technical articles, sign up for a range of free newsletters, and receive exclusive discounts and offers on Packt books and eBooks.

# Other Books You May Enjoy

If you enjoyed this book, you may be interested in these other books by Packt:

**Building Python Web APIs with FastAPI**

Abdulazeez Abdulazeez Adeshina

ISBN: 978-1-80107-663-0

- Set up a FastAPI application that is fully functional and secure
- Perform CRUD operations using SQL and FastAPI
- Manage concurrency in FastAPI applications
- Implement authentication in a FastAPI application
- Deploy a FastAPI application to any platform

**React Projects - Second Edition**

Roy Derks

ISBN: 978-1-80107-063-8

- Create a wide range of applications using various modern React tools and frameworks
- Discover how React Hooks modernize state management for React apps
- Develop web applications using styled and reusable React components
- Build test-driven React applications using Jest, React Testing Library, and Cypress
- Understand full-stack development using GraphQL, Apollo, and React

# Packt is searching for authors like you

If you're interested in becoming an author for Packt, please visit authors.packtpub.com and apply today. We have worked with thousands of developers and tech professionals, just like you, to help them share their insight with the global tech community. You can make a general application, apply for a specific hot topic that we are recruiting an author for, or submit your own idea.

Hi!

I am Marko Aleksendrić, author of Modern Web Development with the FARM Stack. I really hope you enjoyed reading this book and found it useful for increasing your productivity and efficiency in developing interesting web applications.

It would really help me (and other potential readers!) if you could leave a review on Amazon sharing your thoughts on Modern Web Development with the FARM Stack

Your review will help me to understand what's worked well in this book, and what could be improved upon for future editions, so it really is appreciated.

Best Wishes,

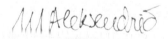

Made in the USA
Las Vegas, NV
09 October 2022

56888585R00188